IMPROVISING THE SCORE

IMPROVISING THE SCORE

RETHINKING MODERN FILM MUSIC THROUGH JAZZ

GRETCHEN L. CARLSON

UNIVERSITY PRESS OF MISSISSIPPI / JACKSON

Publication of this book was supported in part by a grant from
the H. Earle Johnson Fund of the Society for American Music.

The University Press of Mississippi is the scholarly publishing agency of
the Mississippi Institutions of Higher Learning: Alcorn State University,
Delta State University, Jackson State University, Mississippi State University,
Mississippi University for Women, Mississippi Valley State University,
University of Mississippi, and University of Southern Mississippi.

www.upress.state.ms.us

The University Press of Mississippi is a member
of the Association of University Presses.

Copyright © 2022 by University Press of Mississippi
All rights reserved

First printing 2022

∞

Library of Congress Cataloging-in-Publication Data

Names: Carlson, Gretchen L., author.
Title: Improvising the score : rethinking modern film music through jazz /
Gretchen L. Carlson.
Description: Jackson : University Press of Mississippi, 2022. | Includes
bibliographical references and index.
Identifiers: LCCN 2022008543 (print) | LCCN 2022008544 (ebook) | ISBN
9781496840721 (hardback) | ISBN 9781496840844 (trade paperback) | ISBN
9781496840738 (epub) | ISBN 9781496840745 (epub) | ISBN 9781496840752
(pdf) | ISBN 9781496840769 (pdf)
Subjects: LCSH: Motion picture music—History and criticism. |
Jazz—History and criticism. | Jazz in motion pictures. | Motion
pictures—Production and direction—History.
Classification: LCC ML2075 .C3706 2022 (print) | LCC ML2075 (ebook) | DDC
781.5/42—dc23/eng/20220303
LC record available at https://lccn.loc.gov/2022008543
LC ebook record available at https://lccn.loc.gov/2022008544

British Library Cataloging-in-Publication Data available

For my family. I love you 3000.

CONTENTS

ACKNOWLEDGMENTS IX

INTRODUCTION: JAZZ GOES TO THE MOVIES
FROM "AUTHENTICITY" TO INNER CIRCLE 3

CHAPTER 1: WHEN STRANGERS MEET
STRUCTURES, TENSIONS, AND NEGOTIATIONS IN JAZZ/FILM COLLABORATIONS 26

CHAPTER 2: "NOT A LOT OF PEOPLE WOULD GO FOR THAT"
RISK AND EXPERIMENTATION IN THE IMPROVISED SOUNDTRACKS OF BIRDMAN
AND AFTERGLOW 48

CHAPTER 3: "HONEST, TRUE PORTRAYALS"
TERENCE BLANCHARD, SPIKE LEE, AND THE RACIAL POLITICS OF JAZZ SCORING 74

CHAPTER 4: "A FILM DIRECTOR'S DREAM"
DICK HYMAN PLAYS THE PERSONAL FOR WOODY ALLEN 118

CONCLUSION: MILES AHEAD
A NEW WAY OF MAKING MOVIE MUSIC? 144

NOTES 160

BIBLIOGRAPHY 184

INDEX 202

ACKNOWLEDGMENTS

Like the intermedia works in the following pages, this book has come to fruition through the encouragement, collaboration, and feedback of an incredible community of scholars, musicians, family, and friends. I am so grateful to each and every one of you for your invaluable support.

This project would not have been possible without the generosity of my interviewees, whose insights and experiences greatly informed the case studies in the following chapters. I am grateful to Terence Blanchard, Mark Isham, Dick Hyman, and Vince Giordano for taking time out of their busy schedules to speak with me in detail. Thank you also to Mark Lopeman, Adrian Cunningham, Stewart Lerman, Bill Kirchner, and Allison (Geatches) Cantor for sharing your experiences, and providing me "behind-the-scenes" insights into film soundtrack work. All of these incredible artists have encouragingly supported this project, and I hope that it rewards their generosity. I look forward to seeing how these talented individuals continue to shape the world with their creative work in the future.

To my colleagues, mentors, and friends—I am eternally grateful for the continuous support, feedback, and thought-provoking conversations that have helped shape this work. Buzz Jones, Marta Robertson, Paul Austerlitz, John Howland, Lewis Porter, Henry Martin, Scott DeVeaux, Karl Hagstrom Miller, Nomi Dave, Hector Amaya, Bonnie Gordon, John D'earth, Amy Coddington, Courtney Kleftis, Stephanie Gunst, Christa Bruckner-Haring, John Hasse, Kim Teal, Darren Mueller, Phillip Collister, Aaron Ziegel, and Liz Massey—your consistent encouragement and coffee conversations unquestioningly inspired and motivated me as I developed this project.

I am also indebted to the numerous organizations and institutions that have facilitated and supported my research, including Towson University, the University of Virginia, the Institute of Jazz Studies, Rutgers University, Gettysburg College, the Society for American Music, the Jazz Appreciation Network, Rhythm Changes, and the American Musicological Society. Thank you to all the faculty, staff, administrators, and committee members who have provided me opportunities to develop and present my research at these institutions and organizational conferences. It has been an honor to advance and share this work within such dynamic and impressive scholarly and musical communities. Thank you also to the reviewers, board members, editors, and publishing staff that have played a vital role in refining and disseminating my work. Special thanks to Karen Ahlquist and the *Journal of the Society for American Music*, Michael Heller and the *Jazz and Culture* journal, and Craig Gill, Carlton McGrone, and all at the University Press of Mississippi whose invaluable efforts have transformed *Improvising the Score* from a vision into a published reality.

Last, but certainly not least, I want to thank my ever-supportive and unconditionally loving family and friends. You are the foundation that grounds me, inspires me, motivates me, and helps me overcome the challenges. Drew, thank you for everything. From proofreading to picking up carry-out pizza, accompanying me on conference trips, listening to film scores on repeat in the car, and binge-watching pretty much every movie ever made with a jazz soundtrack—you have always supported me, respected me, and loved me. Mom and Dad, you have always encouraged me to pursue what I love, to challenge myself, and to push through times of struggle. Your continual love and support has shaped me into the independent, knowledge-seeking, challenge-loving person I am today. Jay, I am so blessed to have grown up with such an amazing, life-loving, music-loving, movie-loving, and food-loving brother. You always make me laugh, and I am so grateful for your constant words of encouragement and support. Grams, your passions for family, faith, music, and education have been guiding influences in my life. (You also inspired me to follow in your footsteps and write books!) To my extended family, you have all motivated and inspired me in so many different ways. I am blessed to have grown up with such a beautiful, brainy, talented, and loving group of people. My girls—Leslie, Rachel, Emily, Theresa, Kayla, Amy, Courtney, Steph—whether through dance parties, cocktails, movie nights, or just hanging out by the pool, you all have brought so much joy to my life. My Rutgers cohort—Cabo, José, Shawn, Elizabeth, Ben, Ginger, Tony—despite the miles between us, you have always been and remain close. Thank you for all the adventures, and all the support. A.J. and Sarah, Jon and Margaret, Sarah and Carl—you are awesome, brilliant, and have excellent taste in wine, food, and music (and friends). And Todd, thank you for being fantastic, inspiring, and ever encouraging. Our Music Days, karaoke nights, and cruises in the Challenger undoubtedly kept my energy invigorated as I finished this book. This is for you all.

IMPROVISING THE SCORE

Introduction

JAZZ GOES TO THE MOVIES

FROM "AUTHENTICITY" TO INNER CIRCLE

The shrill ring of the telephone cuts through attorney Paul Biegler's office. "Hello?" The operator puts him through. Before we hear a human voice on the other end, a brazen, bluesy brass smear blasts through the telephone receiver, followed by raunchy jazz riffs in full swing. Soon, the invisible caller appears onscreen. The seductive and mysterious Laura Manion appears to be at a club, bedecked in a tight-fitting trench coat, glittering earrings, dark lipstick, and black sunglasses completely obscuring her eyes. She asks Paul to meet with her husband, who is in need of an attorney after being arrested for murder. Laura's voice is simultaneously desperate and commanding, tinged with a flirtatious coyness when she asks, "Would you want me there too, Mr. Biegler?" Throughout the conversation, the sinuous, bluesy musical soundtrack accompanies Laura's presence, complete with a sultry saxophone solo sonically signifying her "femme fatale" nature.

This film is Otto Preminger's *Anatomy of a Murder* (1959), arguably one of the most renowned movies featuring an original jazz score in cinematic history. The musical accompaniment, a tune called "Flirtibird," was composed and performed by Duke Ellington and his orchestra, featuring a scintillating sax solo by Johnny Hodges. The music's representations in the film are ripe for critical consideration (as scholars Mervyn Cooke, Krin Gabbard, and Jans B. Wager have examined),[1] and one could certainly write an extensive tome on the soundtrack's cultural, racial, gendered, and ideological semiotic meanings. The soundtrack itself—which according to Ellington was finalized in "about forty-eight hours"[2]—has been a topic of significant critical analysis and debate among jazz critics and scholars alike. Some responses reveal dissatisfaction; *Jazz Review* asserted that the music was "uncommitted" and "lacking in enthusiasm,"[3] while Ellington himself admitted a lack of satisfaction, stating: "Music in pictures should say something without being obviously music, you know, and this was all new to me. I'll try another one

3

and then I'll show them."[4] Other responses to *Anatomy*'s soundtrack have been laudatory, highlighting the artistry of the score itself, as well as its uniqueness in the context of Hollywood cinematic conventions. Tom Piazza described the soundtrack as "a vernacular American symphony,"[5] while jazz critic Stanley Crouch enthusiastically professed that "the film score not only detailed extraordinary development but showed just how far Ellington and Strayhorn had stretched the language of jazz and just how far they were beyond all contenders."[6] Wynton Marsalis claimed that Ellington's *Anatomy* work is "among the most creative ever heard in jazz or film,"[7] while Terence Blanchard asserted that "Duke Ellington was probably the only composer who got to score film using [jazz] with some degree of integrity."[8]

Scholarly analysis of Ellington's *Anatomy* score has focused primarily on how well (or not) it functioned within the context of the visual narrative, theorizing the broader implications of its effective roles. Krin Gabbard described it as sounding "randomly tacked on," incompatible and ineffective with the on-screen events.[9] Mervyn Cooke read these incongruences differently, arguing that the soundtrack represented "a clear manifestation of modernist leanings in soundtrack design."[10] Similarly, Jans B. Wager argued that the overtness of the soundtrack generated a strategic "alienation effect" that offered "explicit commentary on the ambivalent morality offered by the film," while revealing Ellington's (and Billy Strayhorn's) Afromodernist agendas within the contexts of 1950s Hollywood.[11] Regardless of their conclusions, these scholars all share an analytic perspective that prioritizes the film over the music, reinforcing what Nicolas Pillai has identified as "two assumptions: that jazz and Hollywood narrative are formally incompatible, and consequently that successful jazz films are those which subvert or undermine Hollywood's patterns of classical film narration."[12] The potential pitfall of these assumptions, as Pillai argues, is that they "characterize the meeting of jazz and film, the improvised and the recorded, as a problem to be solved."[13]

Like Pillai, whose groundbreaking work *Jazz as Visual Language* examines interactions between jazz and visual media that have proven "mutually transformative,"[14] I want to move beyond jazz soundtrack analysis that focuses solely (or primarily) on its subjugated or subversive representational relationships to visual narratives. Instead, I want to look at these jazz-film intersections as sites of creative collaboration, development, and experimentation within their unique cultural and social production contexts. Therefore, I go "behind the scenes" with contemporary jazz artists who have recently worked in film, theorizing how their unique collaborations with filmmakers allow us to rethink the possibilities of how jazz and film may integratively shape each other, and provide models for further experimentation in film soundtrack production.

Returning to the Ellington *Anatomy* case study, we can enrich our understanding of the soundtrack and its significance if we move beyond solely considering how it "fit" in the film. Consider the following questions: Why did Otto Preminger hire Ellington to score this particular movie? What sort of value did he believe Ellington's music could bring to his narrative? Why did Ellington agree to work on the project? What was the content of Preminger and Ellington's conversations about what the music should be like? What was Ellington's method for composing this score, and how much creative agency did he retain in the process? How much of his music ended up being used in the film, and was it used as he intended? What interactions and negotiations among Ellington, the musicians, the filmmakers, and the music editors influenced this soundtrack's development?

Ellington is no longer with us. We can no longer ask him about his experiences composing for *Anatomy*, and his own autobiographical comments are brief and not especially illuminating.[15] At this stage, it would be difficult to investigate *Anatomy*'s production circumstances thoroughly, in the absence of detailed records. But we can talk to contemporary jazz artists working in film—a methodology that greatly informed the research for this book. The aforementioned inquiries provide a framework for examining contemporary jazz-film collaborations, leading us to a deeper understanding of how jazz and film can be "mutually transformative." Accordingly, such investigations illuminate the *process* of jazz soundtrack production, challenging us to rethink our understanding of film music as an ancillary component of the overall film, instead viewing it as a site of creative experimentation, negotiation, and personal expression.

We are presently decades removed from jazz artists' peak involvement in the film industry. The "golden era" of jazz soundtracks during the 1950s and 1960s—which featured a proliferation of jazz-oriented scores from artists such as Quincy Jones, Benny Carter, John Lewis, and Miles Davis—seems an idyllic ghost relegated to the annals of history. Contemporary film scores predominantly feature a combination of the neoromantic stylings of John Williams, Hans Zimmer, and Howard Shore, compilation "pop" scores,[16] and increasing forays into experimental electronic soundtracks. Amidst these trends, jazz film scores have been limited. That said, they are not completely absent. While infrequent, jazz's presence has manifested in a variety of film productions within the last fifteen years, including jazz biopics (*Bessie, Miles Ahead, Born to Be Blue, Bolden*), "period" programs (e.g., *Boardwalk Empire,*

Mildred Pierce, Mob City), fictional dramas (*Whiplash, La La Land*), and the oeuvres of directors such as Woody Allen, Spike Lee, and Clint Eastwood. Additionally, there have been several films that feature jazz soundtracks that do not seem to have anything to do with jazz (at least narratively speaking)—several of which make up the case studies in this book. While the diversity and intermittence of these jazz/film intersections hardly intimates a jazz renaissance in cinema, it illustrates that jazz soundtracks are not just a phenomenon of the past but are of value to filmmakers, jazz artists, and audiences in the present. The question is, why? What does jazz have to offer contemporary film production, and conversely, what does film production have to offer jazz?

THE CURRENT STUDY

This book provides vivid investigations into innovative collaborations between renowned contemporary jazz artists and prominent independent filmmakers, theorizing how these integrative jazz-film productions challenge us to rethink the possibilities of cinematic music production. More specifically, I argue that these projects provide models for the ways that jazz can effectively integrate with and transform film/media, functioning as a dynamic site of creative experimentation that illustrates the possibilities of interactive collaboration between filmmakers and composers, and between movies and music.

As discussed, jazz is a rare genre in modern original soundtracks; it does not appear to "fit in" well with standard filmmaking practices. This tension makes these rare intersections particularly ripe for analysis. Why doesn't jazz seem to fit? What happens behind closed doors when jazz film scores are produced? This book addresses these questions, illustrating how jazz/film collaborations can transform how movie music is made. I provide detailed, behind-the-scenes investigations of recent soundtrack productions, demonstrating how they are sites of disruption, experimentation, and creative expression that exceed and transform the films themselves. Specifically, *Improvising the Score* examines the production of soundtracks for films directed by a diversity of influential film directors, including Spike Lee (*Malcolm X, When the Levees Broke*), Alejandro González Iñárritu (*Birdman*), Alan Rudolph (*Afterglow*), and Woody Allen (*Hannah and Her Sisters*, among others). Employing a sociological approach grounded in ethnographic research, I focus specifically on recent soundtrack productions created by professional jazz artists such as Terence Blanchard, Antonio Sánchez, Mark Isham, and Dick Hyman, examining the unique features of their scores, as well as how they negotiated their own creative musical practices and ideologies within the hierarchies and expectations of the film-production process. This work draws on close score and film analysis and personal interviews with several of the composers and film production personnel, examining what they do that is different from conventional Hollywood film composers, and what possibilities their works present for movie music production and meaning in the future.

Just as jazz soundtracks are rare in contemporary film, they have been largely absent from the literature in both jazz studies and film music (though notably, there has been an increase in jazz and film topics within the last few years). The small existing body of scholarship—including Gabbard's landmark *Jammin' at the Margins* (1996), and more recent influential works such as David Butler's *Jazz Noir* (2002), Peter Stanfield's *Body and Soul* (2005), Björn Heile, Peter Elsdon, and Jenny Doctor's *Watching Jazz* (2016), Wager's *Jazz and Cocktails* (2017), and Pillai's *Jazz as Visual Language* (2017)—valuably examines jazz's representations and reception in film as products of (often-problematic) societal perceptions of race, sexuality, identity, and cultural meaning. Similarly, Emile Wennekes and Emilio Audissino's excellent recent anthology *Cinema Changes: Incorporations of Jazz in the Film Soundtrack* (2019) offers a wide diversity of jazz/film analyses that focus on jazz reception and representation within Hollywood and across national cinemas. Consistent with New Jazz Studies criticism (as illustrated through the influential anthologies *Jazz among the Discourses* [1995] and *Representing Jazz* [1995]), these works theorize jazz's representations and influence on diverse media through pointed, interdisciplinary cultural criticism. Largely missing, however, are the voices of the musicians themselves. What roles do jazz musicians play in these productions, and how must they negotiate labor, creativity, and personal ideology when creating movie music? Influential literature in the fields of media and culture industry studies—including Robert Faulkner's *Music on Demand* (1983), David Morgan's *Knowing the Score* (2000), Fred Karlin and Rayburn Wright's *On the Track* (2004), John Caldwell's *Production Culture* (2008), and Matt Stahl's *Unfree Masters* (2013)—addresses these questions on a broad level, offering critical sociological analyses of the cultural practices, beliefs, and complex creative labor that culture industry workers (e.g., film production workers, composers, recording artists) negotiate. However, what these texts do not specifically address is the work of contemporary jazz composers and their unique positions in and contributions to the film world and culture at large.

Improvising the Score engages these diverse scholarly fields in dialogue. I bring contemporary jazz musicians and their work into the conversation on jazz and film. Using the lenses of sociology, psychology, film production analysis, media analysis (e.g., film scenes and musical scores), and what I characterize as "creative labor," I move beyond analysis of jazz's representations in film and instead demonstrate how the process and development of jazz/film soundtracks allows us to rethink the roles and influence of film music and its composers. Ultimately, this book examines some of the most uniquely collaborative film scores in modern cinema, challenging readers to recognize film music composition as a site of creative agency, individuality, and media transformation, while thinking more broadly about how media music can amplify ideological, political, and personal expression.

BEHIND THE SCENES: AN OVERVIEW

As discussed above, one of my primary motivations for examining jazz in film from a "behind-the-scenes" production standpoint is to give voice to the composers themselves. Such an approach provides insight into general film music production processes but also specifically illustrates the unique circumstances informing these unconventional collaborations between jazz artists and filmmakers. The case studies featured in this book examine the film work of contemporary jazz artists who hold the rare distinction of being full-time professional jazz musicians who have also recurrently worked as film composers. Indeed, this list features the major jazz figures working in film today: percussionist Antonio Sánchez, trumpeter Mark Isham, trumpeter Terence Blanchard, and pianist Dick Hyman.[17] Isham and Blanchard are well-established film composers with multiple film credits to their names (i.e., Isham over one hundred, Blanchard over forty), while Sánchez and Hyman have performed several soundtracks throughout their careers, often working recurrently in collaboration with particular directors (as I examine in more detail). All of these artists maintain active jazz performance careers.[18] What makes these collaborations particularly promising for investigation is the seeming tension between the improvisational ideals of the jazz world and the conventionally highly structured and regulated expectations of the film music world, in which the music is often subjugated to the visual narrative. The fact that these individuals have worked recurrently in film despite these tensions—holding a level of status and recognition that very few jazz artists have held in the film industry throughout cinematic history—suggests that they bring something to the table that conventional film composers do not. I examine and theorize the reasons why.

In the following chapters, I investigate the relationships and tensions between these artists' creative autonomy and their "work-for-hire" statuses within the hierarchies and structures of the film industry. How do they negotiate the shifting internal labor markets, business transactions, and power hierarchies that structure film projects? How do they balance film industry conventions and filmmakers' expectations with their own artistic expertise and creative desires? I read such tensions alongside critical examinations of the following phenomena: (1) the artists' relationships with particular directors; (2) the director's goals and interests; (3) risk ideologies within the film industry; and (4) the jazz artists' own creative practices. I challenge my readers to think about the ways that film score production necessitates direct engagements between the jazz and film worlds, and demands a nuanced, critical consideration of how each world's conventions, practices, ideologies, and expectations complexly intersect, and affect its members in turn.[19] These specific examinations of jazz in film contribute to the extant discourse addressing the tensions and complexities between creative agency and labor in cultural industry work.

I employed a multimethodological approach in investigating these artists' experiences working in film soundtrack production, drawing on ethnographic methodologies. A significant portion of this research was accomplished through long-form personal interviews with the musicians themselves, as well as other involved film production personnel (e.g., recording engineers, editors, musicians, assistants). In addition, I had the valuable opportunity to observe live film-scoring and recording sessions. I chose to integrate these ethnographic methodologies into my research approach so that I could engage directly with the people behind the work, providing opportunities for them to speak for themselves. These musicians are complex, savvy, strategic artists, who understand the balance of personal ideology/ creativity and the structures of reality that they must negotiate when working in film (or any industry, for that matter). Beyond personal interviews and session observations, I employed archival work, researching numerous additional interviews and articles that addressed these jazz musicians' involvement in film projects. Drawing on all the aforementioned sources, I theorize these artists' work and influence within their broader sociological, cultural, ideological, and aesthetic contexts. Finally, I employ close analysis of film scenes and musical moments, examining these jazz artists' creative productions in dialogue with the media itself.

In concentrating on these major jazz figures, I have deliberately chosen not to engage with the multitude of nonrecurrent, freelance jazz artists who have contributed sporadically to film or television recording sessions. This is not intended to undermine or erase these artists' experiences or contributions. My focus in this book is examining direct collaborations between jazz artists and filmmakers, examining how these artists engage with (and shape) the filmmaking process and negotiate their own work and creativity within its structures. The aforementioned "peripheral" artists rarely interact directly with filmmakers and are not involved in any filmmaking decisions. Rather, they are hired by music supervisors or contract companies to record the music, and that is generally the extent of their involvement. Therefore, for the purposes of this project, I remain focused on Sánchez, Isham, Blanchard, and Hyman.

Overall, this book's intervention into jazz (and film) scholarship is three-fold. First, it investigates jazz musicians' film work from a sociological per-spective, an approach that is virtually absent in analyses of jazz in film. I provide detailed case studies of jazz musicians' behind-the-scenes labor and production within the film industry, highlighting their unique collaborations with influential filmmakers, and utilizing these examples to illuminate the wide-ranging possibilities of transformational relationships between the two mediums. In bringing jazz studies into dialogue with film production, I treat jazz not merely as sonic style but as the product of a dynamic jazz culture whose conventions uniquely influence its intersections and integrations with other disciplinary networks (i.e., film).

Second, I examine how jazz/film intersections provide opportunities for jazz musicians' creativity in a radically different medium. Jazz critics often ignore this issue, preferring to view the music as an idealized, "autonomous art" existing only within its own world. This view is historically rooted. Scholars such as Gabbard (1996), Scott DeVeaux (1997), Paul Lopes (2002), and Mark Gridley (2003) have shown how the rise of bebop in the 1940s corresponded to a movement in jazz cultural politics advocating for the music's new status as an art form, removed from its commercial associations with swing and mass entertainment. As Lopes argues, "[jazz] enthusiasts . . . were looking to elevate this music as an art form deserving of 'serious' appreciation."[20] This upholding of such "autonomous," creative recordings and compositions as the paragon of jazz production still proliferates in jazz scholarship and criticism today—as evidenced in the canonization of jazz "greats" and cultural support of perceived musical "masters"/innovators.

Because film music is created "for hire"—with obligations to the film's narrative and the filmmakers' tastes—few jazz scholars have taken it seri-ously.[21] Many film composers themselves have internalized their music's subjugation, as evidenced by the assertion of a young composer (who chose to remain anonymous) that "television [or film] is just not the place to stage a musical revolution."[22] I am not interested in such dismissals. Rather, I read these jazz scores within the context of their unique sociological and cultural environments, understanding that the "for hire" aspect of creating film soundtracks is just another structural component that the artists must navigate. On a base level, how is creating music for film different than creating music on the bandstand? (I of course realize that there are numerous differences, but I'm trying to make a point.) Both involve negotiating one's creative impulses within the context of unique structures and expectations—what I refer to as "creative labor." Rather than collaborating and negotiating with other musicians on the bandstand, following the chord progressions of the pieces, and simultaneously attempting to meet audiences' expectations, film composers develop creative works while navigating the structures of the visual media and the filmmakers' desires and expectations. In many ways, such navigation itself is a substantial part of these artists' creativity.

In the following chapters, I examine specifically how these artists utilized their expertise as jazz musicians to develop new, creative works within unfamiliar media contexts, strengthening their own compositional and performance skills as a result. Broadly, this project engages with studies of creativity, labor, and agency in culture industry production. How can musicians be "creative" when they are producing artworks "to order?" How might working within the film industry as a composer generate new possibilities for experimentation and musical development, rather than limiting them? How does collaboration affect and facilitate creative production? These questions are relevant to any discussion of artistic labor within the mass market economy—whether it be focused on pop stars' work in the recording industry or jazz artists' scores for the movies.

Finally, *Improvising the Score* posits larger implications for jazz within the fields of film and media studies. I argue that these unique jazz/film intersections challenge audiences to rethink film music's agency and meanings by providing models of integrative film projects built on mutual collaboration between composers and filmmakers, challenging conventional film soundtrack production methods in unique and innovative ways. These examples illustrate how jazz can effectively interact with and shape visual media and its meanings, as well as how the media (and the expectations of film production) can shape jazz composition/performance in return. Furthermore, these case studies position film score productions as active sites of creative experimentation and collaboration, shaped by intersecting social, cultural, political, ideological, and aesthetic values, beliefs, and motivations.

In the remaining sections of this introduction, I introduce the primary topical threads that inform this study as whole, establishing a framework for the sociological and musical analyses that emerge throughout the case studies.

"JAZZ" IN FILM

My discussion of "jazz/film intersections" implies an established definition of the term "jazz." But how does one define jazz in film—or distinguish it from film music that is not jazz?

Jazz music has a long history of usage in film soundtracks. Early jazz, modal jazz, bebop, "cool jazz," free jazz, fusion, swing—all have been present in film soundtracks at one time or another, in various manifestations. A brief skim through David Meeker's *Jazz in the Movies* (1977) highlights the wide range of jazz musicians who have performed in film soundtracks, from Louis Armstrong to Stan Getz.[23] This wealth of jazz artists and styles that have been represented in film (and their varied cinematic and cultural associations) exists simultaneously in cinema's extensive catalog, complicating any singular readings of what "jazz in film" means.

The tenuousness of this phrase becomes increasingly apparent when we consider how jazz film scores/soundtracks can often be stylistically quite different from recognizable jazz styles. Many jazz/film works are not created in traditional jazz performance methods and instead represent unique musical products that blend jazz and film music traditions. Often, such productions result in fusions of jazz elements with more traditional film-scoring elements. Examples include jazz-style improvisations integrated with lush, orchestral scoring (e.g., Ornette Coleman's score for *Naked Lunch* [1991]), tunes with jazz-style "feels" (e.g., swing, bebop) that feature prominent character themes (e.g., Terence Blanchard's jazz versions of "Malcolm's Theme" in *Malcolm X* [1992]), and soundtracks that draw on jazz practices (e.g., improvisation) but don't necessarily sound "jazzy" (e.g., Antonio Sánchez's improvised score for *Birdman* [2014]). These complications are further compounded by scores that feature jazz elements (e.g., instrumentation, swinging rhythms, bluesy inflections) but are not associated with a particular jazz style (e.g., Alex North's score for *A Streetcar Named Desire* [1951]). How do we contextualize such products? Accordingly, how do we introduce into this argument a discussion of the meaning of "jazz" in cultural discourse?

Within the jazz world, the term "jazz" has often been one of contention. Ake et al. stated, "The lines people draw between 'jazz' and 'not jazz' can at once be both fiercely guarded and very difficult to discern."[24] The recent titles of critical texts such as *Jazz/Not Jazz*, *Jazz in Search of Itself*, and *What Is This Thing Called Jazz?* speak to a nearly century-long proliferation of debates about the definitions of the genre and its cultural meanings.[25] Must jazz include improvisation? Does jazz music have to "swing?" Is jazz a Black music, an American music, an international music, or all of these? Do various forms of jazz "fusions" count as jazz?

Since the early 1990s, scholars affiliated with New Jazz Studies have offered modern insights into jazz historiography, critiquing the established narratives and introducing new ways of thinking about the definition of jazz.[26] Scott DeVeaux—whose seminal work "Constructing the Jazz Tradition" (1991) greatly influenced New Jazz Studies criticism—later argued that jazz scholars should be willing to examine works that exist on the boundaries between jazz and other art forms. Prior to the emergence of New Jazz Studies, jazz scholarship had typically focused on jazz's "core" (i.e., the "great" musicians and their music). DeVeaux has contended that in focusing on the "boundaries," definitions and understandings of jazz are negotiated across these boundaries, and give us the opportunity to think about how these musical works contribute to jazz scholarship.[27]

My readings of contemporary jazz in film align with this new approach. My research focuses on the boundaries of jazz, considering the way jazz works *as* film music. I therefore focus less on musical style per se than on the musicians' sociological self-identification as "jazz musicians." Sánchez, Isham, Blanchard, and Hyman all identify themselves as professional jazz artists, and are recognized as such through their social connections to a larger cultural network of jazz practitioners, institutions, critics, and audiences. Accordingly, if these artists call their film scores "jazz" (which they do), I respect that, regardless of whether or not their works sonically fall within already-established jazz styles. The purpose of this research is not to make value judgments about what does or does not constitute "real jazz"; rather, it is to examine the unique experiences of jazz artists working in film, and the creative projects that they develop within that environment.

"INNER CIRCLES": THE ESSENTIALITY OF DIRECTORIAL INVESTMENT

The role of directorial investment in facilitating opportunities for jazz artists to create film scores cannot be understated. Despite the collaborative nature of film production, directors have the most significant power in making production decisions. The director is the artistic boss, responsible for integrating all of the creative aspects of film production into a comprehensive motion picture. While in some cases executive producers, studios, and financiers may reserve "final cut" of the film, the director is the person most significantly involved in putting all the pieces together. He oversees the determinations about which actors to cast,[28] where/how the scenes should be filmed, what the costuming should look like—and, for our purposes, what music should be used for the soundtrack. Therefore, it is only through a director's approval that a composer's music makes it through the final cut into the completed film.

Certain accomplished film directors have been recognized as the artistic authors of their films, emphasized in what film studies scholars identify as "auteur theory." This theory maintains that a given film reflects the director's personal creative vision, lauding distinctiveness, originality, and the perceived presence of an authorial signature. As a method of film analysis, auteur theory developed out of the critical writings of contributors to the French film magazine *Cahiers du cinéma*, greatly influenced by director/critic François Truffaut's article "Une certaine tendance du cinéma français" (1954), in which he coined the phrase "la politique des Auteurs" (auteur theory). Auteur theory was primarily employed in the discourse surrounding the 1960s French New Wave cinematic movement and later became influential in US film criticism through the writings of Andrew Sarris.[29] This critical theory remains present in film scholarship today—even as its history and acceptance among film critics have been riddled with controversy and polemical debate regarding the potential limitations of grounding interpretation of a film in the director's singular identity/vision (reflecting poststructuralist literary criticism such as Roland Barthes's "death of the author"[30]).

A sociological perspective lends credence to these criticisms of auteur theory. As Pauline Kael argued, filmmaking is inherently a collaborative effort, and the director cannot (or should not) receive full credit as the author of the film.[31] Other opponents of auteur theory have echoed these criticisms, challenging the privileging of the director over other cinematic producers, including screenwriters, cinematographers, and studio executives and producers at large—as well as the inherent fallacies of developing cults of personalities that risk marginalizing a number of potentially valuable filmic works.[32] The sociological study of film production as the cooperative action of a diverse network of organized laborers (as seen in the work of Leo C. Rosten, Hortense Powdermaker, John Caldwell, and Vicki Mayer, among others) further supports these criticisms.

However, what auteur theory usefully highlights is the hierarchies of power within film industry production that make such directorial control possible. If not the author, the director is the authorial editor, whose decisions and preferences ultimately shape the final outcome of the film project, even though the project is ultimately dependent on the collaborative contributions of a host of other personnel (e.g., screenwriters, cinematographers, actors). This is especially true of the particular directors examined in this book, who retain essentially unlimited control over their own films, reflected in the name-based branding of their works (e.g., "a Woody Allen film," "a Spike Lee joint"). Therefore, auteur theory—while inherently problematic—recognizes the hierarchical structures that are already in place in film production, placing the responsibility (and credit) for artistic decisions on top-tier agents.

Howard Becker identifies such hierarchical social distinction in his theorization of art world community and production. He contends that within a given art world, there is an accepted distinction between those personnel who are recognized as "artists" and those who are recognized as lower-rung craft workers. Becker positions the "artists" as the most-respected authors of artworks in the cultural social system, regardless of the works' collaborative production.[33] The Academy Award designations offer insight into these arrangements of distinction and privilege within the film industry. Only those personnel considered to be "artistic" are given award categories (e.g., cinematographer, composer, costume designer), as the more prominent awards receive the most-distinguished recognition (emphasized in their placement at the end of the ceremony). The award for Best Director is one of these most prominent awards.

Accordingly, such cultural veneration for artistry is strongly reflected in the film art world's respect for the identified auteur—the determiner of cultural capital, and (often) the leader of the vanguard in establishing new, artistic directions for the field. These filmmakers are often recognized as "mavericks," art world actors who push against the established conventions of the production field in new, experimental ways, thus paving the path for future art world development. In many cases these maverick auteurs are not integrated studio professionals. Rather, they are often independent filmmakers who retain artistic control of their projects through self-production and independent financing.[34] Yet because of their recognition as the "innovators" of the field, they also can become profitable entities who benefit from additional financing and distribution from the major studios. These positions thus allow them to retain both cultural *and* economic capital within the film industry.

All the directors examined in this book (Alejandro González Iñárritu, Alan Rudolph, Spike Lee, and Woody Allen) have been identified as independent auteurs. Due to their recurrent film successes, the industry lauds their oeuvres and encourages their unique, often unconventional and experimental approaches to filmmaking. Accordingly, these directors have the best of both worlds—largely uninhibited creative control, with the financial, promotional, and distributional resources typically unavailable to filmmakers working outside the studio system. Through such resources and accreditation, they essentially have the "green light" (and the financial capabilities) to do whatever they see fit with their films.

Now, getting back to jazz. Notably, throughout cinematic history it has predominantly been independent, auteur directors who have hired jazz musicians to score their films. Louis Malle hired Miles Davis for *Ascenseur pour l'échafaud* (1958). Otto Preminger hired Duke Ellington for *Anatomy of a Murder* (1959). Bertrand Tavernier hired Herbie Hancock for *Round Midnight* (1986). Despite the diversity of these film projects, the commonality of independent filmmakers choosing to collaborate with professional jazz musicians (who were not film scorers by trade) is too significant to be ignored. This then raises the question, What inspired these collaborations? Is there something about jazz musicians that particular "maverick" filmmakers find appealing, that more conventional studio filmmakers do not? I argue that yes, there is a common thread that permeates all the following case studies: *the directors' perceptions of jazz as a sonic indicator of "authenticity."* In the remainder of this introduction, I theorize this notion and its relationship to the specific jazz/film intersections examined in this book, culminating with an overview of two primary phenomena that undergird these collaborations between auteur filmmakers and jazz artists: ideological and aesthetic notions of "risk" in film production, and the sociological phenomenon of "creative labor." These themes permeate the specific case studies in the following chapters, functioning as frameworks that inform the jazz artists' integrations as part of the directors' go-to networks—their "inner circles."

AUTHENTICITY

A key thread that connects these disparate case studies is jazz's function as a signifier of "authenticity." Iñárritu, Rudolph, Lee, and Allen understand jazz as representative of the concept, albeit in different and very specific ways. For each respective director, jazz signifies "liveness," improvisation, Black experience, and/or raw human emotion. Accordingly, these filmmakers view jazz as a sonic vehicle for injecting authenticity into their films, hoping to utilize it as a means for connecting with their audiences on a more "genuine" level.

The term "authenticity" itself is a source of intellectual controversy. It is complex, polysemous, romanticized, and frankly impossible to define without a litany of qualifications and nuance. It is a notion that is constructed and can be faked, leading to suspicion about whether it is something that exists at all. J. L. Austin usefully recognizes it as a "dimension word," or—as Denis Dutton defines it—"a term whose meaning remains uncertain until we know what dimension of its reference is being talked about."[35] Its potential dimensional meanings are manifold. I find philosopher Peter Kivy's breakdown of authenticity's five primary definitions to be particularly illustrative of these possible dimensions. In his seminal work *Authenticities* (1995), Kivy utilizes the Oxford English Dictionary to identify these definitions as follows:[36]

1. Of authority, authoritative. (Possessing original or inherent authority).
2. Original, firsthand, prototypical. (Opposed to copied.)
3. Really proceeding from its reputed source or author: of undisputed origin, genuine. (Opposed to counterfeit, forged).
4. Belonging to himself, own, proper.
5. Acting of itself, self-originated, automatic.

These diverse definitions illustrate the complexity and polysemy of the term, reinforcing Austin's claim that authenticity is dimensional, dependent on the contexts in which it is being employed and understood. While Kivy theorizes authenticity's functions and meanings in the context of historically informed practice in musical performance, these definitions can also be theorized in any artistic contexts—for our purposes, the usage of jazz in film production.

"Authenticity" is a term that arises frequently in both jazz and film discourse, however problematically. Jazz is entangled with the ideological recognition of authenticity as individual, autonomous creative expression, evidenced in jazz culture's self-identification around the art of improvisation. Influential works such as Paul Berliner's *Thinking in Jazz: The Infinite Art of Improvisation* (1994) and Ingrid Monson's *Saying Something: Jazz Improvisation and Interaction* (1996) reinforce the primacy of this value among jazz's practitioners and critics. Improvisation has often functioned as a "requirement" for inclusion in jazz circles, operating as an ideological parameter by which jazz's gatekeepers have enforced its boundaries. The historical controversies surrounding jazz and its margins (e.g., the "moldy figs" vs. modernists, neoclassicism vs. fusion or avant-garde jazz) feature improvisation and its attendant associations with "authenticity" wielded as ideological weapons in the fight for cultural authority.[37]

Jazz authenticity discourse has also centered on the topic of race. Frank A. Salamone argued, "Throughout jazz history, the concept of 'Africa' has served as an index of authenticity."[38] Scott DeVeaux has further maintained that ethnicity is one of the most significant factors in jazz's historiographical construction, averring, "Jazz is strongly identified with African-American culture, both in the narrow sense that its particular techniques ultimately derive from black American folk traditions, and in the broader sense that it is expressive of, and uniquely rooted in, the experience of black Americans."[39] This association was congressionally legitimized through the Jazz Preservation Act (1987), which declared jazz a "rare and valuable national American treasure," "bringing to this country and the world a uniquely American musical synthesis and culture through the African-American experience."[40] The blues, a distinctly Black American folk tradition, has played a primary role in this authenticity discourse, as evidenced in the writings of Ralph Ellison, Amiri Baraka, and Albert Murray. The recognition of jazz as the sonic expression of authentic Black experience further formed the ideological basis of the development of styles such as bebop, avant-garde jazz (or New Black Music, as branded by Baraka), and the Black nationalist works of artists such as Charles Mingus, Max Roach, Abbey Lincoln, and Archie Shepp.[41] And while it certainly cannot be denied that non-Black artists have significantly contributed to jazz's growth and development (pointedly addressed in the writings of Gene Lees and Randy Sandke),[42] the recognition of jazz as an authentically Black music remains prominent in jazz discourse.

Authenticity discourse has also permeated the field of film production, albeit in different ways. The film industry is first and foremost a commercial industry. Its claims to authenticity are marketing devices, utilized to capture audiences' interests. Films are inherently an illusory medium; they are con-trived representations of reality. Filmmakers attempt to achieve perceived authenticity by utilizing historically or situationally appropriate settings, props, and music, as well as projecting "realistic" scenarios and emotional scenes, attempting to facilitate empathy and personal connection from their audiences.[43] This latter impetus drove the Stanislavsky-inspired approach to Method Acting, a technique that demands an actor's complete emotional and psychological identification with their character, with the intent of deliver-ing dynamic, emotionally expressive scenes, and appearing "genuine" or "authentic" to viewers. Despite controversy regarding the dangers of such psychological immersion, this approach has undergirded dramatic film act-ing techniques since the mid-twentieth century.[44]

These diverse conceptions of authenticity affirm the dimensionality of the construct. Filmmakers and jazz artists alike continually negotiate these potential meanings in their artistic work. In the following chapters, I examine specifically how certain filmmakers' perceptions of the relationships between authenticity and jazz shape their film productions. Iñárritu, Rudolph, Lee, and Allen all seek to represent authenticity in their films through jazz, drawing on the previously discussed authenticity discourse and cultural perceptions. As I stated before, whether or not jazz audiences perceive the music in these films to be "authentic jazz" is beside the point. These filmmakers ideologically view jazz as representative of authenticity in and of itself, thus envisioning the music (and respectively, the jazz artist creating it) as an essential component of the film's message and meaning. It is these viewpoints that led each of them to hire a professional jazz musician to score their films. It is also this association, as I argue, that influenced the significant amount of creative liberty the filmmakers gave to these jazz artists during the film's production. In the remaining sections of this introduction, I theorize how these filmmakers' employments of production risk and facilitation of "creative labor" stemmed from their perceptions of jazz as reflective of innate human authenticity—of genuine human expression—regardless of whether or not "authenticity" actually exists.

RISK

Any study of culture industry production demands an engagement with the fields of business and economics. The film industry exists within a capitalist economy, and therefore all its production decisions are tied to the industry's commercial imperatives. While filmmaking is an artistic endeavor, innovation can also be risky. Filmmakers are aware of this tension. Martin Scorsese once described the internal struggle he faced as a filmmaker at the nexus of the mainstream and the vanguard, frequently asking himself, "How much can I get away with [while remaining commercially successful]?"[45]

Risk is an aesthetic construction, rooted in culturally constituted beliefs about what "works" or "doesn't work" in film. At any given time, the accepted conventions and attitudes of the film industry determine the dominant risk discourse, which in turn shapes further practice.[46] I contend that the film industry's general risk aversion greatly informs its production decisions, and affects the ways jazz has been (or has not been) utilized in film soundtracks. On this topic I have benefited greatly from the limited scholarship that addresses the economic and business aspects of film production. These texts include film scholar Mette Hjort's collected volume entitled *Film and Risk* (2012), economists John Sedgwick and Michael Pokorny's edited collection *An Economic History of Film* (2005), and film scholar Jeff Smith's *The Sounds of Commerce: Marketing Popular Film Music* (1998). Each of these resources considers, through a variety of approaches, how economic considerations influence the decision-making processes of the film industry.

Within this context jazz is especially risky. First, it has a long history of associational codifications in film, dating back to the 1950s. Whether functioning as a musical synecdoche for crime/urban decay, sexuality, Blackness, or urban sophistication, jazz styles hold specific (if specious or outdated) meanings for filmmakers and industry executives. Often these meanings position jazz as a sonic "other" within the narrative—exoticized, sexualized, racialized, and used to draw overt attention to itself and the associations it is meant to exploit.[47] Jazz's sonic signifiers in film have become integrated into the industry's catalog of conventional formulas, much as other musical genres exemplify other ethno-stereotyping (e.g., bagpipes for Scots, drums for Native Americans, mariachi brass for Mexicans). Simon Frith describes such generic conventions as "musical shorthand," cultural codes that inform the semiotic dimensions of the film score.[48]

The semiotic significance of such "shorthand" has thus been limiting for jazz in film. Filmmakers and audiences associate the music with such connotations, thus any unconventional usage of jazz is risky, as it works against them. In many cases it is also the seeming outdatedness of these connotations that leads to jazz's unattractiveness among filmmakers. Accordingly, I posit that studios and filmmaking executives who accept jazz's preestablished cinematic codes are often reluctant to utilize jazz-influenced scores or soundtracks in nonstereotypical or unconventional ways, or indeed at all. Composer/saxophonist Bill Kirchner shares these views: "I think directors are squeamish [about using jazz in their films] . . . unless you have a director who's a big jazz fan . . . when you get something like that, someone [who] is willing to take risks. . . . But you've got to have filmmakers who are willing to do that. It takes an exceptional director to want to take that kind of risk."[49]

Improvisation—perhaps jazz's defining feature—poses a significant threat to typical film score production. Improvised scores are the rarest form of jazz scores in cinematic history, and I contend that this relates to the filmmakers' perceived lack of control over the score's production. Conventionally, film composers write out music to fit short segments of film and "demo" the score for the filmmakers in advance. Such preapproval is not possible for improvised scores. Improvisation is spontaneous. It is not written out and rehearsed ahead of time. It relies on an aggregate of "in-the-moment" influences that make it difficult to interpret the outcome. If "messed up," it costs time and money to be redone. All these elements of uncertainty can be unsettling for filmmakers, whose investment in the success of the film often leads them to want to maintain as much awareness of the production features of their films as possible. Those examples in which improvised jazz scores are utilized in movies are perhaps the most fascinating case studies of jazz artists' work in film, as they represent a very unconventional production approach—and for many, a very risky one.

At one time, namely, "the golden era" of the 1950s–1960s, jazz scores were relatively popular. Their proliferation in a number of French New Wave films soon extended to the US, manifesting in an abundance of film noir productions throughout the 1950s, and significantly informing the "crime jazz" soundtracks that dominated 1960s productions such as *The Pink Panther*, the James Bond franchise, and television series such as *Peter Gunn* and *Mission: Impossible*. This is not the case anymore. Jazz does not hold the same moorings in popular culture that it did sixty years ago; therefore, many filmmakers believe that jazz-influenced scores are not valuable in contemporary cinema. They fear that jazz's semiotic "outdatedness" poses aesthetic risk, lacking engagement for contemporary audiences. This fear is inherently tied to fear of economic risk, for if a film's techniques are not believed to be ideologically successful, the implication is that the film will not be commercially successful overall.

It is in this proliferation of risk discourse in film that the significance of the aforementioned "maverick" filmmakers becomes evident. Working outside the typical conventions and expectations of the industry, these filmmakers are inherently much greater risk takers than the majority of integrated industry professionals. Their statuses as experimental innovators who break out of the mold (with the resources to do so) provide them the opportunity to challenge aesthetic conventions. For these directors, jazz offers possibilities for experimentation and improvisation, for pushing film production in new creative directions. Overall, assessing these filmmakers' strategic employments of jazz soundtracks within the risk-averse, highly conventional milieu of the film industry challenges us to consider the potential ways that jazz in contemporary cinema can be revolutionary, transforming how movie music can be made and understood.

CREATIVE LABOR

For many jazz critics, artists' authorial control may seem to be significantly diminished in film score work. A composer of a film score is hired with the understanding that their work must serve the film narrative and must ultimately meet the filmmakers' expectations. These constraints are inevitably limiting, subordinating the artists' own authorial intentions and creative ideas. Such circumstances potentially facilitate an artist's creative separation from their own work, a phenomenon that Marx theorizes as "alienation" in modern industrial production.[50] Robert Blauner contends that "alienation exists when workers are unable to control their immediate work processes

. . . and when they fail to become involved in the activity of work as a mode of personal expression."[51] Yet in many cases, particularly in culture industry production, artistic workers' labor is not nearly as industry controlled as some critics might have you believe.

Creative agency is a necessary component of effective film scoring. Indeed, it is often for their creativity that culture industry personnel such as film scorers are hired. Film scoring takes place within an industry; but as scholars David Hesmondhalgh, Bill Ryan, Robert Faulkner, and John L. Sullivan have contended, workers in the culture industry experience greater autonomy in their work than industry laborers, given the importance of original and creative products in market success. Film composers necessarily work within industry expectations, but their work is nevertheless creative, and creativity is rewarded. As Robert Faulkner claims, "Hollywood demands both working according to conventions and working according to one's top expertise."[52] While film composers must create music that meets the filmmakers' expectations (particularly with regard to supporting the visual narrative), these artists still employ their own musical knowledge, experiences, and creative insight.

Therefore, throughout the following chapters, I characterize jazz artists' work in film as "creative labor" (borrowing the term from Hesmondhalgh and Baker)[53]—work that is contained by structural and executive expectations but also allows for experimentation and personal musical development. This is a view that places artistic labor within a sociological framework. My treatment of the term "creative," or "creativity," refers to an individual's self-directed transformation of available ideas and materials into a unique artistic product. Jason Toynbee's theorization of musical creativity among popular musicians parallels my conceptualization.[54] Toynbee reads creativity through the lens of Bourdieusian concepts of habitus, field, and positionality, arguing that musicians make creative decisions based on numerous structured "possibles." Their own authorial voices shape musical products within the structures of the social field at large, a formula he identifies as "social authorship." Toynbee states, "The social author stands at the center of a radius of creativity, but the range and scale of voices available to him/her/them will always be strongly determined by the compass and position of the radius on the musical field."[55] Thus, he insists that popular musicians retain "institutional autonomy," the space for creative production within institutional structures.

The term "creative labor" itself theorizes the balance of creative agency and subservient labor inherent in all culture industry work, informed by the tense balance of art and commerce that characterizes the industries themselves. I found Matt Stahl's *Unfree Masters: Recording Artists and the Politics of Work* to be a particularly useful framework for thinking about this balance. Stahl utilizes the term "creative worker" to conceptualize the positions of recording artists in our present-day working, neoliberal society, examining the tensions between their relative autonomy as artists and subordination as the objects of industry control.[56] In my own readings of jazz/film collaborations, I acknowledge the inherent tensions and contradictions that characterize this balance, while recognizing the musicians' own artistic agency and creative (or ideological) development in the process.

I investigate this "creative labor" by engaging directly with the musicians themselves, examining the dynamics informing the development of their jazz soundtracks through the lenses of both film industry expectations (including directorial control) and the jazz artists' own artistic and aesthetic preferences and decisions. In so doing, I analyze their works while engaging with the connections of the scores to the on-screen narrative, the music's own unique artistic merits separate from the films, and its broader recognition within jazz culture. Finally, I integrate my analyses of these artists' creative labor with a consideration of how their work relates to and reinforces concepts of "authenticity" in the films' production and reception.

THE CHAPTERS

Chapter 1, "When Strangers Meet: Structures, Tensions, and Negotiations in Jazz/Film Collaborations," invites the reader behind the screen/stage. It juxtaposes the traditional hierarchies, structures, and methods of film production with those of jazz performance, considering the complex negotiations that must take place in jazz/film collaborations. What adjustments/ sacrifices are made? Who has the power to make the final decisions? These analyses engage the topics of industry risk, authenticity, and creative labor, while laying the groundwork for the in-depth case studies that follow in the remaining chapters.

Chapter 2, "'Not a Lot of People Would Go for That': Risk and Experimentation in the Improvised Soundtracks of *Birdman* and *Afterglow*," investigates the rarest form of film soundtrack: the improvised score. It goes behind the scenes of two very different improvised soundtrack productions: Antonio Sánchez's percussion score for Alejandro González Iñárritu's *Birdman* (2014), and Mark Isham's small-group jazz score for Alan Rudolph's *Afterglow* (1997). In both examples, the directors associate improvisation with the authenticity of "real life" (i.e., improvising one's way through it), therefore explicitly choosing improvising jazz musicians to create soundtracks that sonically evoke the "authentic experience" they attempt to feature in their films. Reading against the concept of filmmaking risk, I illustrate how these scores' production methods significantly uprooted conventional film-scoring practices, generating rare opportunities for the film composers' creative agency.

Chapter 3, "'Honest, True Portrayals': Terence Blanchard, Spike Lee, and the Racial Politics of Jazz Scoring," provides an in-depth look at the ongoing collaboration between filmmaker Spike Lee and jazz trumpeter Terence Blanchard. It situates their relationship at the intersections of shared sociopolitical ideologies and a committed understanding of jazz as representative of authentic Black experience and creativity. I provide close readings of several of their film projects, including *Mo' Better Blues* (1990), *Malcolm X* (1992), and *When the Levees Broke: A Requiem in Four Acts* (2006), as well as Blanchard's own extended creative projects based on the film scores. Blanchard's unique melding of classical film score elements with jazz styles shapes the underlying political and social meanings of Lee's films, while also exhibiting Blanchard's own personal values.

Chapter 4, "A Film Director's Dream: Dick Hyman Plays the Personal for Woody Allen," investigates a different type of jazz score: the compilation soundtrack, featuring historic and recent recordings of early jazz and swing. Examining jazz pianist Dick Hyman's ongoing collaborative relationship with filmmaker Woody Allen, I elucidate how jazz is highly personal for Allen, functioning as the sonic vehicle through which he expresses nostalgia, idealism, and escapism. Allen views jazz as representative of authentic human experiences and emotions (e.g., love, sexual angst) that transcend time. Whether his films are set in 1920 or 1980, they feature Hyman's contemporary, historically informed performances of early jazz styles. As I argue, musical anachronism in these soundtracks, rather than undermining authenticity, is designed to evoke it.

The conclusion, "Miles Ahead: A New Way of Making Movie Music?" addresses the recent increase in jazz-related films within the last five years, theorizing this resurgence within the contexts of cultural ideology and jazz's broader meanings in contemporary society. I address how the book's case studies provide innovative models for transformative developments in the intersections between music and film, positioning these works in dialogue with recent advents in experimental film scoring (e.g., *There Will Be Blood* [2007], *The Social Network* [2010], *Dunkirk* [2017]), technology, and inter-arts/media collaborations. Finally, I posit these case studies' larger implications for jazz culture as a whole, addressing jazz's potentialities for dynamic, inter-arts collaborations, stylistic developments and transformations, and growth, influence, and longevity within our present, media-dominated age (an era that has seen dramatic changes in both the film and music industries due to the COVID-19 pandemic). Ultimately, this conclusion challenges readers to understand film soundtracks as the unique products of dynamic, creative collaborations that are situated within their historical, cultural, ideological, and aesthetic contexts. Jazz—an ever-changing music with a rich, complex history shaped by individual improvisation, collaboration, race, technology, and social change—is uniquely situated to navigate and stimulate transformations in media music as we enter the third decade of the twenty-first century.

Chapter 1

WHEN STRANGERS MEET

STRUCTURES, TENSIONS, AND NEGOTIATIONS IN JAZZ/FILM COLLABORATIONS

Generally, music (jazz, for our purposes) and film operate in very different economic and artistic spheres. Sociologist Howard Becker's concept of "art worlds" is useful for theorizing the structures, networks, collaborations, and negotiations that inform artistic production in both of these artistic fields. Art worlds are "[networks] of people whose cooperative activity, organized via their joint knowledge of conventional means of doing things, produces the kind of art works that the art world is noted for."[1] This chapter provides a behind-the-scenes look at the distinct structures, motivations, personnel, and methods of both the jazz and film worlds, addressing the unique negotiations that must occur in jazz-film collaborations.

The film art world is characterized by a system of executives, producers, and laborers cooperatively invested in the creation and mass distribution of movies. It is a multibillion-dollar worldwide industry with immense financial resources, comprising major and independent studios, as well as multinational umbrella corporations and production companies. The industry employs an "inner circle" of renowned filmmakers, peripheral independent filmmakers, and wide-ranging freelance support personnel, from directors to copyists, and from actors to recording musicians.

The vast majority of—if not all—production within the film industry is in service of developing commercially viable motion pictures. Because of the visual nature of the medium, filmmakers assert a hierarchy of the optical; much attention is paid to how production features such as camera angles, lighting, and set design—along with visually convincing acting, costuming, etc.—enhance the overall narrative. Nonvisual, postproduction features such as music and sound effects are considered decidedly ancillary (although helpful) to the work as a whole. Ultimately, the American film industry constitutes one of the most lucrative and internationally successful culture industries in the world, and many filmmakers' economic and artistic decisions are informed by a desire to maintain this status.

In contrast, the operations, networks, and methods of the jazz art world are distinct from those of film. Composed of a host of musicians, record producers, concert producers, critics, scholars, and fans, the jazz world exists as an eclectic yet small subset of the broader global music industry. According to Nielsen's 2019 U.S. Music Mid-Year Report, jazz accounts for only 1 percent of the total volume of music sales in the United States.[2] It does not have the same financial resources as the film industry, and it includes a limited number of jazz-specific media organizations (e.g., labels such as Blue Note, Verve, Impulse!, and Sunnyside; critical media such as *Downbeat* and *JazzTimes*). While operating within the music industry at large, jazz exists as its own sphere of artistic and economic negotiation. The boundaries of style, what constitutes jazz/not jazz, and what counts as innovative art are constantly in critical flux. To be fair, similar aesthetic and ideological debates occur within the film industry, but its immense commercial capital often leads to heightened assessments of economic risk, and an often-reduced flexibility (at least within mainstream studios) for stylistic experimentation.

The most significant contrast in production between the two art worlds— aside from the obvious difference in medium (optical vs. audial)—is jazz's propensity for and identification with the art of improvisation. The risk-aversive conservatism of the film industry results in high regulation of the majority of production aspects, including the musical score, which is predominantly written out and sent regularly to production executives for approval before being inserted into the finalized film. In jazz performance, however, spontaneous, individualized creativity within the production setting is encouraged and is generally considered to be a central feature of jazz itself. Given this fundamental methodological disjuncture (i.e., improvisation vs. risk-aversive regulation), it is not surprising that jazz has infrequently been utilized in film soundtracks throughout cinematic history. The paucity of this interaction is compounded by the incongruence of the two worlds' production and distribution networks; because the personnel in these networks rarely (if ever) overlap, film industry producers and executives often overlook jazz musicians in favor of composers and musicians within their established systems. Where these intersections do occur is generally in spite of the film industry's conventions.

It is these unique intersections that constitute the focus of this book. Only when influential film personnel (e.g., directors or producers) want jazz in their films do these collaborations occur. It is at these moments that the jazz and film art worlds intersect and interact. But what happens during these collaborations? What adjustments, compromises, and sacrifices are made? How much creative agency do the jazz artists have? How similar is the music to a "regular" jazz performance? Who makes the final decisions?

To successfully analyze jazz's presence in film production, one must acknowledge the hierarchical predominance of the filmmakers. There is not an equivalent balance of authority and influence; the filmmakers are in control. Directors, composers, arrangers, musicians, recording engineers, and editors (among others) all contribute to the finalized film. But the determination of who makes the final artistic calls relies on the socially accepted hierarchies of talent and expertise in the production of the given work. As will be delineated in the forthcoming section, there is a structured order of artistic weight granted to particular members of the film industry. The directors and producers are at the top of this structure; they make the final decisions.

That said, one must also acknowledge that filmmakers generally rely heavily on the artistic expertise of those they commission to produce their musical soundtracks, just as they do for other supporting production roles (e.g., writing, acting, set designing). As evidenced by the numerous Academy Award categories, the film industry recognizes the artistic contributions of sundry personnel, including actors, cinematographers, costume designers, sound editors, and composers (among many others). Many directors (and the film industry as a whole) realize that relative artistic freedom among their independent contractors can greatly influence the overall success of the film. As David Hesmondhalgh claims, "creative autonomy" is essential to cultural industry work because "autonomy itself is bound up with the interests of culture-industry businesses."[3] Such (relative) freedom is what allows creative workers to develop valuable cultural products, whereas restriction of these freedoms potentially impedes productivity.

As such, film-industry contractors such as composers and musicians occupy a paradoxical position in which they are simultaneously support laborers and independent artists. Their relationships to the industry "employers" (e.g., directors, producers, music supervisors) are not equal, and their production is both overseen and owned by the filmmaking executives. Not unlike recording artists (or any artists who create music "for hire")[4], (jazz) film composers and musicians must balance creative autonomy with industry expectations as delineated in their contracts. However, they may also be given significant liberties in the production process—the phenomenon introduced earlier as "creative labor." The jazz figures in the following chapters—Sánchez, Isham, Blanchard, and Hyman—have had particularly unique opportunities for creative liberty in their film works, for reasons I address below.

HIERARCHICAL STRUCTURE OF JAZZ/FILM COLLABORATIONS

Before delving into a more thorough analysis of the intersections between creativity and labor in jazz artists' film works, I want to first outline the general structure of personnel involved in these collaborations. This network is largely reflective of the hierarchical organization that characterizes the majority of filmmaking music departments; the distinguishing factor is that the composers/musicians are specifically *self-identified jazz artists*. I elucidate this structural network to illustrate how the intersections of creativity and labor in these artists' film works operate within a complex milieu of interpersonal and business transactions and relationships.

DIRECTOR/PRODUCER

At the hierarchical zenith of the jazz/film network is the producer or the director. (These positions are not mutually exclusive; there are several examples in which a single person has been both producer and director for a film project). A film producer is responsible for planning and coordinating various aspects of a film's production—from the early development stage through postproduction and marketing. Tasks may include selecting a screenplay writer and director, securing rights and financing, planning schedules and

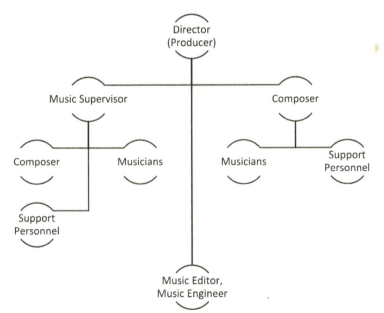

Figure 1.1. Hierarchical model of conventional network relationships in film music production.

budget, and consulting with directors, other creative personnel, and editors. Some films and television programs have multiple producers. In such cases the producers' roles vary in relation to their expertise.

For the purposes of a single film, producers are the industry executives; they are representative of the industry at large (although they also work within it). While the producers can be highly involved in the creative aspects of the film, in many cases they finance and oversee production, while creative control is the domain of the director. The majority of the cases examined in this book feature directors who produce their own films as well. In such cases, production decisions are economically and aesthetically tied to directorial decisions.

The director governs the making of the film, exerting control over many creative and dramatic aspects to produce a completed narrative. Directors are responsible for organizing the cast and crew, and overseeing all the elements of production, among them acting, costuming, music, and editing. According to the Directors Guild of America (DGA), a director "contributes to all creative elements relating to the making of a motion picture and participates in molding and integrating them into one dramatic and aesthetic whole."[5] Ultimately, directors are artistically responsible for the final outcomes of their films; they are the industry executives most directly involved with the day-to-day production aspects of the work. In film music production, either the director or the producer may choose to directly consult with the composer and/or the musicians to discuss their vision for the soundtrack. In some cases, the director/producer may contract a music supervisor to serve as a liaison for these negotiations.

MUSIC SUPERVISORS

In film music production, music supervisors are the next step below directors and producers. They are either chosen directly by the film's director, or their production company is hired, and they take on the supervisory role. The music supervisor is essentially the overseer of the music production, and the liaison between the director, the composers/musicians, and the music engineers and editors. According to film composers Fred Karlin and Rayburn Wright (whose brilliant volume *On the Track* provides a detailed, comprehensive guide to film scoring and navigating film industry structures), "the music executive [supervisor] is responsible for anything and everything having to do with music."[6] These duties might include creating budgets for projects and sessions, conducting preliminary discussions with filmmakers regarding what the music should entail, choosing music, seeking out and negotiating contracts with artists and contractors, attending screenings and spotting sessions, and fundamentally functioning as a liaison between the composer/musicians and the director. To illustrate, saxophonist and film recording artist Mark Lopeman stated, "[The music supervisors are] doing what the director wants them to do. The director is hiring them to essentially procure music for the film. And they can procure it various ways, and one of those ways is to get a soundtrack recording from us—and in another instance, one of those ways is for us to be on camera and play."[7] Renowned period-jazz performer Vince Giordano, who has recorded soundtracks for film and television programs such as *Boardwalk Empire* and *The Aviator*, claimed, "[The supervisor] has his tentacles out there all around, just to try to put it all together."[8] According to prolific recording engineer Stewart Lerman, "A lot of [a music supervisor's responsibility] involves licensing, and figuring out the copyrights and the publishing, as well as the creative side of it, which is picking the material."[9]

Many established music supervisors have a network of "go-to" people for specific tasks (e.g., composers, musicians, recording engineers, music editors); these are generally personnel they are familiar with and can rely on in order to accomplish their projects efficiently. For example, Vince Giordano and his group the Nighthawks have become the "go-to" ensemble for supervisors such as Randall Poster and Stewart Lerman whenever they are seeking music for period films set in the 1920s–1940s. (It is worth noting that Giordano's work in film provides another illustration of jazz as a sonic marker of "authenticity"—in this case, of historic time periods. While beyond the purview of this book [since I am focusing primarily on original jazz film scores and nondiegetic underscoring], Giordano's "historically informed" jazz performances in film and television provide another fascinating avenue for examining the collaborative intersections between jazz and visual media production—one that I intend to pursue in future work.) Dick Hyman—who has simultaneously worked as both music supervisor and composer on a number of Woody Allen's films (and whose work I consider in more detail in chapter 4)—had a select group of musicians that he contracted for many of his film soundtracks. As Robert Faulkner states, "The music contractor must be familiar with the talent available, know the individual skills of the musicians, understand the needs and desires of the composer and conductor, and, on the basis of his experience and bargaining power, hire the best musicians he can."[10] Certain projects might call for certain styles or types of artists more than others, so music supervisors are often in touch with an expansive network of artists to suit different filmmakers' soundtrack needs, as well as budget limitations.

COMPOSERS AND MUSICIANS

Composers and musicians are the specialists within this network and contribute the most substantially to the creation of the film music itself. When composers are hired, they are often brought on during the postproduction stage of the filmmaking process; the scenes have been shot, the dialogue has been recorded, and the film is being put together for the final cut. The composer can either be directly hired by the producer or director (as is the case in all of the following case studies in this book) or be hired by the production company/music supervisor. Contract decisions are informed by the employer's decision to pursue an original score, a compilation score (of previously made recordings), an adaptation score, or some combination of these. This decision determines whether a composer is needed, whether musicians are just needed to rerecord adaptations of songs, or whether the entire soundtrack can be licensed for rights of previous recordings without requiring composers or musicians.

Composers are responsible for writing music that fits specific, predetermined scenes. Often, the composer sits with the director and/or music supervisor in what is referred to as a "spotting session," watching rough cuts of the film to discuss where music should be placed, and what it should sound like. In some scenarios the composers are given musical frameworks on which to base their compositions (e.g., "we want this to sound like Wagner" or "this should sound like your previous work on [insert title])." Other times, composers are granted more extensive compositional freedom and expected to develop music to reflect the emotions, themes, or characters depicted in the films themselves.

Once demos have been approved, composers are then directly involved in the score recording process. In some cases the music supervisor will select the recording ensemble/musicians; in others the composer will choose, having written scores or cues with specific individual musicians in mind. All of the jazz artists discussed in the following chapters have selected their own musicians for their soundtrack recordings. Composer Mark Isham—who has worked on such jazz-based scores as *Romeo Is Bleeding, Afterglow,* and *The Black Dahlia*—stated, "The key to [score writing is that] you try to write for the musicians that you have. You kind of know what you want to achieve, and you cast it. I cast my scores."[11] Naturally the only way to successfully "cast" a score is to have a strong familiarity with the musicians' playing styles and capabilities. As such, these composers rely heavily on artists whom they have worked with before, or whose music they have listened to extensively. The composers develop their own "go-to" networks—just as the music supervisors do.

MUSIC ENGINEER AND MUSIC EDITOR

Two other key players in the film music production network are the music engineer and the music editor. The engineer is responsible for working with and manipulating the technical aspects of sound during the recording, mixing, and reproduction processes. The position is both creative and highly technical, encompassing such activities as balancing volume, adjusting sound fidelity, and so on. Producer, engineer, and mixer Phil Ek has described it as the "technical aspect of recording—the placing of microphones, the turning of pre-amp knobs, the setting of levels. The physical recording of any project is done by an engineer . . . the nuts and bolts."[12] Engineering mixers may do a number of different things, depending on the director's vision for the soundtrack, including overlaying various tracks on top of one another, "looping" tracks, and applying distortion (among many other) techniques. For example, engineers may use their technological expertise to "distress" recording fidelity, making music sound older and appropriate for period films or television programs. These are but a few examples of the possibilities in soundtrack engineering.

The music editor is responsible for compiling, editing, and syncing the music, as well as any other jobs that directly relate to the process of preparing the music to be laid into the film. The editor is in constant dialogue with the composer and music supervisor, as well as the director and the producer in some cases. Editors attend all spotting sessions and keep detailed notes of all music entrances and exits, as well as filmmakers' verbalized expectations of what the music should sound like. They are highly involved with the creation of the temp track,[13] as well as with dubbing after the music has been recorded. As Karlin and Wright describe:

> The job of the music editor is to provide spotting and timing notes for each cue when/as requested by the composer; prepare the videotape or digital video with visual aids such as punches, streamers, and any special click layouts that may be required to assist the conductor at the recording sessions; monitor the recording sessions; provide clicks and other conducting aids as necessary to ensure correct timings; prepare the music for dubbing; attend the final audio mix on the dubbing stage; assist in any adjustments or changes that may be requested at any stage; and keep detailed notes on the whole process.[14]

For film composers, the music editor is one of their most invaluable allies. It is the editor's detailed notes and active communication that allow the composer to write and record the "right" music for the scenes. Without the editor's assistance, the composer could be lost in the dark. The composer is also reliant on the editor for effectively fitting the music into the scenes (after dubbing). Editors favored by composers will try to fit/cut the music in aesthetically appropriate ways. However, unexpected issues can arise. For example, a film editor may cut a film scene three bars short, and the music editor must find a way to manipulate the music tracks to make them fit appropriately with the new scene length. Alternatively, a loud percussion hit or trumpet blast may overshadow an actor's speaking, necessitating editing so that the soundtrack prioritizes the dialogue. Some music editors make these adjustments more successfully than others in terms of musical cohesiveness. Jazz trumpeter and film composer Terence Blanchard (whose work is considered in more detail in chapter 3) offers high praise for music editor Marvin Morris, with whom he has worked on numerous Spike Lee film scores. Blanchard refers to Morris as "the gatekeeper" who makes concerted efforts to keep Blanchard's music as intact as possible.[15] Other editors are less attuned to the musicians' desires. When I asked Vince Giordano about his experiences working with music editors, he informed me that I had hit a very "sore point" and expressed the following:

> I'm very disappointed with some of the editing jobs that I have had to endure in my lifetime—because they're real butcher jobs. They don't make any sense. . . . It reminds me . . . when I was a young kid, they were having these horrific scientific experiments in Russia. They were transplanting dogs' heads. They were taking a German Shepherd and putting it on a Collie, and the Collie on the German Shepherd. And these dogs lived! But what the hell are you doing? What kind of animal is this, and how barbaric! Well, I feel the same way about the music editors. They just take out sections, and I'm like, my god! Yeah, the timing is right, but there's a better way to edit this! There's a better way to make a nice, clean feeling for the scene, versus chopping stuff like that. And I have no control over that, so I just have to say it's not my job, and I'm totally out of control.[16]

The editing process plays a significant role in the inherent tensions and negotiations between creativity and labor in jazz artists' work in film, which will be discussed in more detail later in this chapter.

SUPPORT POSITIONS AND TECHNOLOGY

Numerous support positions also constitute this broader network of film music personnel. One is the orchestrator position. This position is not always utilized; some composers do all their own orchestrating. Yet often composers who are especially busy with multiple projects will lay out basic concepts for their scores and send them to an orchestrator along with mockup audio cues of what the orchestration should sound like. For example, composer Mark Isham works frequently with orchestrator Brad Dechter—who has worked with him on such projects as *The Black Dahlia, The Mechanic, Warrior, The Conspirator, Mob City*, and *American Crime*. Isham sends Dechter an outline of his musical ideas (e.g., form, style, chords) in a Finale (music software notation) sketch, and Dechter fills in the score. Anything Dechter adds, however, he makes easy to take out in the Finale program, in case Isham wants to make changes.

Administrative support positions include secretaries, production assistants, copyists, financial managers, and systems operators for recording/timing programs (e.g., Auricle), among others. All contribute to the ultimate finished product of the film soundtrack. These support positions—while generally assumed to be more technical and interchangeable than the "artistic" positions of composer, music, engineer, etc.—are still integral to the completion of the finalized work. Allison Cantor—Mark Isham's assistant, who is also a film composer in her own right—is responsible for a range of necessary duties that help keep Isham's manifold film projects afloat, including (but not limited to): translating notes from music editors into overview documents that indicate all entrances and music lengths for a given project; handling email correspondence with contract agencies and other film personnel; sketching Finale files based on Isham's score ideas for distribution to orchestrators/arrangers; organizing and scheduling recording and editing sessions; and even writing score cues. Without the presence of thousands of support personnel like Allison, the music film industry would cease to exist.

Technology also plays a significant role in the film music support system. At times, it has even supplanted traditional support roles. Developments in score-notation systems such as Finale and Sibelius have reduced the need for copyists, as the music can just be printed directly from the notation program for each part. In addition, having scores saved on computers eliminates the need for complete reproductions of updated scores when changes must be made spur-of-the-moment during the film editing process. Sequencing and timing programs such as the Auricle Time Processor function as conducting aids by utilizing clicks and/or visual punches and streamers superimposed on video in order to help the composer synchronize the music with the film.[17] Such aids reduce the amount of time spent in the recording studio, by ideally reducing the need for multiple "takes" or rerecordings. The Auricle also fulfills several other functions, allowing tempi and meter manipulation to assist composers in quickly finding the preferred options for hitting cues. Such technology—along with similar programs such as the Streamline Music Scoring System and other sequencing programs—allows for quicker, more efficient score experimentation and correction. Audio workstations and production software (e.g., Logic Pro, Pro Tools, Vienna Ensemble Pro 5) have also dramatically influenced film scoring. These technologies allow composers to create demos (and sometimes full scores) without requiring live musicians. Therefore, these programs reduce expenses and logistics during the production process, as they eliminate the necessity for finding, hiring, and paying live musicians, as well as renting recording space and equipment.

All the aforementioned personnel (and technology) participate in the film art world, significantly contributing to and shaping the industry's extensive production.[18] As illustrated throughout this chapter, their relational structure is certainly hierarchical, yet it is also linearly collaborative. While those who occupy the higher hierarchical rungs give direction and reserve the right to approve and/or demand changes in production, they also can grant an extensive amount of autonomy and creative freedom to the contractors they have hired, relying on the contractors' own expertise to make creative decisions. The level of autonomy granted is greatly dependent on the contractor's reputation, combined with his/her relationships to the filmmaking executives. Both reputations and relationships are enhanced through network development—a key element in any film musician's career.

THE "INNER CIRCLE" AND NETWORKING

The value of networking within the film industry cannot be understated. As Robert Faulkner highlights, the majority of film-scoring opportunities are issued to a small coterie of renowned personnel who receive recurrent film-scoring gigs, surrounded by a semi-periphery of moderately active freelance composers, further surrounded by freelancers who have received only one or two (or no) scoring opportunities.[19] The film industry is composed of an "inner fraternity,"[20] which is built through reputation and industry connections, in which one hand washes the other. Reputations can be built slowly through accumulations of credits or can be established instantaneously—the product of a fortuitous moment of being in the right place at the right time. A composer's agent stated, "Sometimes ability is not enough. It's fate, luck, or personality. There are a million factors that go into who gets trapped and who breaks out."[21]

For most full-time freelance composers, "breaking out" into the inner circle of the film industry network is the primary career goal. Faulkner states, "The real targets of a career line are networks of work relationships: the 'social circles' of ties among employers that result in snowball effects or a credentialing again and again as a sought-after composer. It is the changing of those alignments among producers that is sought."[22] In his text *Hollywood Studio Musicians*, he further argues: "Breaking into the informal web of relations in the studios requires a combination of entrepreneurial zeal, aggressive self-advertisement, ability to handle interpersonal competition with grace and coolness, and performing talent."[23]

Unfortunately, many are not able to break into the inner circle. Networks— while valuable for some—can be exclusionary for others. For instance, such exclusivity is evident in the racial and gender dynamics of the film industry. The film art world and its networks are largely organized around the predominant statuses of whiteness and maleness. Studio systems are overwhelmingly headed by white, male executives, reflected in the racial makeup of the vast majority of producers and directors, as well as throughout the industry. UCLA's Division of Social Sciences' 2019 *Hollywood Diversity Report* revealed that people of color and women are largely underrepresented in every industry employment category (including leads, writers, and creators), constituting only about 12.6 percent of film directors.[24] Networks form and grow among personnel of common backgrounds and interests, resulting in the continued marginalization of workers from minority races, ethnicities, genders, or cultural backgrounds.

Accordingly, several directors of minority status who have attained executive power within the film industry have aggressively worked to facilitate new networks of minority personnel. For example, as I examine in chapter 3, director Spike Lee has actively provided opportunities and advocated for African American involvement in film industry production, to a point that he primarily hires black personnel. Similarly, Mexican director Alejandro Gonzalez Iñárritu has built up a go-to network of production collaborators who share his Mexican ethnicity. Filmmaker Ava DuVernay—presently the highest-grossing Black female director in box office history—has pointedly featured only women directors in her series "Queen Sugar," which airs on the Oprah Winfrey Network (OWN), asserting: "We can create spaces that nourish in our own image, in the same way that our male counterparts have created in their own image for over a century."[25] Recent ideological campaigns within Hollywood such as #OscarsSoWhite (launched in 2015) have demanded increased diversity in industry nominations and awards,[26] while statistical analysis of American film consumption reveals moviegoers' increasing preference for diverse film and television content (a likely result of America's increasingly diverse audiences as a whole).[27] While these recent movements might suggest that we may see increased diversity within Hollywood's upper echelon in the future, to date the "inner circles" of the film industry are still largely composed of white males, who are continually exerting their power and influence on the production decisions and labor allocations of the film industry at large.

Yet racial or cultural affiliation is only one factor in film industry network determinations. Nepotism runs deep. Think of the numerous "Hollywood royalty" families, whose prestige facilitated opportunities for their family members to score coveted industry positions: the Coppolas, the Barrymores, the Fondas, the Garland/Minnellis, the (Will and Jada Pinkett) Smiths, the Baldwins, the Newman/Woodwards, etc. Sometimes collaborations begin through shared experience, particularly during youth. Woody Allen and Dick Hyman established their relationship while being part of the same New York artistic scene. Director Damien Chazelle (*Whiplash, La La Land*) met his go-to composer, Justin Hurwitz, at Harvard University, where they had a pop band together (and collaborated on a senior thesis).[28] Many film networks are also established by reputation. Alan Rudolph hired Mark Isham after picking up and listening to one of his albums from the record store. Alejandro Gonzalez Iñárritu—who had a stint as a radio deejay in Mexico City—knew Antonio Sánchez's music from playing it on his radio programs.

In summary, the film industry is structured in a way that particular "inner circle" personnel have access to networks, job opportunities, and resources in ways that many "peripheral" workers do not. These networks are established at the intersection of a host of factors—reputation, race, connections, and sometimes simply being in the right place at the right time. Throughout the following chapters, I will examine how particular jazz artists attained these coveted inner-circle statuses, further theorizing the uniqueness of their experiences in relation to the vast number of jazz musicians who are not involved in film soundtrack production.

ART AND LABOR

The intersections of art and labor make up a preponderance of the present study. Film music production is commercial work that is simultaneously determined by industry expectations and desires, and composers' and musicians' artistic craft and innovation. Analyzing film music production through an "either-or" approach (i.e., either it is noninnovative, overdetermined work or innovative, individualized "art") is unproductive. The work develops at the nexus of the industry's conventional demands *and* artistic creation—with results varying from project to project. These forces are concurrently in tension and cooperative; without both the film project could not exist. Highlighting the necessity of both forces, Faulkner posits the following rhetorical questions:

> Hired hands—or artists? Are film composers subservient technicians skilled in working against time pressures and within worn commercial grooves, or independent creators able to balance the demands of commerce and creativity? Are they simple pawns in the television producer's master plan, or dedicated professionals who demonstrate their extraordinary range, stay away from "bad" work, and get the job done?—The commercial composer is all of these things.[29]

It is the cooperation of these intersections—art as labor and labor as art—that characterizes a film musician's career experiences. In this section I examine how both structured labor and creativity interact in film music production, highlighting the necessities of and tensions between employment subordination and expressive freedom. Yet I also argue that the "inner circle" of jazz artists involved in film score production are creative workers whose level of autonomy and independence often exceeds the liberties granted in typical employer/employee relationships. These artists' "creative labor" can complicate assumed culture-industry hierarchies, granting them democratic participation in the film production that is informed by a combination of the director/producer's investment in jazz music, the artists' musical expertise, and the music's pertinence to the film narrative.

ART AS LABOR

Ultimately, filmmakers are in business to make money. They contribute to a large film-making enterprise that Paul Hirsch characterizes as a culture industry—a "profit-seeking firm producing cultural products for national [and international] distribution . . . comprised of all organizations engaged in the process of filtering new products and ideas as they flow from 'creative' personnel in the technical subsystem to the managerial, institutional and societal levels of organization."[30] Standardization is common among culture industry distribution systems, born from a combination of convenience and audience expectations. All of the work that goes into the development of a culture industry artwork—for our purposes, a completed film—operates in service of commercial profit.

It is this bottom-line end goal—this art-as-business approach—that has often led to contentious stigmatization of film music within music criticism. This aligns with condemnations of "selling out" that, according to Faulkner, emphasize the notion "of sacrificing one's integrity for the pursuit of higher and quicker economic net returns."[31] Film work often pays well, in many cases better than orchestral or band side work, or freelance gigging and studio recording (with the exception of "star" performers). On this topic Mark Isham—who primarily established himself as a jazz trumpet player before becoming a film composer—confessed, "Obviously, in film composing I could do very, very well [financially]. I don't know of any jazz musician who could quite do this well, just in general."[32] It is not a mystery why composers and musicians are interested in taking these gigs, in terms of economic reward.

But the crux of the "sell-out" criticism attacks artists' creative dignity. As Herbert Gans contends:

> The criticism of the process of popular-culture creation breaks down into three charges: that mass culture is an industry organized for profit; that in order for this industry to be profitable, it must create a homogeneous and standardized product that appeals to a mass audience; and that this requires a process in which the industry transforms the creator into a worker on a mass production assembly line, where he gives up the individual expression of his own skills and values.[33]

The assumption that film artists "give up [their] individual expression" derives from the subservience of their artistic product to the filmmakers' desires. Composer John Corigliano claims, "[Many critics'] image of the film composer is that of a sellout to his art, because he's composing for money in a sense and to someone else's order."[34] Such criticism may be especially prominent among jazz critics, who are inclined to laud jazz for its innovative, avant-garde qualities, and relative freedom from industry expectation or control. These criticisms reflect a strong suspicion of mass culture, grounded in the idealization of individual creative expression, rather than popular accessibility. Within jazz criticism, jazz's authenticity has been assessed at the nexus of ideas about race, class, gender, culture, art, and commerce—where commercial viability has often been debated as a "mark of illegitimacy."[35] Throughout jazz history, a diverse range of prominent artists including Duke Ellington, Herbie Hancock, Miles Davis, Branford Marsalis, and numerous others have been accused of "selling out" as their styles transformed and incorporated mainstream musical influences (e.g., rock and roll, funk, electronic music, pop). In the later twentieth century, jazz "fusion" met with particular animosity in certain circles, vilified for adulterating "pure" jazz by blending with popular music styles. It stands to reason, then, that jazz film music—a genre in which jazz artists' personal expression is significantly shaped and limited in service of a commercial product—might be similarly condemned.

These concerns are not unfounded. Film composers are first and foremost hired as part of a labor organization whose primary function is to contribute to the production of the finalized film according to executives' expectations. They are certainly creating "to someone else's order." While the film musician contributes greatly to the finalized product, he or she is rarely indispensable. As Faulkner described, "The tensions of dealing with business and art simultaneously are particularly severe. . . . Any attempt to fight the contradictions of commercial work—part commerce and part art and craft—results in another colleague getting the assignment, credit 'point', and work connection."[36] Film historian Gergely Hubai's *Torn Music: Rejected Film Scores, a Selected History* offers a fascinating study of the variety of tensions that have led to film scores being disregarded, and the scorers being replaced, including miscommunication, art/commerce clashes, and aesthetic conflict.[37] Accordingly, composers must carefully balance their aesthetic desires against the demands of the industry. Once hired, the film composer is hardly given "free rein," so to speak. Working in cooperation with directors, music supervisors, and editors, composers must negotiate their own creativity with a number of business decisions and expectations, including budget, timeline, and editing (both expected and unexpected).

BUDGETING

Before any soundtrack production can happen, the music budget for a film must be discussed and delineated. In general, the total music budget is worked out by the music supervisor, once he or she has looked at the scripts and been in touch with the filmmaking executives (e.g., producer and/or director). In many cases, the budget decision is made well in advance of any decisions about composers or musicians, because the budget will determine who can be afforded. The factors to consider in determining budget are typically: size and makeup of orchestra; amount (in minutes) of music; amount of extra studio time for prerecording, song recording, and postmixing; difficulty of music (i.e., time to record); and instrumentation. In terms of personnel, the supervisor must also consider expenses for specific composers and/or musicians; obviously, more-in-demand artists will generally have higher fees. Composers who utilize orchestrators will cost more overall, as fees must be paid to multiple people. Utilizing union or non-union musicians must be taken into account. Union musicians, while generally more reliable in terms of professionalism and efficiency, also require specific union pay scales, regulated break times, and benefits (pension, health and welfare, etc.).[38] For soundtracks that require licensing of original tunes, the process can take on considerable expense.[39] Support personnel must also be paid: copyists, assistants, people carting/transporting instruments, etc. All these potential expenses must be taken into account by the music supervisor when determining how to allocate funds and which composers/musicians to hire for the gig. As composer Dick Hyman maintains, "All [these factors] directly affect the kind of music, and the specific music you would use."[40]

Once the budget has been determined, the personnel hired, licensing arranged, and the production put in motion, steps are still constantly taken to mitigate extra expenditure of funds. Recording musicians are expected to be able to essentially perfectly sight-read their parts in a recording session; extra rehearsal or rerecording means more time in the recording studio, which means more cost to the music department. Instrumentalists are also hired only when they are needed. If the strings and the brass are to be recorded separately, they will likely be recorded on separate days, to avoid unnecessary downtime where instrumentalists are being paid but not playing.

SCHEDULE/TIMELINE

Time constraints are one of the biggest burdens for film soundtrack musicians. As score production is often one of the last phases of the film project, filmmakers are notorious for bringing the composers and musicians on board at the last minute. As Karlin and Wright describe, "Because music is the last element in the production chain, the composer's time gets cut short: he is often not given the final cut when promised, while the delivery date remains unchanged or in some cases may be moved forward."[41] They further state, "Everyone agrees that to be a film composer you must be a fast writer and have the physical stamina to work under extreme pressure and still continue to write music for many days with inadequate sleep."[42] Musical artists are usually given anywhere between a couple of months to a mere week to spot the film, come up with concepts, write the music, and record it. One of the shortest time frames for a major motion picture was Graeme Revell's score for *Lara Croft: Tomb Raider* (2001), which was completed in six days.[43] For many artists, such time constraints might impede creativity, as the artists aren't afforded much time to brainstorm, experiment, and edit. Vince Giordano expressed his frustrations in the following comments:

> I think there's a very unrealistic idea in the film industry about how long it takes to do something. To them, it's like making toast—you just put the bread in there and in two minutes, it's done! Or like choosing different tracks on a CD player—I want track 13, I want track 16. And to be very exacting—it takes time! It's like preparing a meal. And to use another food [analogy]—you take a bowl of lettuce, and it's very edible, but there's nothing very special about it. And I try to tell these folks that you can give me three hours or four hours to just come up with music, but I'm just going to show up with a bowl of lettuce. It's edible, but it's not going to be great. If you gave me more time, I'd be able to cut some tomatoes, and put some olive oil, and some little things in it, and present you with this beautiful salad that's very substantial, and a lot more fun than the bowl of lettuce. [The filmmakers say:] "Well, we're going to pay you!" No, that's not the issue—the money is not the issue—it's what I'm trying to do for you, and [I] need time. You need time to do this.[44]

There is no doubt that allowing more time for creativity, experimentation, and editing would likely enhance the overall product. Yet it is also an expected part of the business that in some cases can influence creativity in unexpected ways. Terence Blanchard acknowledges that such a limited time frame significantly influences his creative process—positively as well as negatively. He contended, "It influences me greatly because I don't have time to sit down and ponder . . . the decision. You've got to make a choice and stick with it. So I think in a weird way it makes you concentrate a little more. It makes me at least make sure that I've dotted every "i" and crossed every "t." . . . It's taxing, but it makes me more conscientious—more aware of where I'm going, because I don't have time to make any mistakes and go back and correct any mistakes."[45] These constraints are not unlike songwriting and album deadlines (for recording artists) or publication deadlines (for writers); they are ostensibly very limiting, but there is also an expectation that the artist can work creatively within these constraints. Whether or not they do so, or whether they might have been more successful with more time, is debatable on a case-by-case basis.

I must also draw attention to the fact that these short timelines are not universal. While in general many directors wait until they have a final cut of the film to start reaching out to the music supervisor about soundtrack details, there are always exceptions. Several of the case studies I examine in this book highlight scenarios in which the filmmakers are actively involved with the composers during (or even before!) the shooting process. Blanchard reveals that Spike Lee—with whom he has collaborated on numerous films— is very involved in discussing musical concepts with him throughout filming: "Spike is a dude that is really involved in [the music] process while he's shooting."[46] Composer/pianist Dick Hyman shared a similar level of collaboration with director Woody Allen, who conceptualized the music for his films from the early developmental and preproduction stages. In Antonio Sánchez's work on the *Birdman* soundtrack (examined in more detail in chapter 2), he collaborated with director Alejandro González Iñárritu during preproduction, recording the majority of the film's soundtrack prior to filming. In each of these examples, the filmmakers demonstrated a strong investment in the music itself as essential to the film's meaning. As I have argued and explore more in depth in the following chapters, they understood the jazz soundtrack as representative of authenticity, and integral to their film narratives. As such, they hired their composers as artistic collaborators early in the filming process, rather than as last-minute postproduction creative personnel.

EDITING

The editorial process in film soundtrack production is both highly necessary and potentially highly contentious. The composer does not have final say in how his music is utilized in the final cut of the film. Karlin and Wright state, "It should be stressed here that no composer, no matter how prestigious or how great his track record, is ever contractually granted the right of final decision as to whether his music is used in a film, or in what manner."[47] Composer John Corigliano stated, "They can take your music out, they can put it in other places, they can cut it up, [and] they can add sounds to it."[48] Renowned film composer Henry Mancini once decried that "many a composer's heart is broken in the dubbing room. Sometimes music is severely subdued or cut out entirely. Sometimes it is used under scenes it was not intended for. Cries of 'How can they do this to my music?' have been heard. 'They' [the filmmakers] can, and 'they' do."[49]

Once the music has been recorded, it is spliced/cut/manipulated to fit within the soundtrack, integrated with (and often subservient to) dialogue and additional sound effects. The editing stage is completed by music editors, though their decisions are primarily influenced by the preferences of the music supervisor, who is in conversation with the director and/or producer.

Ideally, the music editor will have been in close communication with these filmmaking executives from early on in the filming process and will have detailed guidance regarding timing lengths and music expectations for particular scenes, to avoid excess recording or unnecessary editing/recording manipulation. Composers are paid to write for the film; it is in the filmmakers' best interests to give them the information they need to make that happen with as little waste of resources as possible. However, changes to the film are constantly being made, and this can often result in scene changes that require unexpected editing of the soundtrack recording. In some cases the resultant editing is less than musically desirable, being cut or spliced in the middle of phrases or even measures. Mark Lopeman—a saxophonist who has performed on numerous film and television soundtracks with Vince Giordano's Nighthawks (including *The Aviator* [2004], *Boardwalk Empire* [2010–14], and the *Marvelous Mrs. Maisel* [2017–18])—revealed that some editing jobs result in "cutting things so that bars are spliced together and not complete, or that the harmony doesn't work out or make any sense anymore."[50]

With artists like Lopeman—who record song adaptations that are also released separately on compiled soundtracks—editing is absolutely necessary. Entire songs are rarely played in the films/television programs they support; however, recording artists are generally expected to record whole tunes for later soundtrack release. As such, the recordings are chopped/edited to fit into given scenes of varying length. Again, this is not always the case for composers, who generally write to fit given time specifications. Yet as indicated above, these specifications are rarely set in stone. Composers are faced with having moments removed that helped fulfill a musical statement, with whole or partial phrases and sections being eliminated. I do not intend to suggest that all music editing jobs are insensitive to the musical work; many editors take great care in making sure the results are musically appropriate. Instead, I address these complications to highlight the conventionally subservient role of music in film production, and the challenges that many soundtrack artists face.

MUSIC RIGHTS

As in any artistic domain, the artists' rights to their music are an important factor—one that varies from project to project. All film music products fit into the 1976 Copyright Act definition of work-for-hire, in which intellectual property of a direct employee or specially commissioned independent contractor is owned by the employer/producer.[51] As Matt Stahl articulates, "Work for hire splits author from creator: if an employee creates a work, then in the absence of a contract to the contrary, work for hire alienates the work from the employee-creator. The employee is the employer's instrument or medium of creation, the work is the employer's: the employer is the author and owner."[52]

The intellectual property rights owned by the producer include all rights of recording, performance, and music publishing. Vince Giordano confirmed his work-for-hire status in his contract with *Boardwalk Empire*, informing me that he has no rights to the music that he and the Nighthawks record for the soundtrack. He stated, "With HBO it's all buy-out. They own everything, and they can do anything they want with it."[53] As an illustration of the producer's all-encompassing rights, Giordano revealed that he has not been able to produce albums that include any of the tracks from the *Boardwalk* recording sessions.[54] Evidently there are many recordings from these sessions that were not released in the three soundtrack volumes that were issued. That music is now stored somewhere in HBO executives' files, and only they can determine what happens to it. Giordano is interested in the music, but he legally has no rights to it.

Composers/musicians for film soundtracks may receive royalties, which fall under a number of categories. These include printed editions, piano copies, foreign printed editions, mechanical license receipts of the original publisher, and, when negotiated, recording artist royalties on sales of soundtrack recordings.[55] In some cases royalties can be very small (Giordano informed me that he once received a royalty check for thirty-two cents); other times they can be more substantial, depending on the success of the sales and the royalty negotiations in place.

LABOR AS ART

To dismiss film music-making as an artistic endeavor solely because of its subordinate role in film is as naive and uncritical as disregarding books that must meet publishers' expectations or albums that must meet record companies' expectations. Film music artists always have choices. It is for their ability to make these artistic choices and decisions that they have been hired. Certainly, these artistic choices operate within the hierarchies and conventions of the established industry; whether they are conventional, risky, innovative, and successful or unsuccessful depends on unique case-by-case scenarios in which all these art world factors are at play.

The assessment of such risks and values continually informs composers' daily decisions and may vary greatly from experience to experience. Ultimately a composer's decision must result in compromise. While "compromise" is generally pejoratively construed, I argue that it can also be a positively valenced term. Faulkner positively reframes compromise's significance in film industry work: "It is all too easy to see such compromise as a lowering of the standards and values the composer begins with, but such a view is usually an inaccurate cliché. The compromise a film composer must achieve is not the result of a process of weakening but of strengthening his own craft—his talent and his ability to function in the Hollywood scene—to balance conflicting demands."[56]

I would like to take Faulkner's comment a step further and suggest that such compromise may also result in the strengthening of a composer's own compositional creativity. Even within conventional limitations—or even because of them—composers can be challenged to develop musically interesting ways of influencing audience emotion. In my numerous interviews with film composers, they have stressed that the primary goal of film composition is to capture the audience's emotions and imaginations in service of the narrative. While Hollywood conventions have established certain sonic signifiers for particular emotional meanings (e.g., lush, melodic strings for romance), such conventions do not necessarily preclude other musical approaches. There may be several possible methods for scoring romance, fear, anger, or nostalgia. For example, both John Williams's repetitive half-step motif for *Jaws* (1975) and Stephen Price's intensely layered electronic score for *Gravity* (2014) sonically evoke suspense in uniquely different and effective ways. Therefore, the compromises that result in the process of commercial film scoring are not all relinquishments of artistic agency (although this can happen at times), but rather complex negotiations of interests and talents in service of the work. This provides a challenge to mass-culture criticism that views culture industry work as solely alienated labor, instead providing an alternative understanding of labor that is simultaneously regulated and individually creative.

In the following chapters, I highlight how particular jazz artists' involvement in soundtracks demonstrates this phenomenon of "creative labor" within the film industry and further contributes to our expanded understanding of film music composition as an active site of creativity, ideology, and collaborative negotiation. By examining these artists' works at the nexus of creative autonomy and industry regulation, I illustrate how jazz/film integrations can be simultaneously hierarchical and collaboratively transformative. It is to these case studies that I now turn.

Chapter 2

"NOT A LOT OF PEOPLE WOULD GO FOR THAT"

RISK AND EXPERIMENTATION IN THE IMPROVISED SOUNDTRACKS OF BIRDMAN *AND* AFTERGLOW

On December 4, 1957, Miles Davis made cinema soundtrack history. At Le Poste Parisien studio in Paris—along with musicians Kenny Clarke, Pierre Michelot, René Urtreger, and Barney Wilen—Davis created a fully improvised film soundtrack for French director Louis Malle's *Ascenseur pour l'échafaud* (*Elevator to the Gallows*). On this now-historic evening, Davis and the ensemble recorded the entire soundtrack while watching rough cuts of the film on-screen. In fascinating staged footage released on the special features of the 2006 Criterion Collection DVD version of the film, we see a depiction of this soundtrack production; Davis stares intently at a large projection of actress Jeanne Moreau wandering forlornly yet seductively through the Champs-Elysées at night, searching for her lover, who she believes has abandoned her. As Davis watches he appears to be spontaneously creating the accompaniment to Moreau's troubled and lonely wandering. His illuminated eyes shift from side to side, surveying the scene, as we hear him improvise a poignant, languid melody punctuated with gravid moments of silence. His bluesy and mournful-sounding phrases emulate Moreau's exasperated sighs and painful recognition of abandonment yet also suggest a sinuousness that heightens Moreau's on-screen seductiveness—her slight raise of an eyebrow, the fluid motion of her hips as she walks, her haunting, pain-filled eyes.

Improvised film soundtracks such as this—in which musicians improvise to a film (or script)—are rare.[1] Despite improvisation's central role in silent film soundtracks in the early twentieth century, its presence in synchronized-sound film scores has been limited. Davis's aforementioned score was one of the earliest known examples, a cinematic harbinger of the French New Wave movement.[2] The New Wave was an aesthetic reaction against Hollywood's domination of the postwar film industry and its commercial film conventions, as well as against the classic "tradition of quality" in French cinema.[3]

48

Figure 2.1. Miles Davis improvising the soundtrack for *Elevator to the Gallows*, taken from the Criterion DVD release's special features (screenshot, 1957).

Along with those involved in the Italian neorealist movement and American independent cinema, New Wave filmmakers sought to introduce new ways of creating movies that challenged the studio-determined, script-driven commercialism of mainstream filmmaking trends.[4] They pursued alternatives to traditional narrative style, emphasizing fragmentation, abstraction, and improvisation over fixed rigidity and overdetermined production. These critical practices resonated with midcentury modernist trends in art, literature, and music, including abstract expressionism, Beat literature, and bebop jazz, all of which emphasized personal creativity, spontaneity (improvisation), and subjective interpretation.

It was in this milieu during the late 1950s and early 1960s that improvisation enjoyed a brief moment of prominence among independent filmmakers. Several New Wave and independent American directors utilized jazz soundtracks in their films, many featuring improvisation. In addition to Davis's score for *Ascenseur pour l'échafaud*, examples include John Lewis's score for Roger Vadim's *Sait-on jamais* (1957), Martial Solal's score for Jean-Luc Godard's *Breathless* (1959), and Thelonious Monk and Art Blakey's collaborative score for Roger Vadim's *Les liaisons dangereuses* (1960). In America a proliferation of jazz-influenced film scores was spearheaded by Alex North's innovative soundtrack for Elia Kazan's *A Streetcar Named Desire* (1951) and expanded through Elmer Bernstein's scores for *The Man with the Golden Arm* (1955) and *The Sweet Smell of Success* (1957), Duke Ellington's score for Otto Preminger's *Anatomy of a Murder* (1959), and Charles Mingus's score for John Cassavetes's *Shadows* (1960).

Yet New Wave filmmaking, abstract expressionism, beat poetry, and bebop are now all historic movements—they no longer represent the contemporary artistic milieu and cultural criticism in the United States and Europe the way they did during the immediate postwar era. The impetus to use improvised scores now no longer aligns with the ideological and aesthetic motivations evinced by late 1950s independent filmmakers. At present, films featuring fully improvised scores are virtually nonexistent.

Within the last forty years, a sprinkling of films have utilized soundtracks featuring jazz improvisation, yet very few of these are fully improvised. Instead, they highlight brief moments/passages of improvisation against the backdrop of precomposed scores. One example is Ornette Coleman's free improvisation over Howard Shore's orchestral score in David Cronenberg's *Naked Lunch* (1991). Here, Coleman's frenetic, squealing saxophone improvisations evoke the disorienting hallucinations of character William Lee in the eccentric and disturbing milieu of the Interzone—reinforcing cinematic associations of jazz (particularly free jazz) with anxiety, unpredictability, and chaos. Another example is Dave Grusin's jazz-based soundtrack for *The Fabulous Baker Boys* (1989), which features a significant amount of improvisation, but within the context of previously composed tunes and ensemble orchestrations. This film focuses on the musical and personal experiences of two jazz-pianist brothers, primarily the more talented (and troubled) of the two, Jack (played by Jeff Bridges). Improvisational passages, as well as the holistic jazz-based score, reflect Jack's career as a jazz musician, in addition to his own exploration of individuality and expression throughout the course of the narrative.[5] It is worth noting that a significant portion of the improvisation that happens in this soundtrack is featured diegetically, corresponding to moments of "visible" improvisation in the film. As such, these musical components are fulfilling specific diegetic functions that relate to the plot of the narrative. Such circumstances, in which jazz improvisation appears on soundtracks to support diegetic moments, account for the vast majority of improvisation (and jazz, for that matter) in film in recent decades. Examples include films such as *Round Midnight* (1986), *Bird* (1988), *Mo' Better Blues* (1990), *Kansas City* (1996), *Whiplash* (2014), and *La La Land* (2016), among others. It is filmmakers' utilization of improvised jazz scores in *non-jazz* films that is especially uncommon, particularly when the scores are improvised in their entirety.

I argue that this dearth is directly related to the incompatibility between commercial filmmaking conventions and improvisation. As Krin Gabbard argued, "The improvising jazz artist, who answers to a private sense of which sounds are right for which moment, is almost by definition incompatible with standard film music practice."[6] In contemporary Hollywood, the rarity of these soundtracks results from institutional attitudes and policies concerning "risk," governed by film companies' commercial impetuses. With economic profit as the end goal, filmmaking decisions are primarily informed by conventional beliefs about what will (or will not) be successful among consuming audiences. Potential sources of risk can include any form of production uncertainty that might negatively influence the expected financial success of the film.[7]

For many contemporary Hollywood filmmaking executives, improvised soundtracks are perceived as risky production ventures. Since improvisation occurs in the act of creation and is not developed before recording, such soundtracks pose a greater risk for "error" in meeting musical expectations during limited (and expensive) recording sessions. Jazz pianist and film composer Dick Hyman—who has extensive experience working in film and media industry recording settings—spoke to this phenomenon from his own experience. He stated, "You don't improvise much in films. It has to be precisely the length to match the scene, or it has to be of such a length that it can be edited into the scene for ambience, and it has to be carefully planned. And more and more, it has to be put together in some form in advance, so that people can make judgments about whether it's suitable."[8] If the director/producer does not approve of the outcome, the soundtrack must be rerecorded in order to meet expectations. Filmmakers do not want to deplete their limited budgets with rerecordings or to waste time (and thus money) requiring composers to redo their scores. They expect the music department to work quickly and productively and to achieve "the sound" they are looking for without much ado. As such, these potential complications have made filmmakers' utilizations of improvised scores a risk many are not willing to take.

Nevertheless, there are a few filmmakers who invite the challenge. They are almost exclusively independent directors, whose work is primarily produced outside of the Hollywood studio industry. Specifically, I focus on the works of renowned filmmakers Alejandro González Iñárritu and Alan Rudolph, and their collaborations with jazz artists Antonio Sánchez and Mark Isham, respectively. These independent directors produce their films without the same constraints experienced by integrated film-industry professionals; accordingly, they experience more freedom and less restriction in the usage of unconventional storylines, film style, and production techniques—including utilizing improvised scores.

It is useful to contextualize Iñárritu's and Rudolph's positionality in Hollywood through the lens of the concept of the *auteur*. As discussed in the introduction, "auteur"—or author—is a designation for distinguished film directors who are recognized for having a distinct originality and artistic authorial signature that manifests in their cinematic works. They are often believed to push against established filmmaking conventions in new, experimental ways, thus paving the path for future cinematic development. Sociologist Howard Becker employed the term "maverick"[9] to broadly distinguish such artistic individuals who "propose innovations outside the limits of what their art world conventionally produces.[10] Film scholar Geoff Andrew employed Becker's concept within the context of the film industry, understanding "maverick" as describing an "attitude or achievement" and identifying "those film-makers who, for some or all of their directing careers, have made movies which in one way or another stand outside the commercial mainstream."[11]

Both Iñárritu and Rudolph have been recognized as auteurs/mavericks. Both have distinctive independent filmmaking styles that have challenged mainstream conventions, and considerable film oeuvres that distinguish them within the contemporary film industry. Additionally, these directors have demonstrated a unique openness to production risk and creative experimentation. This context provides a crucial backdrop for analyses of their unique treatments of music, specifically improvised soundtracks.

While *Birdman* and *Afterglow* are very different films, with very different soundtracks, they share what I argue is the most important factor in recent jazz/film collaborations: *a director who envisions jazz as an integral component of the film itself*. To connect to the broader thread of this book, both Iñárritu and Rudolph understand jazz (specifically jazz improvisation) as representative of a particular form of "authenticity" that is fundamental to the messages of their films. As I examine throughout this chapter, Iñárritu associates jazz improvisation with "liveness"—the perceived authenticity of lived, unadulterated experience. Rudolph associates jazz improvisation with raw, genuine human emotion, the mainspring of his emotionally laden dramatic narratives. Despite the risks—or perhaps because of them—both these directors employ jazz improvisation as the sonic cornerstone of their film narratives.

It is my contention that these directors' recognition of jazz improvisation as representative of a form of authenticity—an authenticity that has an essential function in their films—directly leads to heightened opportunities for their film composers' (i.e., Antonio Sánchez and Mark Isham) creative agency and collaborative influence in the film production process. In other words, Sánchez and Isham, as the ostensible "sources" of authenticity (through the jazz they create), experience much greater opportunities for creative freedom within the "creative labor" structures of the film industry than the vast majority of film composers do. Accordingly, their respective improvised soundtracks challenge conventional production methods, collaboratively integrating musical score and film in groundbreaking, innovative ways.

"DRUUUMMMMMSSS! EUREKA!" ANTONIO SÁNCHEZ'S IMPROVISED *BIRDMAN* SCORE

Alejandro González Iñárritu is a Mexican filmmaker lauded for his innovative filmmaking techniques. As of this writing, he has directed six feature films; five of them were nominated for Academy Awards for Best Picture or Best Foreign Language Film.[12] He holds the distinction of being the first Mexican director to be nominated for the Academy Award for Best Director—which he won in back-to-back years for *Birdman* (in 2015) and *The Revenant* (in 2016). Beyond the Academy Awards, he has received manifold nominations and honors from the Directors Guild of America (DGA), the Producers Guild of America (PGA), the British Academy of Film and Television Arts (BAFTA), the Australian Academy of Cinema and Television Arts (AACTA), the Golden Globes, and the Cannes Film Festival, among others. And while Iñárritu is certainly recognized within the film industry as an accepted member, he produces his films independent from the Hollywood mainstream. He is actively involved in writing and producing his own films and, although he often partners with industry studios for funding and distribution, seeks to maintain independent creative control over his work. In an interview with Lorraine Ali of the *Los Angeles Times*, Iñárritu asserted: "The only way I know how to [make films] is with absolute freedom. I can't understand the conditions of a corporate budget being designed and getting millions. I admire it, it's great, but I don't know how to do that. I have to have the wheel. It's given me an opportunity to experience and explore things. If I had been at an assembly line for films, I don't know if I would be the best driver. I think I would have crashed the car."[13]

Iñárritu's current recognition as a critically acclaimed and commercially successful auteur contributes to his distinction within the film industry, through which he accesses substantial industry support and funding while also retaining creative control over his projects. He is acclaimed for his nontraditional approaches to filmmaking, which have included nonlinear mosaic narratives, graphic realism, remote global location shooting, long film takes, and, recently, a virtual reality film documenting the experiences of migrants crossing the border into America. The critical acclaim he has garnered generates industry support and enables him to continue to successfully push the boundaries of film production with significant financial backing.[14]

Released in 2014, *Birdman* received numerous accolades, including four Academy Awards for Best Picture, Best Director, Best Original Screenplay, and Best Cinematography. There are two primary features of the film's production that have drawn significant acclaim. The first is Iñárritu's groundbreaking method of recording and editing the film so that the narrative is experienced as one singular, uninterrupted shot. There are no cuts, fades, or breaks that take the audience away from the immediate action. Instead the camera follows the characters throughout their daily lives, continually moving with them into new spaces and interactions. Iñárritu described his conception of this form in a conversation with Elvis Mitchell for *Interview* magazine:

> When I conceived it, I knew the form of it. I had a discussion with Walter Murch, the editor, about whether our life is experienced as a handheld [shot], or if it's experienced as Steadicam, the fluidity of it. And I realized that, at 50 years old, our life, everybody's lives, is a continuous Steadicam shot. From the time we open our eyes in the morning, we are navigating our lives without editing. Only when there's urgency are we in hand held mode. Editing time and space comes only when we talk about our life, or the way we remember our life. I wanted to slowly put myself in the continuous experience of somebody else without escaping.[15]

Iñárritu therefore developed the film's form to reflect how humans perceive their lives while they are living them—moving from room to room, place to place, experience to experience. Through this technique he sought to represent "authentic" daily life, attempting to facilitate audiences' connections with the characters and the story through the familiarity of "liveness."

The soundtrack has also garnered significant critical attention. Antonio Sánchez's original percussion score differs substantially from traditional mainstream soundtracks. First, as mentioned, the soundtrack is predominantly improvised. (While six prerecorded works by Mahler, Tchaikovsky, Ravel, Adams, and Rachmaninoff also appear in the film soundtrack, they are generally featured as source music in the film and, according to Iñárritu, are ancillary sonic elements. Interestingly, it was the presence of these precomposed, "non-original" works that precluded the *Birdman* soundtrack for Academy Award consideration for Best Original Score—a snub that many [including Iñárritu and Sánchez] found to be more rooted in the Academy's musical conservatism than in the actual nomination rules.)[16] Second, in featuring predominantly nonpitched percussion, the score forgoes melody and harmony—the conventional features in the majority of film scores. Third, the soundtrack was originally recorded in the *preproduction* stages of the film's development, rather than in postproduction. I examine all three of these unique aspects below.

Sánchez is not a film composer by trade. Although his prolific career boasts more than one hundred albums (including collaborations with such artists as Pat Metheny, Chick Corea, and Michael Brecker) and an immense repertoire of jazz performance styles, film soundtrack work remained outside of his purview until *Birdman*. This project was facilitated by Iñárritu's admiration of Sánchez's work as a jazz percussionist and a fellow resident of Mexico City. Iñárritu described his admiration in the *Birdman* liner notes, along with the circumstances of their first meeting:

> I met Antonio Sánchez [in 2004] at a sublime Pat Metheny concert in Los Angeles. Like me, Antonio is a Chilango.[17] Unlike me, Antonio is one of the best drummers in the world. I became a fan and luckily a friend. At that concert, Antonio, like a human octopus, played a solo that made me wonder how just four extensions of a human body could propel so many beats, emotions, sounds, ideas, and extraordinary rhythms.[18]

As Iñárritu developed his concepts for *Birdman*'s narrative and form, he also conceptualized a soundtrack that conveyed its central themes of emotion, frenzy, spontaneity, and artistic experimentation. Accordingly, he regarded Sánchez's percussion improvisations as an integral part of the story. Sánchez's unfamiliarity with film scoring was largely irrelevant, for it was his experience and skill as an improviser that drew Iñárritu's attention. Iñárritu stated to Sánchez, "I want something that's not scripted, something jazzy. You're a jazz musician. That's what I want."[19] The resulting soundtrack is a fascinating demonstration of Sánchez's ability to channel his improvisational aptitude and command of stylistic and timbral percussion possibilities into an emotional narrative that sonically embodies the themes of *Birdman* itself.

The film's plot documents the struggles of washed-up superhero actor Riggan Thomson (played by Michael Keaton[20]), who attempts to shed his commercial reputation and establish himself as a "true" (read: noncommercial) artist late in his career by producing a Broadway adaptation of

Raymond Carver's *What We Talk about When We Talk about Love*. The film's central themes address Thomson's ego, his career anxiety, and his growing insanity, as well as his complicated relationships with others, including his drug-addicted daughter, his girlfriend, his acting rival, and an influential, antagonistic theater critic. Sánchez's score sonically represents these themes. The frenzied aesthetic of his percussive grooves musically evinces Thomson's anxiety, disillusionment with his career, chaotic life status, and descent into madness. The drums simulate corporeality—heartbeats racing, neurons firing, palms sweating—as well as psychological states of mind, explicitly functioning as the musical embodiment of the characters' emotions. Iñárritu averred, "Sánchez's score . . . was absolutely key and irreplaceable. The intensity of the drum cues almost became a separate character in the film, and an indispensable part of it."[21]

PREPRODUCTION DEVELOPMENT

The uniqueness of the *Birdman* soundtrack lies not only in its improvised creation but in its development during the preproduction stage of filming. Conventionally, film composers record scores during postproduction, after the film has been shot and is in the editing stage.[22] As has been discussed, in the hierarchical structure of film production, scoring is largely subservient to the visual aspects of the film.[23]

Unconventionally, Iñárritu asked Sánchez to score the film *before the scenes themselves were filmed*. His reasoning? He wanted to find and establish a rhythm for the actors' movements that would facilitate his ability to shoot the film in long takes, to create the perception of one singular shot. In the soundtrack liner notes, Iñárritu claimed: "I attempted *Birdman* to be experienced in one continuous and uninterrupted shot. Very much as we live our lives. But not having the possibility to fragment time and space, it is almost a contradiction to the nature of cinema itself. DRUUUMMMMMSSS! Eureka! I thought the drums would help me to find the internal rhythm of the film and the audience [would] flow with it."[24] Using Sánchez's improvised recordings, Iñárritu worked with cinematographer Emmanuel Lubezki to design and block the scenes, calculating each movement and location transition so that it could be rehearsed and performed by the actors with exact precision. Lubezki described the production as a "major choreography with the whole cast and crew."[25]

But how did Sánchez score something he couldn't see? Prior to production, Iñárritu and Sánchez went into the recording studio, where Iñárritu described the scenes based on the scripted screenplay, addressing the action and the energy, setting the thematic/emotional tone, and giving Sánchez verbalized cues.[26] Sánchez guided him in his direction, suggesting, "Sit in front of me, and when you feel like [the character] is opening the door, raise your hand. When you feel that he's turning the corner of the hallway, raise it again. When he's getting to the stage door, do it again."[27] Each time Iñárritu raised his hand, Sánchez would alter the beat and intensity he was playing to reflect the subtext of the scene. He recorded approximately sixty to seventy takes of those improvised segments, which Iñárritu then used for timing during production.[28] The recordings helped determine the pacing for the actors as filming commenced. The music editor then selected and edited the takes into the rough cut of the film as "temp tracks." In a later production stage, Sánchez improvised another version of each track—this time watching the movie as he was drumming—and made the cuts for the final release of the film.[29]

In a significant way, the editing of the film itself revolved around Sánchez's playing. Lubezki, the film's cinematographer, described this unconventional approach as "like an upside-down movie where you do post-production before production."[30] This hierarchical fracturing was echoed in Iñárritu and Sánchez's collaborative relationship on this project; while Iñárritu certainly gave narrative direction (and reserved the right to demand edits or re-dos from Sánchez), he granted Sánchez a significant amount of creative liberty in the score production. He asked Sánchez to create the score spontaneously based on his improvisational expertise and creative instinct. This is a unique opportunity that film composers rarely experience.

STRUCTURE/MOVEMENT/PACING

Iñárritu employed a unique cinematic approach that demanded rethinking the traditional usage of a musical score. The movie was filmed as a single continuous, uninterrupted shot, in which scenes were connected through the movement of the characters from location to location.[31] One of the most challenging aspects of such a technique—aside from the intricate editing challenges in threading the takes together in a manner that appeared seamless and continuous—was discovering a way to aesthetically evoke the transitional nature of the movement. Sánchez's preproduction improvisations provided the sonic framework that linked these mobile, transitional moments together.

An example from the film can help illustrate this approach.[32] In the opening scene, Riggan Thomson floats in the middle of a dirty, dim dressing room in the St. James Theater, backlit by faded afternoon sunlight creeping underneath a half-blinded window facing the New York streets. As he meditates, the voice of his past superhero role, Birdman, haunts him. "How did we end up here?" Birdman taunts. "This place is horrible." Birdman's monologue is interrupted when Riggan's computer rings; his daughter, Sam (played by Emma Stone), angrily appears on his video chat, demanding to know what flowers he wants for his dressing room. The conversation abruptly ends as Sam yells, "I hate doing this job!" and hangs up. Riggan wearily sits down and sighs. As he does we hear a sharp, invasive drum hit, soon layered with a syncopated, militant-sounding drum groove and triplet-heavy ride cymbal overlay. The camera pans to a close-up of Riggan's face—exhausted, disappointed, both?—as he stares at himself in the mirror with a poster image of Birdman looking on. Sánchez's shimmering, hissing cymbal figure symbolically reflects the psychological tremor of anxiety that permeates Riggan's inner thoughts as he thinks about the status of his career, family, and life.

The texture of the improvisation shifts as we hear a voice on the loudspeaker saying, "Riggan, they're ready for you [onstage]." The groove is at once propulsive yet stationary through repetition, sounding as though it is "prepping" to go somewhere, much as a car does when the engine is revved. The groove's tension is soon released after a second encouragement from the loudspeaker, when Riggan visibly jolts out of his contemplative daze, rises quickly, and puts on his pants. The percussion soundtrack remains viscerally present through this dressing scene: a solid 4/4 groove interpolated with polyrhythmic, full drum set improvisations. Tight hits on the snare and bass drum pierce loudly through the scene, the hi-hat clasps the off-beats, the ride cymbal shimmers in and out of the rhythm. Syncopation is rampant; rhythmic motives shift and turn inward and outward on each other, but the groove—with or without the downbeats—is omnipresent.

Following a sharp drum hit that corresponds to Riggan opening his dressing room door, the groove shifts again when he steps into the hallway. The pacing is slightly quicker, more decisive, paralleling the speed with which Riggan moves through the theater corridors. The soundtrack is a syncopated march, reflecting Riggan's pace as he progresses through the hallways toward the St. James stage, as well as the tempo of the inner voices of Birdman and Sam inaudibly beating in his mind. Sánchez's change in groove not only marks the shift in momentum but sonically alerts us to the changes in scenery that are happening on-screen. Even without the visuals, an astute listener can identify where these changes occur. As this example illustrates, Sánchez's improvisations assist in both narrative and structural clarity in the film, making Riggan's internal anxiety more sonically perceptible while simultaneously supporting the continuity of Iñárritu's single-shot cinematic approach.

"LIVE" AESTHETIC

The soundtrack reflects Iñárritu's aesthetic desire to present the film with a perceptible liveness and seeming authentic realness that reflects "[how] we live our lives." The act of improvisation itself corresponds to the "the gritty, live aesthetic of the film,"[33] which is produced in an unglamorous, documentary style that evokes the rawness and unexpected spontaneity of everyday life. Visually, Iñárritu captures Riggan's day-to-day experiences as he maneuvers through the dark, dirty St. James theater, battles his own anxiety within the confines of his dressing room, argues with a play reviewer in a dimly-lit nearby bar, walks through Times Square, and interacts with his producer, fellow actors, and family members in the corridors and rooms of the theater. We as audience members feel as though we are actually with him in the rooms—living his life alongside him. Sonically, Sánchez attempted to portray this "live aesthetic" by adjusting his conventional percussion set-up, utilizing such techniques as putting tape on his drumheads, detuning them, and stacking his cymbals to make them sound more broken in and well used—ultimately giving the recordings a quality of grainy realism (opposed to typical clean, smooth soundtrack recordings). The result is a dominant sonic force characterized by harsh familiarity in the form of crashes, scrapes, percussive scuttling, and driving rhythmic grooves, inviting mimetic participation from all viewers, regardless of musical background. Drawing on Arnie Cox's "mimetic hypothesis" and Miguel Mera's thoughtful discussion of "haptic music" in film, Jonathan Godsall offers a compelling analysis of this embodied response to the *Birdman* score, suggesting that the foregrounded soundtracks "invite us to play along with Sánchez."[34] Audiences' heartbeats escalate to match anxious tempi, bodies jump and shift in response to unexpected percussive hits, and, while perhaps seated, we are not in stasis—corporeally moving (however subtly) through the on-screen rooms in subconscious response to Sánchez's propulsive rhythms.

At two points in the film, the music itself becomes "live," shifting from nondiegetic to diegetic status—and then back again—within the context of the scenes. Here, the music functions "syn-diegetically," as Emile Wennekes describes it, "synthesizing plural diegetic expressions."[35] These two musical tracks are identified as "Doors and Distance" and "Claustrophobia." In "Doors and Distance," nondiegetic score switches to live performance as Riggan and coactor Mike Shiner walk down a street in New York, encountering a drummer performing on a drum set on the sidewalk. The drummer's performance looks accurately synced with the percussion we are hearing.[36] The perceived "liveness" of this performance is further emphasized through the

Doppler effect of the recording production. As Riggan and Mike approach the drummer (we as viewers cannot see him yet), the recording is mixed in the right speaker, moving to middle-balance between the speakers as they pass directly in front of him, and moving away into the left speaker as they pass and move beyond him down the sidewalk.

A similar effect occurs in "Claustrophobia." As Riggan moves through the St. James corridors toward his opening-night performance, he turns a corner that reveals the same drummer playing a drum set in a back room/kitchenette off the hallway—again appearing to be playing the music we have been (and are) hearing. The performance is mixed heavily in the left speaker as Riggan approaches and passes him, since he is coming to him from the right. Once Riggan moves beyond him, the recording is mixed in an equal balance between both speakers again. In both of these aforementioned cases, Sánchez's improvisations begin as sonic reflections of the internal state(s) of Riggan's mind; they are psychological underscores that simultaneously generate the pulse of Riggan's physical momentum as he moves through various milieus. Yet both tracks momentarily transform into diegetic performances, as Riggan passes a drummer ostensibly performing the exact music that is being heard. In these tunes the fluidity between underscore and "live" diegetic performance parallels Riggan's own conflations of internal thought and reality throughout the film. These moments also draw attention to the score in ways that demand recognition of it as an integral part (or even character) in the story—just as the voice of Birdman is. They become present components of the narrative, forcing audiences to directly acknowledge the music as they watch it being performed on-screen, further enhancing the authenticity/realism (even in psychological nonrealism) that Iñárritu is trying to convey.

SEMIOTIC MEANINGS

An analysis of the *Birdman* soundtrack is incomplete without consideration of the score's semiotic significations. Specifically, in its recognizable associations with improvisation and jazz, the soundtrack adopts layers of meaning rooted in cultural and social perceptions of what these concepts represent. Improvisation, for instance, is generally associated with spontaneity, experimentation, and freedom. The frenzied improvised aesthetic of Sánchez's performances therefore reflects Riggan's own impulsive, reactive, and unpredictable approaches to pursuing his creative dreams and establishing a new artistic identity, as well as his efforts to escape the structure and associations of his mainstream persona and personal ghosts. Furthermore, in its recognition as an act of spontaneous creation, improvisation functions as a representative vehicle of unfiltered expression—an ideal medium for projecting *Birdman's* "gritty, live aesthetic."

The soundtrack's semiotic meanings through its relationship to jazz are also significant. Jazz is an idiom that has largely developed around the art of improvisation.[37] Jazz culture lauds individual, creative autonomy and experimentation and has therefore come to represent the notions of freedom and spontaneity that are associated with improvisational performance. However, jazz's significations in popular culture also abound. Whether functioning as a musical synecdoche for crime/urban decay, sexuality, Blackness, or white urban sophistication, jazz styles have held a variety of specific meanings for filmmakers, advertisers, and consumers throughout the twentieth and twenty-first centuries.[38] Simon Frith describes such generic conventions as "musical shorthand"—cultural codes that inform the semiotic dimensions of the musical work. Examples include bluesy saxophone as denoting a "fallen woman" or "femme fatale," lush, soaring strings representing romance, and so on.[39]

The way the soundtrack reflects Riggan's internal anxiety, fear, and purported madness draws heavily on discursive formations of jazz as representative of psychoses and neuroticism. This relationship's earliest manifestations in film were arguably initiated by Alex North's raunchy, jazz-inflected score for *A Streetcar Named Desire* (1951), where the tragic Blanche Dubois's psychological instability and anxiety is reflected in unsettling harmonic dissonances, harsh brass timbres, and aggressively syncopated themes, interwoven with sinuous, eroticized, blues-laden scoring that enhances the narrative's undertones of lust and seduction (for example, Stella Kowalski's "sexy walk" down the stairs in response to her husband Stanley's infamous impassioned cries). North's score drew heavily on a legacy of jazz's codification in cinema as a racialized, sexualized, and exoticized sonic force, representative of erotic desire, immorality, and decadence—adapting these connotations to reflect internal decadence in state of mind.[40] These sonic tropes continued to develop throughout the 1950s in a bout of film noir and social-problem films and manifested in the emergence of the Mancini-esque "crime jazz" soundtracks that proliferated in film and television throughout the 1960s.[41]

Another semiotic consideration is the percussion-based instrumentation of the soundtrack. Percussion—drums specifically—hold their own associational meanings in the media industry. Drums, like jazz, have been racialized, exoticized, and sexualized, problematically employed as sonic markers of primitivity, impulsivity, corporeality, and sexuality.[42] In late nineteenth- and early twentieth-century American popular culture (minstrel shows, cartoons, films, vaudeville floor shows), drums were largely used to represent "exotic Africa"—sonic signifiers of the racist ideology that portrayed Black Americans as primitive, emotional, physically aggressive "others."[43] Furthermore, drums' associations with militancy and war reinforce their connection to the notion of aggression. In the context of *Birdman*, the percussion soundtrack reflects these associations, sonically embodying Riggan's impulsivity and irrationality. In addition, it simulates corporeal passion, reflecting the physical aggression that he both inflicts and experiences as a manifestation of his own psychological frustration. He anxiously runs through hallways, slams doors, violently throws objects around his dressing room, clenches his hands in frustration and desperation, screams profanities, and even aggressively attacks one of his costars. Throughout the film, Sánchez effectively employs drums and auxiliary percussion to capture these physical displays of emotion through gritty drum rolls, surging crescendos, explosive drum hits and cymbal crashes, and shifting tempi and rhythmic directions. Ultimately, therefore, Sánchez's percussion-based soundtrack both draws on and reinforces the associations between drums and impulsive corporeality, while also establishing the rhythm of the characters and the film itself.

SÁNCHEZ'S CREATIVE LABOR

Sánchez has revealed that working on *Birdman*'s score pushed him into new creative territory. It required him to improvise according to unique narrative and visual structures and gave him the experience of working in a film-production environment. In an interview with Steve Pond, Sánchez stated, "It was an amazingly fun challenge. Being a jazz drummer, I am used to improvising, but I usually don't do it with imagery."[44] Throughout the soundtrack, Sánchez incorporated a variety of grooves and tempi to capture the themes and emotions represented on-screen. He also experimented with his drum set's timbral and textural capabilities, utilizing a variety of mallets and sticks (and his hands), and playing in both traditional and nontraditional ways (i.e., hitting the rims, playing on the sides of the drums, etc.).[45] Even in the absence of the film itself, Sánchez's improvisations sonically reflect the themes of anxiety, internal conflict, and frustration that permeate the characters' emotional states.

One example of Sánchez's creative approach is how he navigated and supported the narrative dialogue. Dialogue has often been a point of contention for many film scorers. Many have found their scores edited/rearranged/cut (sometimes inartistically so) to prioritize it. Yet Sánchez's soundtrack is not only featured clearly during the dialogue but also seems to be a critical part of it. A specific illustrative example is the scene "Just Chatting." Riggan walks through the theater corridors, arguing with his producer/lawyer, Jake (played by Zach Galifianakis), that the first preview of the play must be cancelled due to the inadequate talent of one of the lead actors, Ralph, who has recently been injured by falling overhead equipment. Jake fights back that they would have to refund a full house, and that Ralph would also have the right to file a lawsuit. Sánchez's percussive, clipped phrases and hits effectively simulate the fast-paced, energy-laden and quarrelsome dialogue between the two characters. The call-and-response interaction between the lower-pitched, syncopated snare and bass groove and the interruptive cymbal and tambourine hits illustrates the dialogic, yet combative, nature of the conversation.

The music begins with a syncopated drum roll on brushes, capped by a hi-hat hit that sets off a dynamic conservational interchange among bass drum, snare, and cymbals. A steady, medium-tempo quarter note pulse drives the rhythm, but a relentless, sixteenth-note subdivision stimulates an internal, anxious propulsion—reflecting Riggan's own nervousness after "causing" Ralph's injury. His nervous energy belies his attempts to casually leave the scene. In spite of his large, rhythmic strides, everything inside him—from his brain to his heartbeat—is rushing. This anxious hurriedness is mirrored by Jake, who immediately thinks of the potential lawsuit that Ralph could bring against them. Together, the paced rhythm of their intentional, long strides down the hallway and the quicker, more syncopated palpitations of their internal concerns are manifest in Sánchez's multilayered percussive dialogue.

Sánchez's improvisations sonically and structurally capture the nuances of Riggan and Jake's argument as they hurry through the theater hallways to Riggan's dressing room. This is a segment from the beginning of their dialogue:

JAKE [after Ralph has been hit by the falling equipment]: That's going to be a fucking lawsuit. [To Riggan:] OK, where are you going? They're starting to be ready [for rehearsal] in less than five minutes.
RIGGAN: . . . We're going to have to cancel the first preview.
JAKE: But it's a full house! We would have to refund the entire—
RIGGAN: Just do it. Just do it.
JAKE: Fucking wait! [as Riggan continues to hurry down the hallway]
RIGGAN: Listen to me. It was going to be a disaster. That guy's the worst actor I've ever seen in my life. The blood coming out of his ear is the most honest thing he's done so far.
JAKE: He's not that bad. [Pause, Riggan turns back to look at him incredulously.] OK, he's fucking terrible.

Despite the worry on his face, Riggan's replies to Jake are direct, pragmatic, and relatively unemotional. His voice is low and monotonic; he does not employ emotion-laden pitch/range changes or inflections. Instead he keeps repeating his primary argument, albeit with different support: "We have to cancel the first preview." "Just do it." "It was going to be a disaster." "He's the worst actor I've seen my life." Riggan's mind is made up, and he remains consistent—both in content and expression—throughout the conversation. Jake, in contrast, is highly emotional and reactive. His voice is much higher in range, further exaggerated through the high-pitched screechiness that accompanies emotional speech. His phrases are clipped and abrupt, reacting both incredulously and pleadingly against Riggan's forceful assertions that the preview be cancelled (and, later, that Ralph be replaced).

Sánchez supports this dialogue through timbral choices as well as the cyclic yet varied structure of his improvised performance. Riggan's low-pitched, repetitive arguments are represented by the lower-range drums—the snare and bass drum. Jake's high-pitched, emotional pleas are reflected in the abrupt, shimmering splashes of higher-range auxiliary percussion—various cymbals, hi-hat, and tambourine. These separate voices engage in a cyclical call-and-response with each other. Riggan's "drums" are fundamentally repetitive within each cycle—reflecting the consistency of his responses to Jake's cries. Yet the rhythm/syncopation within each cycle is slightly varied, indicating Riggan's own variations and reassertions throughout the dialogue. Jake's "cymbals" are much more irruptive; each figure is different from the one before it, representing Jake's desperate efforts to say anything that will make Riggan change his mind.

All the while, the groove pulsing through the improvisation aligns with the pacing of Riggan and Jake's movement throughout the St. James Theater corridors. The rate of exchange in the percussive call-and-response impressively reflects the pacing of the dialogic interchange between the two characters—at times even directly aligning with their voices in the film soundtrack. The end of the percussion track poignantly corresponds to the movement of the on-screen action. Right after Riggan argues that Ralph is the worst actor he's ever seen in his life, Jake exasperatedly argues, "He's not that bad!" Riggan stops abruptly, turning to stare at Jake as though he can't believe he said it aloud. Sánchez, who had been solidly improvising Riggan's groove on drums, cuts to a short, syncopated tambourine figure, which abruptly cuts into silence. The tambourine figure represents Jake's pathetic attempt to argue for Ralph's talent—resulting in the cessation of not only sound but on-screen movement—in an awkward moment of incredulity. Sánchez's music does not "Mickey Mouse,"[46] but rather compliments the dialogue, operating as yet another essential voice in the conversation, providing more depth to our understanding of Riggan's state of mind.

In this example Sánchez employs his own expertise as an improviser in a creative negotiation with the programmatic demands of film—structure, theme, emotion, dialogue, and the director's narrative vision. By utilizing sonic metaphors, varying percussion timbres and rhythms, and developing unique, movement- and dialogue-inspired structures and forms, Sánchez innovatively explored and pushed the boundaries of jazz improvisation (and his own creativity) at this intersection with cinematic production. Interestingly, *Birdman* continues to provide a platform for Sánchez's own creative development. Since the movie was released, Sánchez has toured the world accompanying the film live. In an interview with *JazzTimes*, he claimed: "Iñárritu wanted the score to be improvised and very organic, so that's what I do live. I try to maintain the dramatic effect that was achieved originally, but every performance is completely different."[47] What is striking about these continued *Birdman* performances is the way that Sánchez uses the recorded film as a continuously negotiable creative site. Each performance is unique, and the film's meanings are distinctively (if subtly) shaped every time Sánchez takes the stage. Such performances sharply challenge the notion that the film is a stagnant artifact—the province of Iñárritu's sole auteur vision. Rather, it is an organic media product that functions as the foundation for Sánchez's continued collaborative experimentation and creative development.

Holistically, the significance of Sánchez and Iñárritu's unique collaboration on this production is that *Birdman* is a movie that is built on the foundation of improvisation. Sánchez's score was the sonic framework that both informed and underpinned a film developed around the concepts of authenticity, liveness, and improvising one's way through life in reaction to both internal and external circumstances. *Birdman*'s production itself was a dialogue rooted in improvisation. Sánchez improvised in reaction to Iñárritu's spoken (and motioned) ideas in the studio. The actors' movements and pacing responded to Sánchez's recorded improvisations. The filming, in order to generate a "live aesthetic," followed the actors in their movements throughout the set. The actors themselves—a formidable core cast of Michael Keaton, Emma Stone, Edward Norton, Naomi Watts, and Andrea Riseborough—brought their own improvisational acumen to their characters. In an interview with National Public Radio, Ed Norton even compared the production to a choreographed dance that left room for individual improvisation: "Once people have gotten the dance—and it's a dance—it's like a complex choreography with a lot of people—but once it has been built as a foundation, I think that's the enormous pleasure of working with people like Michael

Keaton and Zach Galifianakis, people with an astonishing ability to, even within a set choreography, do a backflip that you weren't expecting."[48] (This notion of choreography is a useful framework for theorizing how integrative, collective art making can successfully work. Like jazz improvisation, the "ensemble" establishes a basic structure and context for production and then improvises within those structures, experimenting and adapting in response to the other members of the ensemble.) Finally, Sánchez's rerecorded improvisations to the finalized film brought the creative dialogue full circle. The effective permeation of improvisational technique throughout this film's production illustrates how the collaborative intersections of jazz and film—albeit complex—can lead to new developments and artistic directions in both mediums.

"NO WAY, SHAPE, OR FORM THAT THIS ISN'T A JAZZ SCORE": IMPROVISED SOUNDTRACK PRODUCTION IN *AFTERGLOW*

Alan Rudolph's unique career as an independent filmmaker has earned him such descriptions as "pioneer," "iconoclastic," and "unconventional." Distinguishing himself from the Hollywood mainstream, Rudolph has called himself "Captain Autonomous-Anonymous," highlighting his outsider status and independent production methodology.[49] His films—which have never reached significant mainstream success—often feature melodramatic romances focused on quirky, isolated characters; elements of fantasy and artifice; and underlying philosophies on topics of love, chance, culture, and paradox. This former protégé of director Robert Altman has become a text unto himself, known for his unconventionality and commitment—despite a lack of commercial success—to his own artistic visions. Even recently, fifteen years after his last film, *The Secret Lives of Dentists* (2002), he has reemerged with a new romantic drama production, *Ray Meets Helen* (2017).

In 1996 film composer Mark Isham, who had already established a successful career as a jazz trumpeter and genre-crossing electronic and improvisational artist, recorded the score for Rudolph's emotional relationship drama *Afterglow*, produced by Robert Altman. Rudolph and Isham collaborated together quite frequently prior to the release of this film and have made eight films together throughout their careers.

The origin of their collaboration offers insight into their unique relationship. Rudolph is highly involved in the music selection process for his films. He has stated, "I like to know the music before I shoot a film, because to me the music is the most influential part of any film, except for maybe the

Table 2.1. Mark Isham's film soundtracks for Alan Rudolph's films	
Film	Year
Trouble in Mind	1985
Made in Heaven	1987
The Moderns	1988
Love at Large	1990
Mrs. Parker and the Vicious Circle	1994
Afterglow	1997
Breakfast of Champions	1999
Trixie	2000

actors."[50] He has further claimed: "Music to me is like the hub of the wheel. It's visible, it works in your senses and emotions, and that seems to be where I reside. To me, music and emotional responses are twins, and if you want to establish emotional tone in a film then music is the number one way to do it."[51] Clearly, music is an integral component of Rudolph's creative process during film production.

In a documentary about the development of *Trouble in Mind* (Rudolph and Isham's first collaboration), Rudolph revealed that he went to the record store looking for music that would fit the emotional themes of the narrative. He came across Isham's *Vapor Drawings* cassette on the Windham Hill label and noticed on the back cover that Isham recorded all the instruments himself. Rudolph purportedly recognized the financial value of Isham's self-sufficiency, stating, "This guy is my guy—he plays all the instruments! We can afford him!"[52] Isham himself expressed interest in working with Rudolph and was soon hired to score the film.

Regarding his inspiration for filmmaking, Rudolph has contended that he's "more influenced by John Coltrane than John Ford."[53] He is fascinated by jazz and its fluidity and resonances with emotion. He is interested in tonal color and spontaneous performance and how these elements evoke life and human relationships. In his words: "There's something about jazz—you know it when you hear it, or you feel it."[54] These assertions strongly reflect the "authenticity" discourse that permeates jazz's representations in popular culture, investing the music with emotional and spiritual authority. Rudolph has further revealed that one of the largest sources of inspiration for his filmmaking was Miles Davis's album *Kind of Blue*. In a recent interview, he stated: "I'd walk around Manhattan [with a Walkman] and watch a movie unfold on the sidewalks listening to how it was scored in my head. But it's funny, the number-one album was always *Kind of Blue*. Without that album, I'm not sure I would have been able to make films. *Kind of Blue* was my film school."[55]

Accordingly, Rudolph enjoyed working with Isham, whose trumpet playing reminded him of Davis's.[56] Isham's experiences as a jazz trumpet player and electronic composer have informed his unique improvisational, emotion-driven approach to film composition, which made him particularly attractive to Rudolph. Isham stated that his discussions with Rudolph about soundtrack production were frequently permeated with such terms as "jazz" and "improvisation"—reflecting Rudolph's desire to incorporate these elements into his works. Isham has further revealed that of all his film credits, Rudolph's films are the only ones in which he never views the movie as he is creating the music.[57] Instead, he develops his scores solely based off Rudolph's description of emotion and thematic content.[58] This method of film composition is truly novel, as it disrupts the conventional hierarchy of the visual image and on-screen narrative in favor of musical authority.

AFTERGLOW

Isham's most comprehensively improvised film score was for Rudolph's *Afterglow*. Tellingly, Rudolph claims that he conceived *Afterglow*'s script while listening to Isham's *Blue Sun*, a quintet album with a predominantly "cool jazz," Miles-esque flavor. Rudolph sent the script to Isham, telling him, "*Blue Sun* is the accompaniment to this—that's [the kind of music that] I want for the score."[59] Therefore, even in its inception, *Afterglow* was developed around Isham's improvisational style.

Afterglow's narrative follows the relationships of two couples: an older couple, Lucky (Nick Nolte) and Phyllis (Julie Christie), and a younger couple, Jeffrey (Jonny Lee Miller) and Marianne (Lara Flynn Boyle). Their marriages are unhappy, characterized by betrayal, loss, emotional incompatibility, neediness, jealousy, and callousness, leading them to seek comfort and/ or satisfaction through adultery with the spouse in the other relationship (they don't find out until later that they are all interconnected). The narrative is rife with emotion—love, lust, distress, and pain—which is enhanced by the underscoring. As in *Blue Sun*, the soundtrack features a range of jazz styles, including slow, minor modal ballads and up-tempo, frenetic bop tunes. This diversity corresponds to the array of emotions experienced by the four primary characters. Frantic bebop improvisations channel Jeffrey's inner rage and jealousy when he discovers that his wife is cheating on him. Manifold scenes characterized by seductive romance and somber loss echo the longing minor melodies heard on tracks such as "Lazy Afternoon" and "In More than Love" from *Blue Sun*—featuring Isham's self-described "mournful trumpet sound."[60]

As an example, let us consider a specific scene. When we are introduced to Phyllis, we see her at home with Lucky at the end of the workday. Their relationship is strained, for reasons that we discover throughout the course of the film. In this particular scene, Phyllis has just heard about the death of a former costar (Phyllis is a former B-movie actress). She is also aware that Lucky has just returned from a home-repair job that likely included more than appliance maintenance. Lucky is a philanderer, and she knows it. Lucky tries to flirt with her, but she is not fully receptive, deflecting with passive-aggressive statements such as, "How was work today—unclog a few tubes?"

The music effectively underscores and reflects the dynamic unfolding onscreen. We first hear it when Lucky and Phyllis come together physically—when he sits with her on the couch and begins massaging her foot. The tune establishes a 3/4 waltz groove. Two solo instruments represent the two characters—muted trumpet for Lucky, and violin for Phyllis. Characterized by languid, minor melodies, the two instruments contrapuntally interact in an ebb and flow that reflects the back-and-forth of the couple's conversation. Periodically the two lines come together in homophonic harmony but consistently break apart once again. The intertwining melodic lines evoke a sense of longing while the rhythm section maintains the slow waltz groove—an ever-circling, melancholy dance that sonically embodies the characters' strained relationship.

While this particular scene might appear to be a conventional application of soundtrack techniques (i.e., establishing mood, accompanying individual characters, representing jazz's established semiotic associations), in reality it is significantly more unique. The script was inspired by Isham's *Blue Sun*, which in turn influenced the film soundtrack, which was composed without Isham viewing the film footage. Like *Birdman, the film was developed around the music, not the other way around.*

Regarding the development of the soundtrack as a whole, Isham averred, "There's no way, shape, or form that [this score] isn't a jazz score by pretty much any definition."[61] He described the score's conception and development as follows:

> I took a look at the script and picked the five basic emotions that were hit—betrayal, distress, whatever they were—and charted a jazz lead sheet that exemplified those emotions. And then I assigned every character—because it was a small ensemble cast—an instrument. For example, we have Nick Nolte and Julie Christie and betrayal—so the

violin and the [trumpet] have to play that piece for that scene. And [I] literally just made a little chart for every scene, and what the emotion was, the subject, and the characters—and lined it up.[62]

Isham played demos of a few of the charts for Rudolph to confirm that the music captured the emotional aesthetic Rudolph wanted. When the demos were approved, Isham determined which musicians he wanted to hire. Drawing on his jazz networks, he assembled a small group featuring Charles Lloyd on saxophone, Geri Allen on piano, Billy Higgins on drums, Gary Burton on vibes, Jeff Littleton on bass, and Sid Page on violin.

Isham was confident in the musicians' abilities to successfully create the music without strict regulation of notation or timing. He stated, "I mean, you don't give *these guys* a click track. . . . And you don't give them the picture [film]. You just say, 'All right, I'm going to trust that they're going to give me great material.'"[63] Isham distributed lead sheets, set the tempo for each tune, then started recording the performance. The arrangement was sparsely notated, and the majority of the choruses were improvised. Isham revealed, "There were a couple of [pieces] where I did some arrangements because I knew we had to build, but I really didn't limit the number of choruses that anybody would play. . . . I just went out, played the click through the microphone so everybody heard it, and I said, 'Billy, count it off.' I turned the metronome off. And his time was so great—I mean, everything was spot-on where I had figured out that it would hit."[64] The soundtrack was completed in one recording session. Isham stated, "That's a jazz score, because . . . it was done like a jazz record. And that's the only time I've ever really done that."[65]

Once the recording was completed, Isham worked directly with music editor Steve Borne to take the recordings and edit them into a score for the final film release. "We did the [recording] session two weeks before we had to mix, so that we could cut. And it just became a big editing job. I just sat down with a music editor for two weeks, and took all the material that we created, and cut it into a score."[66] This work was primarily done without supervision from the director or a producer; Rudolph left these preliminary decisions to Isham—although he reserved the right to require changes once Isham gave him the preliminary cut.[67] Here, it is interesting to consider how the process of editing the improvised score affected its improvisational nature. One might argue that Isham and Borne's editing process diminished it. Yet the improvised quality of the recordings remained intact. While portions were cut in order to accommodate the film, the performances themselves were unaltered, maintaining their improvised essence.

In a highly unconventional move, Rudolph also allowed Isham to make suggestions about how the film itself might be edited in relation to the score. Isham recalls that at least twice during postproduction, he called Rudolph and asked if the visual scenes could be edited to fit the length of a musical cue that he thought worked best. He stated, "I think twice I called up Alan and I said, 'Look, I'm going to send something—can you move the picture two seconds later here?' And he said, 'Sure!'"[68] This is also not the first time that Rudolph has edited a film in service of music. His thriller *Remember My Name* (1978) prominently featured music by blues/jazz singer Alberta Hunter. Rudolph claims that after listening to her sing in New York and deciding to incorporate her music in the film soundtrack, "The first thing that I did was eliminate at least a third of the dialogue and even entire scenes because she's more articulate than I could ever be."[69]

Overall, the unique conceptualization and production of this score challenged traditional conventions of film soundtrack development. As with *Birdman*, this case study illustrates the significance of auteur directors with both economic resources and a determined interest in featuring improvised music in facilitating such unique jazz/film collaborations. *Afterglow*'s producer, Robert Altman, also shared Rudolph's interest in utilizing an improvised jazz soundtrack for the film.[70] Isham expressed awareness that without Rudolph's and Altman's enthusiasm, the perceived risk of the project may have prevented it from coming to fruition. He stated, "[This project was] something I'd never done before—or may never do again—not because it wasn't successful, but just because it's risky, and not a lot of people would go for that. But Robert Altman producing, Alan Rudolph—they were totally game."[71]

CONCLUSIONS

My goal in this chapter was to examine the rare phenomenon of improvisation in film from both a sociological and methodological perspective, situating these two soundtracks' development at the interfaces of the distinct cultural mediums of improvised jazz performance and film production. The *Birdman* and *Afterglow* case studies illustrate unique disruptions of the conventional relationship between soundtrack and film, in which the productions are developed on a foundation of improvised music.

As illustrated, the core of these collaborations is the personal relationships between the directors and the jazz composers. Both Iñárritu and Rudolph envisioned improvised music as a fundamental element of their films. And not just any improvised music; they specifically chose Antonio Sánchez and Mark Isham based on their previous performances and improvisational aptitudes. Both directors sought to evince on-screen "authenticity" (e.g., emotion, liveness, realism) in their films, supported through the spontaneity of the improvised score—albeit through different methods. On a broader level, these directors were improvising themselves, carving out new territory through innovative approaches to filmmaking. Malle, Iñárritu, Rudolph—all experimented with new ways of making movies; Malle was on the cusp of an independent filmmaking movement that privileged improvisation (i.e., the French New Wave), while Iñárritu and Rudolph have paved the way for new, collaborative improvisational techniques in future film production (e.g., continuous-shot documentary-style films, writing scripts to fit scores, etc.). By "riskily" building their films around the aesthetic of improvised music, they arguably transformed them into integrative jazz/film collaborations.

These directors' liberal attitudes toward risk, and receptiveness to improvisation, opened spaces for Sánchez and Isham to experiment more freely with their own creative production. The level of collaboration between the musicians and the directors was highly reciprocal. Rudolph rewrote portions of the script to accommodate Isham's compositions. Iñárritu required *Birdman*'s actors to time their movements to fit the tempo and feel of Sánchez's recorded improvisations. The films themselves were edited around the scores. These types of reciprocal collaborations rarely happen in other film productions.

Tensions certainly exist. The artists in these case studies had to negotiate their own independent creativity and personal artistic goals within the hierarchical structures and regulations of the film production process. Certainly, Sánchez and Iñárritu, and Isham and Rudolph, did not agree on every creative decision, and ultimately the directors had the authority to make the final call. Jazz artists' self-identification as part of a musical culture that highly values improvisation, individuality, and creative agency makes their navigation of these tensions especially rich for analysis. Yet, as these case studies reveal, the relationships between the jazz artists and film executives are not always "clashes." To the contrary, both examples display high levels of collaboration and creative freedom between composer and director. Therefore, this study contributes to the critical dialogue regarding the potentials of musical freedom within the labor expectations involved in culture industry work. Accordingly, it examines how these musicians' work in film provides opportunities for them to bring their creativity into contact with new mediums, technologies, and modes of production.

Such jazz/film production opportunities have also furthered several jazz artists in their own creative development. A prime example of this can be seen once again in Miles Davis's soundtrack work on Malle's *Ascenseur pour l'échafaud*. As scholars such as Gary Giddins have noted, the modal experimentations that Davis employed in this soundtrack are the first recorded examples of the modal style that would later be featured on *Kind of Blue* (1959).[72] Antonio Sánchez has claimed that his work on *Birdman*'s score was a significant learning experience for him as well—in terms not only of learning how to create music that can be integrated into film, but also experimenting with the programmatic potential of solo percussion improvisations as part of a narrative, capturing emotions, themes, and movements. Sánchez has also continued to work on other film soundtrack projects, including Iñárritu's *The Revenant* (2015), Don Cheadle's *Miles Ahead* (2015), *The Hippopotamus* (2017), and the Epix television series *Get Shorty* (2018). In his work on the *Afterglow* soundtrack, Mark Isham explored the possibilities of developing jazz lead sheets and leading a small-group "jam session" based on a film script, allowing opportunities for individual improvisation and creative collaboration. This experience continued to inform his own artistic development as both a jazz musician and a full-time Hollywood film composer.

Overall, these case studies allow us to envision new creative collaborations between jazz and film that are aesthetically influenced by both mediums. The differing critical receptions of *Birdman* and *Afterglow* don't necessarily provide an indication of improvised soundtracks' potential future. *Birdman* was a hit, and based on critical responses, the unique timbral and rhythmic elements of the soundtrack had a lot to do with it. *Afterglow*, in contrast, was not nearly as popular, and there is very little critical discussion (or even awareness) of the improvised nature of its soundtrack. But the significance of these productions is less about whether or not they are harbingers of an improvised film soundtrack movement and more about what they have accomplished artistically. Both Iñárritu and Rudolph used improvised soundtracks because improvisation was central to their films' concepts. While we may not see a proliferation of improvised soundtracks in mainstream Hollywood, these examples highlight the potential of an integrative jazz/film medium that is rooted in jazz aesthetics, as well as lay a foundation for what such collaborative integrations might look and sound like.[73]

Chapter 3

"HONEST, TRUE PORTRAYALS"

TERENCE BLANCHARD, SPIKE LEE, AND THE RACIAL POLITICS OF JAZZ SCORING

Since Spike Lee began making films in the 1980s, jazz has played a significant role in his soundtracks. Lee's film oeuvre, rife with racial politics and personal ideology, reflects an investment in bringing diverse stories about Black experience to a wide range of film audiences, articulated in his assertion, "I want to be remembered for honest, true portrayals of Afro-Americans and for bringing our great richness to the screen."[1] Viewing filmmaking as a comprehensive integration of visual and audial elements of creative production, Lee believes music plays an integral role in supporting his depictions of Black experience. In addition to permeating his soundtracks with commercial recordings of significant Black performers (e.g., Ella Fitzgerald, John Coltrane, Sam Cooke), Lee employs contemporary jazz scores to represent a range of sonic expression of diverse Black culture and creativity—both past and present. As for the directors considered in the previous chapter, jazz, for Lee, represents authenticity. However, his understanding is rooted in the discourse that positions "Blackness" as jazz's essential authenticating factor. His personal investment in and appreciation for the music (informed by his [albeit fraught] relationship with his father, jazz musician Bill Lee)—combined with his desire to expose Black audiences to what he believes is a significant feature of their cultural heritage—make Lee one of the most prominent filmmakers to recurrently use contemporary jazz scores throughout his film work.

Jazz musician Terence Blanchard—who has presently composed for seventeen of Lee's films—shares this understanding of jazz as a diverse musical idiom rooted in Black culture, which holds immense potential to support various types of film narratives. In this chapter I examine Blanchard and Lee's collaborations, situating their relationship at the intersections of shared sociopolitical ideology and commitment to jazz as representative of Black experience and creativity. I offer close readings of Blanchard's score work for two of their most powerful collaborative projects: *Malcolm X*—a biographical account of the title character—and *When the Levees Broke: A Requiem in Four Acts*, a documentary highlighting the horrors of those suffering in New Orleans in the aftermath of Hurricane Katrina. Within these readings, I examine how Blanchard works within the production expectations of Lee's directorial vision yet also branches out beyond the films to assert his own creativity in individualized, extended recording projects—*The Malcolm X Jazz Suite* and *A Tale of God's Will: A Requiem for Katrina*. Through these analyses, I illustrate how film scores themselves can be transformed into artistic concept albums that function autonomously from the visual medium, facilitating new creative projects that expand the original films' reception and meaning.

Terence Blanchard was born in New Orleans, Louisiana—a diverse haven of cultures, peoples, and musical expression. As a youth he studied music alongside fellow New Orleanians Wynton and Branford Marsalis, attending such institutions as NOCCA (the New Orleans Center for Creative Arts), and studying with local musicians Roger Dickerson and Ellis Marsalis Jr. Blanchard has sustained a prolific jazz performance career as a trumpeter since the 1980s. His early tenure included performing with Lionel Hampton, participating in (and eventually leading) Art Blakey's Jazz Messengers, and coleading a quintet with saxophonist Donald Harrison. To date, he has over thirty album credits to his name, has been nominated for fourteen Grammy Awards (he has won six), has received multiple nominations for his score work (having composed over forty film scores),[2] and travels extensively to gig both nationally and internationally.

Blanchard's musical projects often directly reflect his commitments to social justice activism and advocacy, particularly for members of the Black community. His recent album *Breathless* (2015) is titled in response to Eric Garner's final words ("I can't breathe") while in a chokehold by an NYPD police officer, condemning larger issues of police brutality and societal racism. Blanchard published a companion essay with this album entitled "Using Music to Underscore Three Words: I Can't Breathe," in which he pointedly stated:

> It feels like every week there's another YouTube video going viral of police brutality, or civil rights being sent back to the 1800s. Breathless is my attempt to draw more attention to that. This is our E-Collective [the band's] version of a protest album, without the firebrand lyrics of Phil Ochs, but in mood and purpose. Much in the same way John Coltrane's tune "Alabama" captured the immense pain and suffering

of a nation as it mourned the death of those four little girls lost in the firebombing of that Birmingham Church.[3]

Beyond his instrumental albums, Blanchard has spearheaded the "jazz opera" genre, coproducing vibrant operatic productions featuring Black stories sonically depicted through his unique operatic jazz compositions. *Champion* (2013)—coproduced with librettist Michael Cristofer—addresses the life and experiences of African American boxer Emile Griffith in relation to his race and homosexuality. The recent *Fire Shut Up in My Bones* (2019)—cocreated with librettist Kasi Lemmons and based on Charles Blow's memoir of the same name—is a poignant account of a young Black man growing up in a segregated rural Louisiana town. An outspoken advocate of civil rights, racial justice, and the recent Black Lives Matter movement, Blanchard frequently utilizes his compositions and performances as formats for facilitating engagement with these issues among his listenership. This activism has also manifested in many of his film scores (and extended concept albums based on these scores), including *Malcolm X* (1992), *Clockers* (1995), *4 Little Girls* (1997), *When the Levees Broke: A Requiem in Four Acts* (2006), *Miracle at St. Anna* (2008), and *Da 5 Bloods* (2020), among numerous others. I examine Blanchard's activism through his film music projects in more detail throughout this chapter.

Blanchard first became involved in film work when he was hired as a session man for Spike Lee's *School Daze* (1988). He was not hired by Lee directly; as Michael Schelle described, "Spike wanted an orchestra, and his father [Bill Lee], who's a jazz musician, hired a guy by the name of Harold Vick to do the contracting. By him being a jazz guy, he hired nothing but jazz musicians."[4] Blanchard returned for more session recording work on Lee's next film, *Do the Right Thing* (1989). The following project, Lee's *Mo' Better Blues* (1990), marked a significant breakthrough for Blanchard in film work. Dubbing the trumpet solos for the lead character in the film (played by Denzel Washington), Blanchard recorded a large number of prominent solo tracks, while also composing a portion of the soundtrack (as detailed later in this chapter). Blanchard has since worked in a continuous collaborative relationship with Lee for the past thirty years (see table 3.1 below). Their most recent project is *Da Five Bloods*, released in 2020.

Aside from Lee's films, Blanchard has completed score and recording work for a number of other films, including Leo Ichaso's *Sugar Hill* (1993), Mattie Rich's *The Inkwell* (1994), Gina Prince Bythewood's *Love and Basketball* (2000), Darnell Martin's adaptation of *Their Eyes Were Watching God* (2005) and *Cadillac Records* (2008), Anthony Hemingway's *Red Tails* (2012), Kasi

Table 3.1. Terence Blanchard's film soundtracks for Spike Lee's films	
Film	**Year**
Mo' Better Blues	1990
Jungle Fever	1991
Malcolm X	1992
Crooklyn	1994
Clockers	1995
Get on the Bus	1996
4 Little Girls	1997
Summer of Sam	1999
Bamboozled	2000
25th Hour	2002
Jim Brown—All American	2002
She Hate Me	2004
Inside Man	2006
When the Levees Broke: A Requiem in Four Acts	2006
Miracle at St. Anna	2008
Chiraq	2015
BlacKkKlansman	2018
Da 5 Bloods	2020

Lemmons's *Eve's Bayou* (1997) and *Harriet* (2019), and Regina King's *One Night in Miami* (2020), to name a few. Many of these filmmakers are young African Americans who have emerged on the scene since Spike Lee gained recognition in the 1980s. Blanchard's continually expanding recognition within the film industry is a direct result of his integration within these "inner circle" networks.

SPIKE LEE: IDEOLOGY AND ENTREPRENEURSHIP

"CAPTURING THE RICHNESS OF AFRICAN-AMERICAN CULTURE"

Spike Lee is a uniquely independent auteur whose film career has been punctuated with much controversy. A preponderance of his work has targeted the conventions of the Hollywood industry, particularly with regard to the employment, recognition, and on-screen portrayals of African Americans. He rails against what he perceives to be an inherent systematic racism within filmmaking networks, criticizing the dearth of African Americans in positions of authority (e.g., as directors, producers, lead actors), the lack of recognition of Black talent at prestigious awards ceremonies such as the Academy Awards,[5] and the racist portrayals of Blacks in numerous commercial films (which will be examined in more detail momentarily).

When Lee was growing up, African American cinematic history reflected this paucity of Black power within the Hollywood system. Although actors such as Sidney Poitier, Dorothy Dandridge, and Harry Belafonte received significant recognition during the 1950s and 1960s—with both Dandridge and Poitier attaining the first Oscars for Best Actress and Best Actor among African Americans—they retained little (if any) control over their representations in the films, fulfilling the roles determined by white screenwriters, directors, and producers. Aside from acting, African Americans were largely absent from the production side of industry filmmaking. The primary exception was Oscar Micheaux, who maintained a prolific career as a filmmaker, producing and directing over thirty films spanning from 1919 to 1948. Yet Micheaux was not directly involved in the Hollywood studio industry; instead, he organized his own independent production company, the Oscar Micheaux Corporation, in order to be able to greenlight and direct his own material. The first Black filmmaker to direct a feature-length motion picture for a Hollywood studio was Gordon Parks, whose racially sensitive coming-of-age story of a young Black boy, *The Learning Tree*, was not produced until 1969. Even in the 1970s—when Black faces dominated the silver screen in the so-called Blaxploitation era— white filmmakers were at the helm, drawing on the industry's recognition of militant Black ideology as a theme attractive to African American consumers, just as they reinforced "Black buck" racial stereotypes in representing the films' antiheroes as violent, angry, sexually aggressive Black men (sometimes women), fighting against the white establishment.[6] Rooted in the legacy of minstrelsy, these exaggerated representations were more reflective of white audiences' fascination with Black culture (per Lott's *Love and Theft*) than Black culture itself. As David Sterritt aptly contends, "'Black movies' [in the 1970s] were almost always made by white men who unambiguously aimed to redirect African-American energies, talents, subjects, and subjectivities toward the explicitly commercial aims of an industry almost entirely dedicated to the purpose of filling white men's pockets with money."[7]

Even since the 1970s, the Black-directed films that are most prominently greenlit are those that the studio executives ideologically believe will appeal most directly to Black consumers (and their pocketbooks)—tragic films that address racism, drugs, economic struggle, and social oppression (e.g., John Singleton's *Boyz in da Hood* [1991], Lee Daniels's *Precious* [2001], Steve McQueen's *Twelve Years a Slave* [2013]), or highly comedic romances/family films (e.g., Tyler Perry's *Why Did I Get Married?* and the *Madea* franchise). Yet these are not the only African American stories out there—and certainly not the only ones that Black audiences can identify with. When Spike Lee emerged on the filmmaking scene in the late 1980s, he sought to usher in new ways of telling Black stories on-screen that challenged these representational stereotypes.

As Thomas Edison once stated, "Whoever controls the motion picture industry controls the most powerful medium of influence over the people."[8] Vladimir Lenin similarly acknowledged the inherent political and social power of such technology in his famous quotation to his commissar of education Anatoly Lunacharsky: "Of all the arts, for us the cinema is the most important."[9] Like Edison and Lenin, Lee recognizes the power of the film industry in shaping public perception. He is determined to counteract the ways African Americans are both being represented on-screen and participating in the industry's decision-making processes. Believing that the majority of white filmmaking executives lack cultural knowledge or sensitivity to African American experience (a belief sardonically depicted in his pointed satirical drama *Bamboozled*), Lee jump-started his own independent filmmaking company, 40 Acres and a Mule Filmworks (in reference to the US government's broken promise to provide previously enslaved Blacks with their own property following Emancipation). He launched this company with the intent of producing a diverse array of visions of African American life for audience consumption. He has stated, "I think that when I decided I wanted to be a filmmaker, I wanted to attempt to capture the richness of African American culture that I can see, just standing on the corner, or looking out my window every day, and try to get that on screen."[10] This richness includes a variety of African American people (men, women, young, old, light-skinned, dark-skinned, mixed-race), relationships (family, friends, lovers, enemies, coworkers, etc.) and situations (careers, family life, artistic passion, interracial romance, jealousy, bigotry, racial and class discrimination, the law, and so on).

In representing these stories on-screen, Lee hopes to raise hard questions about racial, social, and political issues confronting contemporary Americans—particularly Black Americans—that he feels are neglected within conventional Hollywood films. Much of this marginalization is likely the result of the film industry's ideological risk-averseness, which historically has tended to favor stereotypes and narrative formulas that position African Americans as largely two-dimensional outsiders to white narratives.[11] Counteracting these representations, Lee seeks to show Black culture as *human culture*—not as a culture of "otherness." Yet in the process, he introduces contentious issues that criticize various facets and behavior within African American culture, demanding a sociopolitical awareness informed by his own middle-class conservatism. As articulated in the closing and opening words of his films *School Daze* and *Do the Right Thing*, respectively, the proclamation "Wake Up!" aptly summarizes Lee's primary message of communication to his audiences. He is severely critical of drug culture, Black-on-Black violence, and what he calls out as "ignorance" about self-responsibility and building a better, stronger Black culture. He strongly advocates for education and self-responsibility among members of the African American community. Drawing on the example of his cultural role model—Malcolm X—Lee has argued: "Malcolm said we're the only ones who are gonna do something positive about our lives, so we have to take responsibility for them. You can't blame it all on the white man—that's part of our problem too. In fact, I think education of our younger brothers and sisters is totally on us and up to us now."[12] One of his largest criticisms concerns Black complicity in perpetuating racist stereotypes in entertainment through neo-minstrel performance, which he recognizes in a number of performances from gangsta rap to the grossly hyperbolized representations of Black women in such films as *Big Momma's House, Norbit*, and even Lee Daniels's *Precious*. This criticism is most aptly demonstrated in Lee's satirical film *Bamboozled*, in which he contentiously submits that certain African Americans in contemporary entertainment are involved in their own cultural self-destruction through the perpetuation and revival of racist caricatures from both past and present—with dire implications for the Black community as a whole.

Lee's work is certainly ideological in nature and functions less as a repository of solutions than a visual representation of his own personal concerns. He addresses those issues that matter most to him, without necessarily presenting any answers to the problems. Instead, he focuses on awareness—on educating his audiences about the issues he wants them to be knowledgeable about. As Dan Flory articulated, "When Lee incites controversy, he does so because he wants people to reflect seriously and discuss the matter at hand—whether it be misunderstandings of race and xenophobia or the need to take responsibility for one's actions—and come to a better understanding than they previously have had."[13] Lee himself has contended that he holds no misconceptions that his films will eliminate racial tension or prejudice, rather claiming, "I think the best thing my films can do is provoke discussion."[14] Many of his films are open-ended, not offering conventional wrap-ups or final solutions to the conflicts represented in the narrative. Many leave audiences wondering what the outcome will be or trying to determine what Lee meant for the endings to insinuate. This trope of ambiguity, and Lee's disruption of what he identifies as "Hollywood script structure,"[15] results in unconventional narratives that challenge audiences to engage and try to understand what is happening onscreen. Lee has reported, "More often than not, I let the audience do some work."[16]

Certainly, not all audiences agree with the issues that Lee chooses to present—or the ways he presents them. Scholars such as bell hooks, Michelle Wallace, and Wahneema Lubiano have critiqued a number of his films through allegations of misogyny, sexism, and homophobia.[17] He has recurrently been accused of being racist or prejudiced—particularly against white Americans. Barbara Grizutti Harrison's cover story of Lee for *Esquire* in 1992, entitled "Spike Lee Hates Your Cracker Ass," aggressively encapsulates a perpetuated perception of Lee as an angry Black man who hates white people. While this is certainly not an irrefutably accurate or nuanced engagement with Lee's ideological relationships to whites, his depictions of white characters in his films do not easily let him off the hook. For example, the white characters in *Malcolm X*—about which Harrison's article was written—are entirely two-dimensional, with the vast majority stereotyped as evil, selfish, and manipulative.[18] His depictions of the Jewish Flatbush brothers in *Mo' Better Blues* are even more stereotypically grotesque; the brothers are represented as sniveling, greedy, money-grubbing club owners who don't care about anyone or anything but themselves and their pocketbooks.

Additional scholars level criticisms at Lee's self-contradictions, hypocrisy, and the manner in which he represents African American narratives and experiences on-screen. A particularly prominent example is Amiri Baraka's "Spike Lee at the Movies," in which Baraka criticizes Lee as "the quintessential buppie, almost the spirit of the young, upwardly mobile, Black, petit bourgeois professional."[19] Through this claim Baraka attacks Lee for his middle-classness, capitalist ideology, and social conservatism, arguing that this class position influences Lee's erasure of the economic and social struggles of lower-class African Americans. One can certainly counter Baraka that one's class position does not necessarily make him inattentive to the struggles of the lower classes, particularly since Baraka himself was from an (upper) middle-class background. However, Baraka is but one of many scholars and critics who have challenged Lee for his ideological conservatism and how it influences the ways he depicts Black experience and culture on-screen.

Lee has dismissed many of these allegations and acknowledged some (particularly admitting that he needs to work on his portrayals of women).

But he stands firmly by his right to present his films in whatever way he sees fit. He attempts to alleviate the cultural responsibility of his film work by repeatedly averring, "I have never, ever, felt that I was a spokesperson for Afro-Americans in this country."[20] Yet his unique position as one of the few independently-successful African American filmmakers in cinematic history (and certainly the first to work so overtly against the Hollywood establishment) demands his recognition of the cultural stakes of his work. He himself has repeatedly stated that he wants his work to bring crucial issues to the attention of audiences, so he understands the power that his on-screen representations potentially have. He has also claimed, "I've been blessed with the opportunity to express the views of Black people who otherwise don't have access to power and the media."[21] In this statement, he is clearly accepting responsibility for telling the stories of those who are not able to—a burden not to be taken lightly, or dismissed nonchalantly. Spike Lee's oeuvre must be examined critically; it is imperfect, full of contradictions, and largely biased by Lee's own personal viewpoints and attitudes. That said, his body of work must also be acknowledged and examined for the merits of his auteur approach in bringing diverse representations of African American culture on-screen, and inciting audiences to intellectually engage with the issues he is presenting—whether we agree with them or not.

BLACK ENTREPRENEURSHIP IN THE FILM INDUSTRY

Lee firmly advocates for self-achieved Black entrepreneurship and creative control as the antidote to the film industry's structural racism. He is convinced that the only way to break through the informally established "glass ceiling" is for Black artists to get in "gatekeeping" positions of power themselves.

> The gatekeepers—these are the people that decide what goes on in television, what movies are made, what gets heard on the radio, what's getting written in the magazines—I can tell you those are all exclusively white males. These are the guys making the choices for all of Western Civilization. . . . And we've got to get in those positions. And that's when you'll start to see some change.[22]

Change has started to emerge. Lee made the aforementioned quote in 2000; since then a growing number of African American studio industry executives, independent producers (with their own production companies), and filmmakers have become established forces in the Hollywood scene—including

Stephanie Allain, John Singleton, Effie Brown, Ava DuVernay, Tyler Perry, Jordan Peele, and Oprah Winfrey. However, African Americans make up a very small percentage of these gatekeeping executives, which likely greatly accounts for the limited number of Black-oriented stories in commercial film production. Accordingly, Lee is convinced that the primary method for making sure that Black stories are told the way Black people want them told (or at least how *he* wants them told) is for Black filmmakers to be in positions of power. He views filmmaking as both an art and a business, and is not reluctant to identify himself as a capitalist who seeks both financial power and creative control, which he views as inextricably linked. In an interview with David Breskin, he revealed, "Am I a capitalist? We all are over here. And I'm just trying to get the power to do what I have to do. To get that power you have to accumulate some kind of bank. And that's what I've done. I've always tried to be in an entrepreneurial mode of thinking."[23]

This "entrepreneurial mode of thinking" has manifested in a multitude of business ventures. Aside from initiating and using his own production company (rather than working as a contract director for Hollywood studios), he has also established his own recording studio (40 Acres and a Mule Musicworks), a merchandise store that sells products related to his films (Spike's Joint), and retail lines (e.g., clothing lines, Air Jordan shoe lines). In addition, he has issued multiple publications "demystifying" the development of his film projects,[24] including detailed texts examining the production of each of his first five films (e.g., *Spike Lee's Gotta Have It* [on the making of *She's Gotta Have It*], *Uplift the Race* [on the making of *School Daze*]). His establishment of the moniker "A Spike Lee Joint"—which he typically uses in the opening credits of his self-produced films—pronounces his overt declaration of ownership and entrepreneurship against the conventions of the Hollywood studio system.

As an independent filmmaker, Lee demands ultimate creative control of his film projects, maintaining rights to have the "final cut" before each film is released. He does utilize Hollywood backers—appealing to major studios for financial and distributional support—yet he stipulates in his contracts that he has the rights to all final decisions. In several cases he has had to seek financial and distributional support elsewhere. For his early films, he relied on the support of family (particularly his grandmother), friends, and other local investors. As he gained recognition within the African American community, he also received financial gifts and investments from prominent/wealthy Black figures—Michael Jordan, Janet Jackson, and Oprah Winfrey, among others. Paula Massood has referred to Lee as "the quintessential inside/outside man,"[25] highlighting his propensity to operate independently from yet in collaboration with major film industry studios. Spike has shared, "I think I have the best of both worlds because I'm an independent film-maker with complete creative control of my films. I hire who I want. I have final cut. But at the same time, I go directly to Hollywood for financing and distribution. I find it's best for me to work within the Hollywood system. It's an individual choice, and you have to make up your mind."[26] For this reason, Lee has been criticized as inconsistent, rendered suspicious for his direct industry involvement. While he advocates that African Americans should develop their own production and ownership networks separate from the Hollywood industry, he draws heavily on their resources for economic sup-port. Lee certainly demonstrates business savvy and has clearly figured out ways to play the Hollywood system that allow him to retain control over his film productions; yet one must also think critically about how his economic dependence on various industry entities can influence his filmmaking pro-cess, even though he retains final cut.

Regarding facilitating Black ownership, production, and creativity in filmmaking, Lee's word and actions are most prominently consistent in his personnel hiring. Many currently well-known African American actors cut their teeth in early Spike Lee films, including Samuel L. Jackson, Laurence Fishburne, Halle Berry, Wesley Snipes, Jada Pinkett Smith, and Denzel Wash-ington. Beyond hiring Black actors, he is an avid advocate for facilitating behind-the-scenes opportunities for African Americans as well—including roles in cinematography, costume design, and score composition, as well as others. His contracts demand that African Americans be hired, and he has also worked to make sure that many of his crew members have become estab-lished in unions. Lee has claimed, "It is harder for blacks in the industry. But we have to create our own jobs and make our own films."[27] Accordingly, he built up a consistent, "inner circle" coterie of actors and crew he has worked with regularly throughout his directorial career.

BLACK CREATIVITY AND ARTISTIC EXPRESSION

Lee has maintained, "To me, Black people are the most creative people on this earth."[28] He values his film projects for facilitating the opportunities to bring Black creative artists together, collaboratively weaving stories inspired by their own unique experiences. While one should not state that these art-ists are inherently more creative than any other filmmaking crew members solely on the basis of race (as Lee tries to do), it should be acknowledged that the cooperation of such a number of Black artists in singular, commercial film projects had been virtually unprecedented prior to Lee's emergence on the mainstream stage. Many of these artists directly reference Black culture and heritage in their artistic products, utilizing the films as a platform for sharing it with broader audiences. For example, Ruth Carter's costume design is inspired by her knowledge and research of African American fashions. Ernest Dickerson's cinematography is informed by what facets of Black expression and life he wants to illuminate through his camera. And Terence Blanchard's musical compositions directly stem from his experience and expertise performing an idiom firmly rooted in African American musical traditions—jazz.

Lee's films draw on these various forms of Black cultural expression in experimental ways. For "experimental," I utilize Mia Mask's definition, which describes experimental filmmaking as "encompass[ing] a range of styles that are opposed to—or at least dissimilar from—mainstream commercial feature filmmaking and even documentary moviemaking."[29] Mask explains that the goal of such experimental filmmaking is "to place the viewer in a more active and more thoughtful relationship to the film by provoking spectators to question the meaning of these techniques as they relate to the subject."[30] Lee's oeuvre demonstrates a significant amount of experimentalism—from his postmodern mixing of genres within the context of a single narrative, to his experimentation with various lighting, camera angles, and direct-to-camera addresses, to his "signature shot,"[31] which is designed to disturb the "realism" of the film through a technique that depicts his characters as 'floating,' transcending the ostensible realities in which their characters are rooted.

Beyond these production techniques, Lee's prominent utilization of direct references to African American creative heritage set his films apart from the majority of mainstream motion pictures. He liberally draws on a store of Black cultural references—including literature (e.g., Alex Haley, Zora Neale Hurston), visual arts (African American memorabilia), popular culture (e.g., clothing, sports teams, advertising, television, music videos), and music (featuring historic recordings and commissioned works from a vast number of African American musical artists). Paula Massood characterizes Lee's wellspring of cultural signification as a "polyphonic system of cultural and political references."[32] The intertexuality of his works reflects a cross-media commitment to the African American trope of "signifyin(g),"[33] in which he references, expands, criticizes, and transforms various elements of cultural production to inform his diverse narratives, injecting them with additional, complex layers of potential meaning (ranging from significant references/parallels to Ralph Ellison's *Invisible Man* in *Bamboozled*, to strategic pastiche of Francis Ford Coppola's *Apocalypse Now* in *Da Five Bloods*, among numerous other references to film history, popular culture, and politics throughout the entirety of his works). While one might argue that his postmodern approach to incorporating diverse cultural references within a singular work can be disorienting/disjointed, critical study of these references provides deeper insight into the sociopolitical message(s) that Lee is attempting to convey.

Beyond signifyin(g), Lee also implements production techniques that draw on a characteristic component of African American musical performance—improvisation. He has stated, "I guess [that jazz has influenced my filmmaking] in the sense that I never try to restrict myself. I just let my imagination go very free. And I like to improvise."[34] Such improvisation manifests in his uninhibited approach to screenplay writing, in which he does not adhere to conventional scripting or narrative development. His scripts are bare-bones, and he instead relies heavily on the work of the actors to bring scenes and situations to life. While he does write key dialogue (and certainly maintains a directorial role in all the shooting), he also leaves opportunity for improvisation among the actors. A poignant example is what has been dubbed the "War Council" scene in the film *Jungle Fever* (1991), in which a group of Black female characters (one being the main character's recently jilted wife) discuss their frustrations about Black men and interracial fascination with white women. Lee opened this scene up to the female actors, giving them the premise of the discussion, and letting them create the rest. He stated, "It was completely improvisational. We did between twenty and twenty-five takes. I find the more you talk the more honest you get."[35] These are but a few of the ways that Lee employs a wealth of African American cultural practices, heritage, and experiences in creating his own film projects. Now, I want to turn to examine a particularly prominent aspect of Black culture in his films—and the broader focus of this book—the music.

LEE'S JAZZ

Music—particularly Black music—plays an integral role in Spike Lee's films. He has revealed, "I start thinking about the music for my films at the same moment I'm writing the script. It's part of my creative process. I pay as much attention to the music as I do to the cinematography, casting, and production design."[36] Alex Steyermark, Spike's longtime music supervisor, has claimed that Lee is "incredibly knowledgeable about music. I think music is very important to Spike generally. . . . He devotes a lot of time to it and a lot of resources—the scores on his films are usually very well-budgeted."[37] Lee's film soundtracks draw heavily on Black musical genres, including blues, gospel, R & B, jazz, and hip-hop. They are composed of both licensed popular recordings and commissioned performances and scores—boasting contributions from artists as diverse as Ella Fitzgerald, Public Enemy, Sam Cooke, and Mos Def, as well as composers Bill Lee (his father) and Terence Blanchard. Lee's music selections are crucial in supporting his narratives that voice a diversity of Black experience, history, and culture, promoting Black artists for mass consumption as well as cultural acknowledgment. Just as the films represent a differentiated panoply of African American characters interacting on-screen, they are interwoven with a sonic tapestry of varied African American musical styles, interacting and alluding to the rich history of Black music.

But it is jazz that is most consistently prominent in Lee's soundtracks, particularly in the films' original scores. Lee has addressed this prominence, stating, "Jazz has been an integral part of all my movies."[38] His love for the music runs deep. The son of renowned jazz bassist Bill Lee, Spike grew up listening to and appreciating the music from infancy. Bill Lee himself composed the scores for Spike's first four feature films (*She's Gotta Have It, School Daze, Do the Right Thing*, and *Mo' Better Blues*), as well as several student films Spike produced during his graduate school days at NYU.

But Spike's relationship to jazz is also complicated—a reflection of his troubled relationship with his father, with whom he had a falling-out in the mid-1990s. This relational separation was the culmination of years of unresolved friction and emotional tension (e.g., conflicts about Bill Lee's heroin use, financial instability, and, purportedly, his second, interracial marriage (which may have been the inspiration behind Spike's *Jungle Fever* [1991]), aggravated by Spike's perceptions of his father's lack of familial responsibility and financial reliability in favor of artistic integrity. (Bill Lee, while once an in-demand jazz bassist, refused to play electric instruments despite the potential opportunity for increased gigs. He viewed this as "selling out" and expressed strong disdain for contemporary popular music [e.g., Motown, the Beatles]). In an interview with NPR, Spike discussed how this decision affected their family, revealing his own internal conflict. On one hand, he asserted that he didn't resent his father's decision, stating, "Even today, I don't hold that against my father. I mean he—his integrity—said 'I cannot play electric bass. I'm not going to do it. I can only play acoustic bass.'" On the other hand, Spike claimed: "But when he made the decision that he was not going to play electric bass, my mother had to become a teacher. You know, in a lot of ways, I looked at my father's integrity. But on the other hand, he had five kids. But to him, it didn't matter. He wasn't going to play electric bass."[39] Spike's semi-autobiographical *Crooklyn*—which he cowrote with his siblings Joie and Cinqué Lee—provides insight into his troubled perceptions of his father (and perhaps more broadly, jazz musicians in general). The father in the film, Woody, is a struggling jazz musician (played by Delroy Lindo) who is financially unreliable and, though loving, adds tension and economic strain to the family's life, including added pressure and frustration for the mother Carolyn (played by Alfre Woodard), who, like Spike's mother, worked as a schoolteacher to help support the family. Consider this particularly revealing dialogue between Woody and Carolyn:

> CAROLYN: Woody, we need to make some changes. The money I'm bringing in [from teaching] is not making ends meet. I need your help.
>
> WOODY: You want me to, uh, pick up a guitar and play some rock and roll?
>
> CAROLYN: [emphatically]: YES!

I argue that this tension is essential to understanding the ways that Spike views and represents jazz in his films: a music of integrity, Black creativity, and "authenticity," while at the same time a music sometimes performed by troubled artists who have difficulty maintaining successful relationships while they are devoted to their art.

When interviewed regarding his first feature, *She's Gotta Have It*, Spike claimed, "I feel that jazz is a higher form of music."[40] His assessment of jazz as a "higher form" reveals a complex dynamic that lauds Black creativity with a racial essentialism yet simultaneously positions the music within a high-low artistic hierarchy characteristic of white European assessments of culture. In asserting this hierarchical status, Lee makes proclamations to aesthetic superiority that he hopes will aid jazz's cultural legitimacy within the white cultural establishment, while also presenting his personal proclivity for jazz idioms. While it is unclear exactly what other forms of music Lee is arguing jazz is higher than, I contend that by using the term, he is attempting to spatially elevate the art form's perceived value and, by extension, the perceived value of the films the music is accompanying. To his viewpoint, utilizing "high art" music to accompany the lives and experiences of Black characters on-screen challenges conventional representations of African Americans in film and asserts that the narratives themselves represent valuable culture that should be recognized. Furthermore, I believe this assertion reflects the belief that was instilled in him by his father from a young age: jazz is a music of integrity, not commercial compromise.

The ways Lee utilizes jazz in his films challenges the music's typical Hollywood representations. As examined throughout this book, jazz's semiotic significations in popular film are manifold, ranging from criminality/deviance/sexual promiscuity, to internal anxiety, to sophistication, to markers of historical period. Jazz has been used to underscore narratives featuring both Black and white characters (and occasionally other ethnicities), but its range of uses is consistently rooted in the racialized legacies of the music's representational histories. Jazz is predominantly "othered"; its presence in the sonic background of the film draws attention to itself, alerting the viewer to the specific associations it is trying to trigger. When we hear a bluesy saxophone solo as a mysterious woman slowly walks through corridors in chiaroscuro lighting, we immediately associate her with seduction, loose morals, and deception. As we listen to Antonio Sánchez's percussion improvisations in *Birdman*, innovative as they are, they draw up associations with the "anxiety jazz" that corresponded to characters' internal psychoses in the noir films of the 1950s. As will be examined more in the following chapter, Dick Hyman's performances of classic Great American Songbook standards behind elegant New York penthouse party scenes in Woody Allen's films draw on a parallel history of jazz—the elegance, glamour, and sophistication associated with jazz's "golden age." The soundtracks in Lee's films work against these conventional associations. They do not attempt to reinforce conventional Hollywood signifiers, employing the aforementioned sonic clichés. Instead, they feature jazz as a "natural" part of the sonic backdrop, enhancing the emotional content of the narrative and accompanying the primarily Black characters as they navigate through everyday situations.

For Lee, jazz is the sonic embodiment of Black musical tradition and cultural creativity, an authentic site of Black musical artists' most profound innovation and individual expression. While he acknowledges the musical value of early rock and roll, R & B, soul, funk, and hip-hop artists, Lee prefers jazz, arguing that it "lends a sense of tradition and timelessness" to his films.[41] This investment in jazz as tradition permeates Lee's broader filmmaking ideology that seeks to expose Black (and also other) audiences to the richness of African American culture and history. He believes jazz is an integral part of Black heritage, and that modern-day Black audiences should understand and engage with the music—an engagement that he contends is sorely lacking among younger Black generations. Echoing several African American jazz artists' (and critics') concerns with the small percentages of Black audiences purchasing jazz and attending performances,[42] Lee lamented, "The sad thing . . . is that we have whole generations of black people who know nothing about jazz. . . . Jazz music is black music and that's what we're projecting in my film."[43]

Certainly, jazz is not solely Black music—its rich development through the contributions of whites, Hispanics, Africans, Asians, and many others speaks to that fact. However, jazz's rootedness in Black culture and significance in

African American history cannot be denied. Its associations with creativity and freedom reflect its historical value as the voices through which an overwhelmingly marginalized African American population could speak. Throughout jazz history, artists such as Louis Armstrong, Billie Holiday, Duke Ellington, Dizzy Gillespie, Miles Davis, Charles Mingus, and John Coltrane challenged racism and cultural oppression through musical activism. Accordingly, Lee weaves these jazz voices into the variegated tapestry of Black experience he seeks to represent on-screen, injecting his film with direct connections to Black musical heritage, as well as providing the opportunity for present-day jazz musicians to continue developing their own voices and sharing them with (and beyond) Black audiences.

Throughout his filmmaking career, Lee has employed a number of performing jazz musicians to participate in his soundtracks. While Bill Lee and Terence Blanchard are the obvious examples, his soundtracks have included an array of prominent jazz artists, including the Branford Marsalis Quartet (featuring Kenny Kirkland, Jeff "Tain" Watts, and Robert Hurst), Kenny Baron, and many others. "Jazz" for Lee—as for many who are familiar with its vast diversity of styles—encompasses a wide range of musical expression. His films feature the blues, bebop, swing, modal jazz, jazz-rap fusion, hard bop, and jazz-orchestral scores. To illustrate this diversity, I need only turn to one of his films—significantly, a movie about a jazz musician, as well as the first film that launched Terence Blanchard's film-scoring career:[44] *Mo' Better Blues*.

MO' BETTER *MAKES IT MO' BETTER*

> I always knew I would do a movie about the music. I'm talking about jazz,
> the music I grew up with. Jazz isn't the only type of music that I listen to,
> but it's the music I feel closest to.[45]
> —SPIKE LEE

A brief reading of Lee's film *Mo' Better Blues* (1990) highlights the director's complex personal relationship to jazz. This film is an excellent case study of Lee's usage of jazz as a projection of his ideological desires to represent the music as authentic Black culture/creativity and tradition/cultural heritage, while also illuminating his conflicted personal perceptions of how jazz musicians might struggle with successful relationships in service of their art. Additionally, it illustrates his impetus to counteract traditional Hollywood jazz narratives, and to present jazz as a modern and valuable art form (particularly among Black audiences). The film certainly has its problems (as I address below), but it is also the only film Lee ever made about musicians, and the best representation of how his relationship to jazz music informs his film work.

The film's premise follows the character of Bleek Gilliam (Denzel Washington), a jazz trumpet player committed to his art who navigates his own musical commitment alongside his relationships with his father, two different female love interests, his bandmates, and his irresponsible best friend/manager, Giant (Spike Lee). Throughout the narrative Bleek demonstrates a passionate dedication to his performance, the development of his craft, and the integrity of his music. This artistic commitment has negative consequences, manifesting in frustration from his childhood friends (in the beginning of the film), conflicts with his lovers, and jealousy and tension with bandmates. (It is worth noting that in a scene between Bleek and his lover Indigo [played by Joie Lee], Indigo states that her mother warned her, "Don't marry a musician".) Toward the end of the film, when Bleek's ability to play is finally jeopardized (he gets hit in the mouth with his own trumpet as he tries to protect Giant from violent gambling-debt collectors), his separation from his art clearly shatters him and his sanity. It takes the replacement of his love for his music with love for his family (a wife and child) to help him move beyond the devastation. The script was inspired by Lee's own observations and experiences as a witness to his father's career as a jazz musician who refused to compromise his art. Spike has stated, "Everything I know about jazz, I know from my father. I saw his integrity, how he was not going to play just any kind of music, no matter how much money he could make."[46] Lee projects this integrity and musical commitment onto his depiction of Bleek's character, who navigates similar elements of artistic ideology, stylistic preference, and understanding of music as an integral component of self-identity. (At the same time, he highlights how this "integrity" puts a strain on personal relationships.)

The narrative itself contrasts with conventional Hollywood representations of jazz artists as drug-inflicted, disturbed, and irresponsible. Lee stated, "I did not want to make another typical story of a jazz musician who's an alcoholic or who's hooked on heroin."[47] He produced the film soon after the release of two prominent jazz films, Bertrand Tavernier's *Round Midnight* (1986) and Clint Eastwood's *Bird* (1988), both of which darkly represent depressing illustrations of the lives of jazz musicians. These films were but the more recent manifestations of decades of dark cinematic depictions of the Black (and also white) jazz artist—evidenced since the 1950s in such films as Michael Curtiz's *Young Man with a Horn* (1950), Otto Preminger's *The Man with the Golden Arm* (1955), Leo Penn's *A Man Called Adam* (1966),

Herbert Danska's *Sweet Love, Bitter* (1967), and Sidney J. Furie's *Lady Sings the Blues* (1972).[48]

Determined to work against these stereotypes, Lee chose to illustrate Bleek's life as one characterized by both creativity and (later) social/familial responsibility—perhaps the ideal that Spike wished for from his own father. He stated, "I wanted to show a man who could make decisions, who had a family life, who wasn't a drug addict or alcoholic."[49] Contradictorily (or perhaps not), it is Bleek's jazz career and commitment to his music that renders him indecisive, immature, and selfish. It is only after he gives up performing (out of necessity due to his injury) that he becomes a fully responsible, mature family man. Jazz scholar Krin Gabbard similarly notes that Bleek's renunciation of jazz allows him to reclaim his masculinity through responsible fatherhood, avoiding the destructive pitfalls (i.e., metaphorical castration) of the jazz life.[50] Through such representations Lee reinforces Hollywood's conventional associations of jazz with decadence and irresponsibility more than he might like to admit. That said, Bleek's portrayal as a jazz artist sharply contrasts with the dark depictions of Rick Martin (in *Young Man with a Horn*), Charlie Parker (in *Bird*), and Dale Turner (in *Round Midnight*), instead appearing meticulous, passionate, and fairly heroic—not a pitiful creature lost in the throes of his own drug-induced self-destruction.

Lee wanted to depict an "authentic" Black character who appeared relatable, creative, likable, and real. Bleek isn't perfect, but he isn't hyperbolized. He is not represented as a spectacular "other"—a genius, incomprehensible artist who lives in a cyclic pattern of excess and self-destruction. He is shown laughing while playing catch with his dad, sharing "real" intimate moments with his lovers, hanging out and bantering with his bandmates, and getting in arguments and experiencing conflict and frustration much as everyday people do. The film highlights Black creativity, culture, camaraderie, and familial and friendly love in ways that neither *Round Midnight* nor *Bird* demonstrates. As Lee himself contended, "Both were narrow depictions of the lives of Black musicians, as seen through the eyes of White screenwriters and White directors."[51] With the exceptions of the main character roles themselves, neither of these films engaged with any other Black characters on any substantial level, instead focusing on the protagonists' relationships with their white acquaintances. Lee instead sought to represent Bleek as a fundamentally good, if flawed, Black musician, one whose commitment to his craft—and whose eventual commitment to his family—was aspirational.

Again, the characters represented in *Mo' Better Blues* are not perfect. For a good portion of the film, Bleek has the propensity to be a selfish, preoccupied jerk. He takes advantage of both of his lovers and often seems to be quite callous in his treatment of them. The women themselves are highly stereotypical and two-dimensional. Indigo (Joie Lee) is a responsible schoolteacher, while Clarke (Cynda Williams) is a seductive, aspiring jazz singer. This love triangle reinforces conventional film stereotypes that represent Black women as either Madonnas or whores—particularly in love triangle scenarios. Both women are relatively pathetic characters, pleading for love and affirmation from Bleek and (generally) turning a blind eye to his infidelities.[52]

His representations of the Jewish club owners in the film—Moe and Josh Flatbush—also leave a lot to be desired, as discussed earlier in this chapter. In depicting them as greedy, selfish, and manipulative tricksters who are screwing over Bleek and his ensemble in their financial contract, Lee seems to imply that all Jews (and all white people for that matter, since they are the only whites in the film) are out to oppress and take advantage of others (especially Blacks) for their own gains (depictions that ultimately incited controversy from the Anti-Defamation League [ADF]). As discussed in my assessments earlier in this chapter, Lee has often struggled with the ways he represents women and non-Black characters, and he has been criticized heavily for it. These criticisms should not be dismissed, and Lee's audiences should be careful to assess the ways his depictions of certain types of characters both reinforce conventional stereotypes and potentially introduce new ones. Yet, taking the good with the bad, audiences must also acknowledge how his films potentially introduce us to a diversity of ostensibly realistic Black characters whose stories are rarely shared on-screen. In the case of *Mo' Better Blues*, that is the depiction of a Black jazz musician—one who practices, challenges himself, works/hangs out with other Black jazz musicians, and has made a steady, responsible career of playing music.

In his commitment to represent Bleek as a realistic Black jazz musician, Lee invested a significant amount of research and production into portraying the musical elements of the narrative with as much fidelity to "real life" as possible. He drew heavily on information from his father, Bill Lee, Terence Blanchard, and several other jazz artists to develop an "authentic" portrayal of the musicians and their experiences. For example, he conducted a particularly long interview with saxophonist Branford Marsalis, who performs on the soundtrack (dubbing the parts for Shadow, the on-screen saxophonist played by Wesley Snipes), because, "since Branford is part of the young generation of jazz musicians that inspired the film, [Lee] thought his views on the music . . . would be helpful in bringing Bleek to life."[53]

One of the strongest depictions of "authentic" jazz musicianship is Bleek's continual musical development through solitary practice, an element of musicianship that is so germane and vital but is rarely (if ever) represented in films about musicians. Several scenes depict Bleek air-fingering parts, singing licks, practicing scales and technical exercises, and figuring out harmonies at the piano while muttering chord changes to himself. These depictions work against the "creative genius" or primitivist narratives that permeate conventional Hollywood depictions of Black artists, in which the musicians appear to be imbued with magical musical gifts that require no training or development. Bleek takes his art seriously, and he works at it. In the scene where we first meet Clarke—Bleek's second lover—he reprimands her for coming to visit him during his regularly scheduled practice time. She retorts, "Everything with you is so damn regulated. A certain time to do this, a certain time to do that. Everything's on a schedule or timetable." While Bleek looks like a jerk in this scene, this does not inaccurately portray how some successful jazz musicians may approach their practicing—with a rigorous, consistent daily schedule.

Lee also gives ample screen time to the nuances of jazz performance. Several pieces were written for the film by Branford Marsalis and Bill Lee, including "Say Hey," "Beneath the Underdog" (alluding to Charles Mingus's autobiography), "Pop Top 40," "Again Never," "Knocked Out of the Box," the eponymous "Mo' Better Blues," and an updated arrangement of W. C. Handy's "Harlem Blues." In many cases, the pieces are performed in their entirety by the Bleek Gilliam Quintet onstage at their local jazz club. Cinematographer Ernest Dickerson fluidly moves through a variety of shots during the performance. Viewers are offered close-ups of the musicians' faces and bodies while they are performing, and are granted witness to the nuances of them breathing, drumming, fingering the trumpet valves or saxophone keys, and plucking the bass strings. The camera engages with the performance from multiple angles—close-ups from above, below, and to the side, wide shots looking down from the club balcony, "over the shoulder" shots behind the band members looking down at their instruments or out into the audience, and "flying shots" closing in from wide to close-up.

We are also privy to the more subtle interactions often present in jazz performances. We see bassist Bottom Hammer (Bill Nunn) moving his lips along with the bass lines he is playing, as many bassists do.[54] We perceive the musicians physically internalizing the music, bobbing their heads and tapping their feet. Additionally, bandstand camaraderie is displayed through a number of ways; the ensemble members encourage each other through physical gestures (e.g., clapping on the back), visual gestures (e.g., nods, smiles, eye contact), and verbal cues (e.g., "Yeah!"). These depictions give audiences a closer look at the creation of the music (informed by the scenes throughout the film that show the characters practicing, writing music, discussing how they want to play the charts, etc.), the interactions between the musicians onstage, and the aesthetics of witnessing a live jazz performance.

The realism of these moments is compounded by Terence Blanchard's involvement in the film. Lee wanted all the diegetic performance scenes—of which there are many—to look as authentic as possible. He claimed, "I did not want jazz critics . . . nitpicking about the realism of the music scenes. I can hear them now: 'How can Spike Lee, son of a famous jazz musician, Bill Lee, present jazz music inaccurately, especially after he criticized Clint Eastwood's film?' Give me a break, guys!"[55] Accordingly, he hired professional jazz musicians to not only record the music but also to tutor the actors in convincingly emulating the performance of the recordings. Blanchard worked with Denzel Washington, while artists such as Branford Marsalis, bassist Michael Fleming, saxophonist Donald Harrison, and Spike's father, Bill, worked with the other members of Bleek's Quintet, which included Shadow Henderson (Wesley Snipes), Left Hand Lacey (Giancarlo Esposito), Bottom Hammer (Bill Nunn), and Rhythm Jones (Jeff Watts, who performed for himself).

The music coaches each employed their own unique approaches, meeting with the actors five days a week to help them solidify their techniques. Lee states, "Every time we shot a musical sequence [the musicians] were there, watching their pupils and making sure the fingering, mannerisms, and breathing were accurate, or at least believable."[56] Blanchard collaborated extensively with Washington, teaching him to memorize the fingering, as well as to mentally "sing" the melodies, so that his fingering aligned with the musicality and phrasing of the tunes, regardless of whether or not the pitches were correct. Terence shared his methods here:

> I made a videotape of myself playing Bleek's trumpet parts,[57] and sent it to Denzel in California so he'd have something to work with before he came to New York to begin rehearsals. It would have taken too long for me to show him every note and every scale, so I had him memorize the fingerings to each song. . . . I [later] had Denzel put the trumpet down, listen to the track, and learn to "sing" his part. Once he memorized a song this way, it was easier for him to follow the playback track. He could press any valve on the trumpet, even if it wasn't the right one. And as long as he pressed with confidence, and in sync, while blowing into the horn, his execution was believable.[58]

Lee expressed his confidence in Blanchard's—and by extension Washington's—work. He stated, "Next to my father, Terence had the most impact on how we captured the music on screen. And because of his involvement, I'm

Figure 3.1. Bleek Gilliam (Denzel Washington) performing in *Mo' Better Blues*.

sure we've done it, to the best of our abilities, with utmost integrity. Terence made it his personal crusade to see that Denzel looked real on-screen—his trumpet techniques, mannerisms, attitude. He wanted Denzel to come across nothing short of a real-life musician."[59] I personally was impressed with the convincing manner in which Denzel portrayed a performing jazz musician—a welcome relief from an extensive history of cinema in which the actors do not remotely appear to be playing the music that is heard in the soundtrack (e.g., *Bird*). Denzel's breathing is right in time with the musical phrasing, his valving is (or at least appears to be) accurate, and the intensity of focus on his face while he plays aptly depicts a jazz trumpeter dedicated to his musical craft. Wesley Snipes, who plays saxophonist Shadow Henderson, is not quite as convincing. He moves around a bit too aggressively while he solos to facilitate proper embouchure or breath support, and there are close-ups during one of his solos where he clearly should have been taking breaths but didn't. That said, Denzel's performance—along with the performances of Bill Nunn on bass and Jeff Watts on drums (a simpler task, considering Jeff himself is a drummer)—was quite impressive.

A key framework of *Mo' Better Blues* is Lee's commitment to and respect for jazz music itself as a sonic reflection of Black cultural creativity and heritage. Largely due to his exposure through his father's career, Lee is well versed in jazz music, its historical recordings, and its contemporary artists. He claims that when he wrote the screenplay for *Mo' Better Blues*, he already knew that he wanted the Branford Marsalis Quartet[60] to record all of the featured music. Aside from the original feature tracks, the film's soundtrack is interspersed with a number of classic jazz tunes composed and performed by renowned Black jazz artists, including "All Blues" (Miles Davis), "Tunji" (John Coltrane), "Mercy, Mercy, Mercy" (Joe Zawinul), "Footprints" (Wayne Shorter), "Lonely Woman" (Ornette Coleman), and "Goodbye Pork Pie Hat" (Charles Mingus), among others. The most significant licensed recording of the film is Part I of John Coltrane's *A Love Supreme*, "Acknowledgment."[61] Lee combines this full recording with a montage revealing the "supreme love" of family, as Bleek romances Indigo, gets married, has a child, and celebrates the child growing up. This audio-visual placement evokes Coltrane's own spirituality and recognition of jazz music as a healing, universal element that also draws on its roots in Black expression.

Ultimately, *Mo' Better Blues* is Lee's (fraught) love letter to jazz, as well as his proselytist platform. His primary goal with this film was to encourage more audiences (particularly Black audiences) to connect with jazz. "So much good jazz goes unheard. . . . If people are exposed to jazz through this film, that's wonderful. I hope that *A Love Supreme* sells two hundred thousand more copies because of [this movie]."[62] For better or for worse, for the "music he feels closest to," *Mo' Better Blues* is Lee's capstone homage.

TERENCE BLANCHARD: POLITICS AND PERSONAL EXPRESSION

In many ways, Blanchard and Lee share an ideological commitment to high-lighting Black experience and creativity, working against the erasures of African American culture and authorship within American culture industries. While Lee's platform of expression is through filmmaking, Blanchard's is through musical composition and performance. As described earlier in this chapter, his body of works reflects a fervent activism that manifests in his album titles, the content of his performance projects, and his own musical expression. Blanchard maintains, "I've always felt that [in] being an artist, you have to be socially conscious. . . . As artists, part of our job is to document our environment, our community, as we're experiencing it, and hopefully shine a light on it."[63]

Blanchard positions his own activism within a historical lineage of Black jazz artists who have overtly expressed their political ideologies through their musical projects.

> John Coltrane wrote a tune called "Alabama" for the four little girls that were killed [in 1963's 16th Street Baptist Church bombing]. I take my cues from those guys, and I stand on their shoulders. Those are the

dudes who inspire me. Max Roach wrote the Freedom Now Suite. It's incumbent upon me—or at least, I feel like it is—to keep the discussion going in my realm of the world. . . . If me writing a song, or writing some music to help push [agendas] forward can help, so be it.[64]

Like Lee, he believes in the effective potential of the cinematic format to bring issues to the attention of mass audiences. He thus views his compositional work for Lee's soundtracks as an opportunity for musical activism. He too has uttered contempt and frustration with the lack of diverse African American stories within the film industry and loathes the preponderance of stereotypes that taint Black representations when they are present: "I have strong emotions about some of these movies being made about Black life and Afro-American culture that are very one-dimensional. I'm worried that a lot of directors aren't respecting the Afro-American audience as they should. They think we only want to see one type of film. It's like the 1970s, the [Blaxploitation] period of *Superfly*. It's not the truth."[65] He has further expressed frustration "about African Americans being pigeonholed into this stereotype of what we are. I know the diversity of the culture, so my whole plan was to not give in to that easy stereotype and, instead, to try to build up [Black film] characters in other, unusual ways: To say that they're just like anybody else. They have the same issues of family, loyalty, responsibility, and all that."[66]

Blanchard works against such myopic representation in his jazz scores, focusing on the "authentic" humanity and emotion of the on-screen characters. As examined earlier in this chapter, jazz scores have often been utilized in reinforcing associational links between sonic tropes and transgressive or "othered" character traits. In contrast, Blanchard utilizes jazz elements in ways that dispel these associational myths, drawing on the richness of jazz musical expression to tell Black stories in nonstereotypical ways. He argues that the possibilities of jazz composition and performance well exceed the musical stereotypes that we have come to recognize in conventional Hollywood films. Accordingly, he has claimed,

> One of the things that I'm trying to do [in my writing] is bring the music I love to film. Duke Ellington was probably the only composer who got to score film using [jazz] with some degree of integrity. I get tired of seeing downtrodden figures, and all of a sudden you hear saxophones swinging. Jazz can be funny, can be sad, can be serious, . . . You don't have to hear drums all the time or hear a bass walking all the time. There's a lot of room for this music to be used in very creative ways. It can bring something very fresh to this industry.[67]

This freshness comes in the forms of his cross-genre and cross-ensemble compositions, in which he draws on a diversity of musical elements from jazz, Romantic-style orchestral scoring, folk music, and other popular, classical, and electronic styles. He experiments widely with utilizing a variety of orchestral and ensemble timbres, interweaving contrapuntal lines of strings, horns, and woodwinds, and often writing pieces that employ small jazz groups and large orchestras simultaneously. Blanchard himself has explained, "One of the great things about this business is it gives me a chance to write some of the craziest shit for the most outrageous orchestrations and ensembles—music I wouldn't get a chance to write just being a jazz musician."[68]

The unifying thread in his compositional style for film scores is his strong emphasis on clear, poignant melodies, designed to support the emotions of the on-screen characters. He has been known to incorporate aspects of the blues, swing, funk, and Latin rhythms into his film compositions. Additionally, his scores represent a diversity of engagements with various rhythms, grooves, and syncopations—fresh, yet evident indicators of his jazz experience. It is in these ways that Blanchard's scores differ significantly from either conventional classical Hollywood scores *or* jazz scores. In integrating all these different musical elements, Blanchard challenges film score conventions, problematizing genre boundaries and pushing "jazz" beyond its traditional and associational limits. He utilizes a wide range of timbral, rhythmic, and tonal possibilities for jazz composition and performance, exceeding regimented expectations of genre and style.[69] He declared to me,

> Everybody has just assumed that film scores involve a certain thing, but what jazz hasn't been used for is exploiting all of the different colors and tones within the music which comes from a different rhythmic base—which, when combined with film, can give you something unique from what most people are accustomed to hearing. . . . . Jazz can be humorous, it can be sad, it can be triumphant, it can be heroic. It's all about the composer and how he can envision the music being utilized. There are no limits.[70]

Divorcing himself from stereotypical jazz tropes in film, Blanchard creates scores that contribute new meanings to the images and themes they are accompanying on-screen, supporting both his and Lee's interests in providing film audiences with "authentic," diverse representations of African American experience and creativity.

Now, it is certainly important to recall that due to the hierarchical structure of film production, Blanchard's music is composed and utilized in service of the film—or, more specifically, Lee's aesthetic desires. Blanchard and Lee may not always see eye-to-eye politically or aesthetically, but Blanchard must ultimately adhere to Lee's decisions. One example of a disagreement between the two pertained to a scene in *Jungle Fever*, in which the Good Reverend Doctor (Ossie Davis) shoots and kills his crack-addicted son Gator (Samuel L. Jackson) in front of his wife. Blanchard maintained, "I saw that scene with no music—to draw right into the mother's pain. . . . But [Spike] wanted to a put a hymn there. It works, but it's a little distracting for me because it kind of takes you out of it."[71]

That said, Blanchard has lauded their collaborative relationship, claiming that Lee largely grants him artistic freedom and often allows him to make the preponderance of the musical decisions. Blanchard has claimed, "Since he trusts me so much, he likes to get [right] in the [recording] studio. . . . And then he tweaks here and there—just minor stuff, not major. He never cuts my music. Out of all the films I've done with him, I think only one scene has been cut."[72] Blanchard has not received nearly the same level of independence from other directors he has worked with, in which his scores have been more significantly edited, chopped, moved around, or even omitted entirely.[73] With Lee—as a result of Lee's personal confidence in Blanchard's work as an artist, their shared ideological commitments, and their extensive collaborative history—Blanchard has achieved a level of creative autonomy that exceeds typical film scoring labor and has only rarely occurred in some of the key director/composer collaborations in cinematic history (e.g., Steven Spielberg/John Williams, Tim Burton/Danny Elfman, Sam Mendes/Thomas Newman).

Blanchard uses his work for Lee's films as a platform for his own artistic and ideological expression. Creatively, he finds working in film (and other mediums) to be a welcome challenge to his own artistic development. He has claimed, "[Working on film scores] is liberating for me because the limitations bring about a certain kind of creativity—you have to be creative because you only have a certain amount of space [and time] to work with."[74] This has provided him opportunities to channel his improvisational and compositional talents into efficiently producing scores that are not only coherent, but also support the emotions and themes of the film narratives. Blanchard shared with me, "[My experience in film] has helped [my jazz performance] because, while thinking quickly on my feet, the music stays within the context of the story—it doesn't go all over the place and meander."[75] Film scoring also allows him to experiment with new musical forms, orchestrations, and tone colors; the work often provides him with the financial and personnel resources to compose for large numbers of musicians and instruments—giving him opportunities to experiment with orchestral arrangements that are not possible when he is composing for his own small jazz group.

Ideologically, Blanchard's collaborations with Lee have also afforded him the opportunity to translate his political reactions to particular historical events, racial injustices, and Black experiences into intentional musical statements. Several of these projects—*Malcolm X* (1992), *4 Little Girls* (1997), and *When the Levees Broke: A Requiem in Four Acts* (2006)—are particularly significant. In fact, the themes and messages of these films were so politically important to Blanchard that he extended his musical responses in expanded, self-led musical projects. His two extended albums to date—*The Malcolm X Jazz Suite* and *A Tale of God's Will: A Requiem for Katrina*—illustrate how Blanchard used Lee's films as creative springboards for developing his own musical and political voice.

MALCOLM X

Malcom X is a controversial figure in American history. He was a man of passion, conviction, and contradiction—of revolution, evolution, and spiritual conversion. Many Americans associate him with the Black militancy, supremacy, and separatism he espoused as a minister for the Nation of Islam throughout the 1950s and early 1960s, but his full history reveals a more complicated past—one permeated with multiple shifting and transforming stages of ideology and political action.

It was nearly thirty years after his death before a feature film was made about Malcolm's life. There had been attempts—screenplays written, producers hired—but none came to fruition. There are multiple speculations why none of these endeavors panned out, not the least of which was the subject matter. Malcolm X has often been associated with antiwhite Black militancy, a topic that white filmmakers were likely not readily willing to risk producing, given its ostensibly limited commercial appeal and controversial nature. As Jason Vest claimed, "Fears that Malcolm's stridency would put off viewers (particularly white viewers) affected studio thinking about Malcolm X's financial viability."[76] So, despite film producer Marvin Worth's acquisition of the rights to Alex Haley's *Autobiography of Malcolm X* in the late 1960s[77]—and attention paid by such filmmakers as James Baldwin, Arnold Perl, David Mamet, Charles Fuller, and Sidney Lumet—the film did not become a reality until the 1990s.

Initially, Warner Bros. was interested in having director Norman Jewison direct the film, as he had produced an Oscar-nominated documentary about Malcolm in 1971. Spike Lee was incensed by the circulating news, believing that only an African American (specifically him) would be able to "properly" make a film about such a significant Black figure. He passionately claimed, "We—I gotta make our own Goddamn films. Fuck having these white boys fuck up telling our stories. We gotta tell our own as only we can."[78] This statement reinforces Lee's condemnations of how the white-controlled film industry has appeared generally insensitive to the stories and experiences of Black people on-screen, and has (in Lee's view), consistently determined how Blacks are represented with sole regard to lining their own pocketbooks. He averred, "Too many times have white people controlled what should have been Black films. And there is a reason for this. They still feel—I'm talking about the major Hollywood studios—that white moviegoers here in America are not interested in films with Black subject matter . . . the studios have no respect for the buying power of the Black market."[79]

In a concerted effort to prevent similar treatment of Malcolm X's story, Lee relentlessly pursued the project, eventually negotiating with both the studio and Norman Jewison in order to obtain the rights to the film.[80] Once he was commissioned, he rewrote the Baldwin-Perl screenplay, incorporating aspects of Haley's *Autobiography* and Lee's own interviews with Malcom's living family and associates—including Betty X (Malcolm's wife), Minister Louis Farrakhan, and members of the Nation of Islam who had worked closely with Malcolm in his lifetime.[81]

The Malcolm X we see on-screen is very much Lee's idealized Malcolm. He himself has confessed this point, stating, "Malcolm X is my artistic vision. The film is my interpretation of the man. It's nobody else's."[82] Yet it is not truly "nobody else's"; the contributions of many others greatly inform the final outcome of the film. Most prominent is Denzel Washington, whose commitment to researching the role (e.g., reading texts about Malcolm, listening to his speeches, watching live films) came to impressive fruition in his portrayals. The screenplay itself, while rewritten and adapted, was substantially informed by the original Baldwin-Perl script, with the bulk of the rewriting occurring in the third act.[83] A multitude of external influences (including pressure from Malcolm's family and others regarding how he should be represented) likely influenced the final production in unquantifiable (and perhaps subconscious) ways. Additionally, a whole host of creative production personnel (e.g., cinematographers, actors, costumers) contributed to the film's final release. Lee is an auteur, yes, but he is not a one-man show. One especially influential contributor was Terence Blanchard, whose work on the *Malcolm* soundtrack I will now turn to.

MUSIC FOR MALCOLM: THE MALCOLM X JAZZ SUITE

The *Malcolm X* soundtrack features a combination of licensed commercial recordings and original score. The commercial tunes include an expansive number of performances by popular Black recording artists, helping situate the passage of time over the forty-year span the film addresses. As the line producer for the film, John Kilik, stated, "The music, the songs that are . . . on the soundtrack, not only tell the history of Malcolm X from 1925 until 1965, but much history of Black music during that forty-year period."[84] These recordings include recognizable pieces by such artists as Lionel Hampton, Billie Holiday, Louis Jordan, John Coltrane, Ray Charles, Aretha Franklin, and Sam Cooke.

Beyond these recordings, the remainder of the musical soundtrack is composed of Terence Blanchard's original instrumental score. One might argue that this soundtrack is a "typical" Hollywood film score. Blanchard's poignant compositions guide us through the various stages of the narrative, enhancing the situations on-screen through musical evocations of emotion. His approach is clearly representative of what Claudia Gorbman would identify as the "classic model" of film-scoring conventions.[85] This model is rooted in Romantic orchestral idioms, and draws heavily on conventional connotative musical elements (or *codes*) that function as signifiers of milieu and mood.

Gorbman delineates seven primary conventions in film music, "whose combination and recombination constitutes an easily recognized discursive field."[86] They are:

(1) *Invisibility*: The technical apparatus of nondiegetic music must not be visible

(2) *Inaudibility*: Music is not meant to be heard consciously. As such, it should subordinate itself to dialogue, to visuals, that is, to the primary vehicles of the narrative

(3) *Signifier of Emotion*: Soundtrack music may set specific moods and emphasize particular emotions suggested in the narrative, but first and foremost it is a signifier of emotion itself

(4) *Narrative Cueing*: (a) *referential/narrative*—music gives referential and narrative cues, for example, indicating point of view, supplying formal demarcations and establishing setting and characters; (b) *connotative*—music "interprets" and "illustrates" narrative events

(5) *Continuity*: Music provides formal and rhythmic continuity— between shots, in transitions between scenes, by filling "gaps"

(6) **Unity:** Via repetition and variation of musical material and instrumentation, music aids in the construction of formal and narrative unity

(7) A given film score may violate any of the principles above, providing the violation is at the service of the other principles.[87]

Blanchard's score exhibits many of these formulas, falling within this longstanding Hollywood tradition. Structurally, it is subordinated to narrative form, marking transitions, underscoring montage scenes, and aiding the overall continuity of the film. While noticeable, it does not overpower the dialogue or the story, but rather supports it.

Emotional affect is one of the key functions of Blanchard's work. In a poignant flashback scene, a group of Ku Klux Klan members storm Malcolm's parents' home with torches. As Malcolm and his family frantically run through the house—issuing blood-chilling screams as the walls are engulfed in vibrant flames around them—Blanchard heightens the tension with explosive cymbal crashes and wrenching, dissonant string figures. In another significantly powerful scene, Malcolm leads a massive group of Black activists to the hospital to confirm (and demand) that a friend of theirs who had been beaten—Brother Johnson—is getting proper care. Their confrontational determination and outrage at Johnson's situation resounds in the score's militant march-style percussion that captures the aggressiveness of their movement. These drums are featured throughout the entire scene, first accompanying a syncopated, brass-heavy reprisal of "Malcolm's Theme," ever growing in dynamic intensity and supported by forceful string and brass figures. The drums continue (solo) as Malcolm confronts the police chief guarding the hospital; each snare roll captures the welling intensity burning beneath Malcolm's cool but threatening demeanor. This militant march concludes only when Malcolm is finally satisfied that Johnson is being cared for, and dramatically disperses the crowd with a point of his finger. This leads to the incredulous police officer uttering, "That's too much power for one man to have." These are just a few examples of how Blanchard's score effectively contributes to the emotional elements of the narrative. From romance to sorrow, awe to horror, Blanchard's orchestrations draw audiences into Malcolm's story through affective emotional experience.

Another primary function of this score is its contribution to the unity and contextual coherence of the (quite lengthy) film. This is largely accomplished through Blanchard's focus on several primary melodic themes, interwoven throughout the story. Key characters are associated with their own leitmotif themes—including Laura (Malcolm's girlfriend in his early years), Elijah

Muhammad, Betty X, and Malcolm himself. Gorbman maintains, "The major unifying force in Hollywood scoring is the use of musical themes. . . . The thematic score provides a built-in unity of statement and variation, as well as a semiotic subsystem. The repetition, interaction, and variation of musical themes throughout a film contributes much to the clarity of its dramaturgy and to the clarity of its formal structures."[88]

The theme that is most frequently reprised in the *Malcolm X* score, aptly called "Malcolm's Theme," appears in various stylistic manifestations over the course of the three-and-a-half-hour film. In its first iteration, it is heard during the opening credits, underscoring a vitriolic voiceover of Malcolm (Denzel) condemning and charging the white man for racial injustice (e.g., "I charge the white man with being the greatest murderer on earth . . . kidnapper on earth"). The scene is set against the backdrop of an American flag juxtaposed against violent footage of Rodney King being beaten by police officers. Blanchard's theme is somber and militant; a solo trumpet cries out the melody against combative, dirgelike bass drum hits and minor harmonic string accompaniment. The composition integrates a wordless choir toward the end, as the American flag burns away to leave a red, white, and blue X on the screen.

From that point onward, the theme represents Malcolm, signifying his character development throughout various periods of his life. As he navigates through diverse stages, from being a young criminal in Detroit, to a devout follower of Elijah Muhammad, to a militant Nation of Islam leader, to a loving family man, permutations of the theme reflect different moods and atmospheres that parallel the character's dynamic evolution. When Malcolm first meets Elijah Muhammad, the theme is featured as a majestic French horn solo supported by high tremolo strings that sonically capture Malcolm's simultaneous anxiety and reverence for the moment. Snippets of the theme are introduced with a Middle Eastern flavor in the scenes where Malcolm visits Mecca and Egypt, through the utilization of oboe melody, sitar, high woodwinds, percussion such as finger cymbals and tambourine, and traditional Middle Eastern modes and rhythms.

Audiences also hear jazz-oriented versions of the theme. In one scene we are treated to a swinging big-band orchestration of the tune, as Malcolm escapes in a car from a formidable Harlem gangster, West Indian Archie, with his lover Sophia and his friend Shorty (Spike Lee). Beyond the Ellingtonian feel of the main theme's arrangement (particularly in the sectional interplay), we hear bluesy, improvised solos on both trumpet and saxophone. Later in the film, Blanchard offers another, slower big-band arrangement of the theme, underscoring Malcolm's meeting with Shorty after he (Malcolm) has become a devout follower of Islam. The two discuss their present lives, and Shorty fills Malcolm in on what has happened to everyone they used to know during their hustling days. The bluesy soundtrack theme is accompanied by a medium-slow swing shuffle groove, featuring "cool" improvised solos by Blanchard himself on trumpet. In both these instances, jazz accompanies Malcolm's involvement in (or reminiscences on) his decadent, impetuous former life as a misguided criminal. In overtly connecting these jazz-style permutations of the theme to Malcolm's deviant past, the score reinforces conventional cinematic codes that align jazz with criminality and corruption.

Yet there are distinct jazz features of the score that do not merely reinforce conventional Hollywood codes. First and foremost is the evident influence of the blues. Malcolm's melody is a sinuous exploration of the C minor blues scale,[89] with primary emphasis on the key tones from a Cmin7 chord (with occasional 4ths and a particularly powerful b9 prior to the final cadence). The theme itself intimates a jazz trumpeter's lyrical solo, supported by orchestral strings rather than a jazz ensemble. This "jazz solo" quality is also noticeable near the end of the tune, where Blanchard briefly ad-libs over the final cadence.

Improvisation also plays a prominent role throughout the score. While the soundtrack itself is not fully improvised, Blanchard opens up solo spaces in many of his arrangements to feature improvised solos from the jazz players in the recording ensemble (himself included). In addition to solos featured in the "big band" arrangements described above, there are a few other pertinent examples. Early in the film, Malcolm has a romantic moment with his girlfriend Laura as they walk and kiss on the beach. "Melody for Laura" is highly conventional at first listen—soaring strings and a beautiful oboe melody representing the passion and love shared between the two characters. Yet in the second iteration of the melody—now featuring French horn—one notes the pianist improvising in the background, further introducing jazz-flavored harmonies to the tonal tapestry. Later in the movie, a jazz waltz accompanies Malcolm and Betty on their "ice cream date," underscoring their coy flirtations with improvised piano and a mellifluous soprano saxophone solo (bearing resemblances to John Lewis's "Skating in Central Park," featured in *Odds against Tomorrow*).

Therefore, while Blanchard's score for *Malcolm X* is in some ways highly conventional, it also directly and uniquely reflects his grounding in the jazz idiom.[90] Blues-based melodies, jazz harmonies, swing and jazz waltz styles, improvised solos—all these elements permeate this soundtrack in ways that challenge one to rethink how jazz may be utilized as effective underscore, transforming film and its meanings in the process.

• • •

For Blanchard, composing the *Malcolm X* score was a significant undertaking. He, like Lee, found inspiration in Malcolm's life and teachings. Therefore, he felt an ideological obligation to contribute to this film's production, while also feeling personal pressure to successfully engage audiences through his soundtrack. He stated, "To me, all the time and effort that went into the making of this score [would] have been for naught if the viewer and listener [didn't] come away with an emotional attachment to Malcolm X and his struggles."[91]

Blanchard's explanation of how he developed this score is worth examining. His creative process was driven by his relationships to the characters, particularly Malcolm. He has revealed, "When it came to writing the theme for Malcolm, I went back to all the fears, frustrations, and anger that I felt as a kid and combined that with what I felt when I read the autobiography. And from that, I was able to create the musical identity for Malcolm."[92] Much of this reflection manifests in Blanchard's musical representation of Malcolm's solitude—articulated through the featuring of solitary melodic instruments such as trumpet, French horn, and oboe.

Blanchard's work for *Malcolm X* also served as a creative starting point for his continued musical exploration of his own relationship to Malcolm's history. He has described his interest in Malcolm's legacy at length:

> To me, Malcolm X was a person in search of something. His quest to unravel the truth about human injustice and to acquire human rights in the U.S. and abroad never wavered. Malcolm was a very sincere person who put everything out front for everybody to see, which leads me to believe that he had a large sense of humility. See, that's what I love about his story because if the humility wasn't there, then you don't leave yourself open to change. . . . So for me, my level of respect for Malcom at that point [admitting he was wrong] goes sky high. That's what life is supposed to be about. Those are the principles and values that we're taught as kids but forget as grownups. So it was really inspiring to see a person who maintained those kind of values throughout his life.[93]

Accordingly, he determined to create an extended suite paying homage to the story of Malcolm X's life, appropriately entitled *The Malcolm X Jazz Suite*. This stand-alone concept album is an impressive jazz rearrangement and exploration of several of the themes presented in Blanchard's orchestral score for the film. It is performed by a small-group jazz ensemble, featuring Sam Newsome (tenor saxophone), Tarus Mateen (bass), Bruce Barth (piano), and Troy Davis (drums). Comprehensive in form, the suite builds a musical reflection of Malcolm's history through a succession of themes that parallel his biographical development, from his relationship with Laura ("Melody for Laura"), to his introduction to Elijah Muhammad's teaching ("Theme for Elijah"), to his involvement in the Nation of Islam ("The Nation"), to his relationship with his wife, Betty ("Betty's Theme"), to his pilgrimage to Mecca ("Malcolm Makes Hajj"), to his assassination ("Malcolm at Peace"), to his immortality through his legacy ("Perpetuity"). Additionally, the album interpolates reiterations of "Malcolm's Theme" in various stylistic formats.

The album's distinctiveness from the film soundtrack is immediately obvious. The first track, entitled "The Opening," begins with an extensive one-and-a-half minute bass solo. When the main Malcolm theme enters, featuring Blanchard on trumpet, the solo is much jazzier than in its appearance at the opening of the film (and also is played in F, instead of C minor, as in the film). Blanchard utilizes half-valve smears to elicit a vocalized bluesiness, while the solo is accompanied by piano fills, bass, and drum extemporizations. There is no evident time signature at this point; the ensemble members are engaged in a free improvisation, directed by Blanchard's fluid, rubato performance of the theme. Only at two minutes and forty-two seconds in does the bass player break into a syncopated rhythmic groove, which the remainder of the rhythm sections joins. Blanchard and Newsome harmonize the main theme, then engage in a collective improvisation over the rhythm section. The entire tune sounds uninhibited—a musical platform for each member of the ensemble to express his reactions to Malcolm through his own voice, in his own time.

Numerous jazz styles are featured throughout the album—each movement distinct from its precursor. "Melody for Laura" is a contemplative, bluesy jazz waltz, providing ample room for solo choruses from Newsome, Barth, and Blanchard. This transitions directly into "Theme for Elijah," an intense bop tune flaring at Parker/Gillespie speeds and featuring impressive improvised solos. "Blues for Malcolm" begins with a lengthy drum solo, eventually featuring a waltz with melodic echoes of Wayne Shorter's "Footprints." "The Nation" is a light, fast-paced bop tune, immediately followed by a samba-style variation of "Malcolm's Theme," which features quotes of "Footprints" by both Blanchard and Newsome at the end. "Betty's Theme" slows the tempo down with a somber, bluesy jazz waltz, beautifully reflecting Betty's sorrow and strength throughout her life—particularly when Malcolm was assassinated. "Malcolm Makes Hajj" returns to the frenetic, fast-paced bop style, featuring solos by Newsome, Davis, Blanchard, and Barth. "Malcolm at Peace" begins with a reflective, expressive piano solo that draws on numerous themes from the suite, including "Theme for Elijah" and "Malcolm's Theme," and continues with the introduction of a Middle Eastern–influenced rhythmic groove, emulating the theme heard in the film when Malcolm is in Mecca. "Perpetuity" returns to the fast-paced bop style that reemerges frequently throughout the album, while the final track, "Malcolm's Theme" [reprise], integrates samba grooves and medium swing beneath this final iteration of the primary melody. Blanchard and Newsome collectively improvise over the rhythm section while the tune fades out, implying that the performance is still going (just as Spike Lee suggests that Malcolm X's legacy lives on). All these musical movements representationally weave together Malcolm's complex, multilayered identity—a result of his relationships, experiences, and transformations.

The Malcolm X Jazz Suite was highly acclaimed among jazz critics, reaching #23 on the Top Jazz Album charts of 1993. Geoffrey Himes described the album as an "extraordinary landmark," identifying Blanchard as "Wynton Marsalis' only real rival as a modern composer of jazz suites in the Ellington mode."[94] Scott Yanow describes it as "one of Blanchard's finest recordings."[95] The album is simultaneously a reflective engagement with the life and legacy of Malcolm X and an impressive comprehensive performance for Blanchard and the members of his quintet. Each member of the ensemble demonstrates soloistic virtuosity within an abundance of jazz styles—from ballads, to samba, to blues, to frenetic bop. Blanchard himself demonstrates an incredible range and mastery of the trumpet, a chameleonic aptitude that allows him to transform his reprised themes both stylistically and emotionally. Between his score for Lee's film and his work on the *Jazz Suite*, Blanchard channeled his ideas about Malcolm, his ideology, and his musical talents into two fascinating works of contemporary jazz that greatly informed both his film and jazz oeuvres, as well as the film itself.

WHEN THE LEVEES BROKE *AND* A TALE OF GOD'S WILL

In the late summer of 2005, the devastating effects of Hurricane Katrina permanently silenced nearly fifteen hundred inhabitants of New Orleans. Katrina, now charted as one of the five deadliest hurricanes in the history of the United States, inflicted extreme destruction along the Gulf Coast. The highest death toll occurred in New Orleans, compounded by the failure of the levee system after the hurricane itself had passed through, greatly affecting areas like St. Bernard Parish and the Lower Ninth Ward (where approximately 92 percent of the population is African American). Although many had evacuated the city following weather reports and Mayor Ray Nagin's mandatory evacuation order, others did not—particularly those members of poorer communities who did not have the financial resources to obtain travel and leave their homes. This greatly affected many lower-class African American residents of the city, as well as poorer white communities living in the affected areas. When disaster struck, many cries for help went unacknowledged. Delayed governmental responses, on both the local and national levels, left countless New Orleans residents homeless, without possessions, separated from family members, and suffering in the summer heat.

Attempting to bring these people's suffering into public consciousness, Spike Lee immediately produced the HBO documentary *When the Levees Broke: A Requiem in Four Acts*—a poignant tapestry of images and the voices of those affected by the experience. He began filming in late September 2005, directly following the devastation. It aired one year later on HBO, attaining great critical acclaim.[96] This four-hour documentary highlights the manifold experiences and stories produced by the disaster and its aftermath, focusing primarily on the plights of the lower-class Black communities and their struggles for their cries for help to be heard. It is composed of news video footage, graphic still photos of the death and devastation in New Orleans, and many interviews with both residents and nonresidents of the city.

The documentary's primary function is to illustrate the suffering endured by many New Orleans residents (mainly African American) in the aftermath of the hurricane and the levees' implosion, as well as to highlight their will to survive, overcome, and rebuild their beloved city and communities. Spike Lee himself said of the film: "New Orleans is fighting for its life. These are not people who will disappear quietly—they're accustomed to hardship and slights, and they'll fight for New Orleans. This film will showcase the struggle for New Orleans by focusing on the profound loss, as well as the indomitable spirit of New Orleans."[97]

The second theme of the documentary is its political critique of perceived governmental failure (on both local and federal levels) in both preventative and responsive areas. The film suggests that the levee breakage was preventable, occurring as a result of faulty engineering by the United States Army Corps of Engineers. In the aftermath of the breakage, both local and federal relief was delayed, leading to poignant accusations of the government's indifference, particularly on a racial level. The fact that the majority of those whose lives (and homes) were devastated by the storm were poor African Americans has further compounded these beliefs, echoed in such statements as Kanye West's infamous "George Bush doesn't care about Black people" comment, which he presented during "A Concert for Hurricane Relief" broadcast on NBC in the immediate hurricane aftermath.[98]

The documentary is largely an activist response to what Lee (and many of his interviewees) views as distinguishable racist and social oppression of New Orleans's lower-class residents. Amidst these political threads, Lee's documentary engages directly with the losses and experiences of the people themselves, forgoing voice-overs to present the variety of unique voices that each tell their own story. Like New Orleans musical culture, the voices presented in this documentary constitute an explicitly constructed visual and sonic "gumbo"—a diverse variety of interviewees from different backgrounds and locations, each with articulations of their own detailed experiences.

A powerful component of the documentary is the musical soundtrack. While the voices of the interviewees dominate the sonic landscape of the film, Terence Blanchard's original score evocatively underscores and transitions

Figure 3.2. "Levees" theme (2006), author transcription, 2016.

Figure 3.3. "Wading Through" theme (2006), author transcription, 2016.

Figure 3.4. "The Water" theme (2006), author transcription, 2016.

Figure 3.5. "Funeral Dirge" theme (2006), author transcription, 2016.

between the images and personal stories through poignant, sentiment-laden melodies. Four primary melodic themes weave in and out of the four-hour montage, strongly evincing the emotions of fear, longing, sadness, and frustration that are reflected through the subjects' words and expressions. These pieces—nominally identified as "Levees," "Wading Through," "The Water," and "Funeral Dirge"—each draw on a diverse wellspring of the blues, New Orleans funeral marches, military dirges, and lush, Romantic-style string orchestrations to musically convey the aforementioned emotional themes.

These four themes manifest in varied permutations throughout the documentary. The transcriptions indicated above are only approximations—the melodies are never played exactly the same way twice. They sometimes appear holistically, and sometimes in fragments. They emerge through melodic improvisations featuring saxophone, trumpet, violin, piano, and other solo instruments. They weave in and out of audibility, underscoring an assortment of visual moments from photo montages to news clips, from film of the destruction to conversations with politicians and residents alike. While the iterations of each theme are continually varied, they remain recognizable. As such, they help bring thematic unity to the scrapbook-style documentary, connecting the vast array of stories and footage together with recurrent, emotion-laden musical statements that sonically support the sentiments evinced onscreen.

Blanchard had a limited amount of time to put the score together, given its unplanned inception and Lee's determination to immediately release the documentary as a call to action for aid for the people of New Orleans. When the hurricane hit, Blanchard and Lee had been working on postproduction for the feature film *Inside Man* (2006). Interestingly, the "Wading Through" theme used in *Levees* is prominently featured in *Inside Man*. In his commentary on the *Levees* DVD, Lee recounted the circumstances: "Terence, you're not going to have a lot of time. I like these themes from *Inside Man*, so let's use them [for the *Levees* film]." Blanchard did, however, compose the remainder of the themes for the documentary and would later go on to greatly expand his musical work from the soundtrack through an extended concept album—*A Tale of God's Will: A Requiem for Katrina*—which I discuss in more detail.

Blanchard's connections to the New Orleans disaster ran deeper than his professional relationship with Lee. A New Orleans resident himself, he was acutely affected by the tragedy, as many of his friends and family members suffered greatly in the destruction. One of the most powerful scenes in *Levees* features Blanchard returning with his mother to her obliterated Pontchartrain Park home. Upon entering the premises and looking at the water damage and destruction, she breaks down in tears, collapsing into his chest and sobbing: "I knew there was devastation, but I didn't know it was this bad. Lord, have mercy!" In a recorded interview on the documentary, Blanchard states, "It's like I can't go home," as he chokes up with tears and grows silent.

The personal effects of the post-Katrina circumstances led Blanchard to expressive activism through his own voice—his music. "When I looked at all those people struggling . . . it's not like I [just] felt like I needed to make a musical statement about it. I felt like I needed to be a megaphone for the voiceless. In my little corner of the world, I could bring attention to what was happening to people who didn't have resources. Of course I have to say something. Of course I have to do something."[99]

Taking the themes he composed for *Levees* as a starting point, he expanded his musical ideas in a concept album inspired by his own personal responses to the events. Blanchard shared with me that he felt that he had more to say musically about the situation than he had been able to produce for the documentary. "I felt like I had done my job in terms of creating music for the score, but not creating music that was totally based on how I wanted to express myself regarding those issues. So with *When the Levees Broke*, I just felt like I wasn't finished making a statement about it—that's how *A Tale of God's Will* came about."[100] The full album, *A Tale of God's Will: A Requiem for Katrina*, was released on Blue Note records in 2007, featuring Blanchard's quintet,[101] Seattle-based symphonic orchestra Northwest Sinfonia, along with prominent solos by Blanchard himself. The album is composed of a combination of rearrangements of the four primary themes from the documentary, as well as a number of original pieces composed by Blanchard and the ensemble members alike.[102]

The four primary themes—"Levees," "Wading Through," "The Water," and "Funeral Dirge"—are not simply redistributed from the documentary soundtrack to this album. Instead, Blanchard, the quintet, and the orchestra greatly expand on and embellish the themes. The brief melodies are transformed into comprehensive five-minute-plus performances composed of orchestral features, lengthy solo choruses, new countermelodies, and newly introduced rhythmic grooves. Blanchard's own voice—his solo trumpet—remains firmly tied to his Black cultural heritage through its predominantly blues-inflected utterances. Just as in the documentary, the sonic expressions of jazz and the blues highlight the suffering of African American people in New Orleans yet also emphasize their resilience in challenging their predicament, maintaining their spirits, and rebuilding their lives. Allow me to illustrate in greater detail on one tune in particular—"Levees."

"Levees"

Before a storm hits, the weather cools. The winds are gentle. New Orleans feels big and easy. My hometown is known for food, music, and summer heat so oppressive that you almost don't feel like eating and dancing. But before a storm hits, the weather is calm and beautiful. The city seems to move at a laid-back pace like the tempo of "Levees."[103]

Following an ominous, trembling open fourth interval, the piece begins with haunting strings sequentially "rocking" between dissonant minor second intervals, evoking a sense of precarious calm, of unsettled fear, and of impending threat. It aurally represents the calm before (and after) the storm. Moving legato contrapuntal lines beneath the high sustained notes evoke a sense of longing and anxiety, reflecting the emotions of those trapped and displaced after the levee breakage, further represented through the descending scalar motion of the melodies and the ebbs and swells of the strings' dynamics. The melodic and harmonic intervals of seconds and fourths are unsettling, demanding resolution that never comes. The repetitive harmonic motion, shifting back and forth between variations on A minor and G minor chords, elicits a sense of stagnancy, an inability to escape.

> That calm is a warning. A cry. Listen to the trumpet. . . . These are the people the trumpet is crying for. For the 72-year-old man I met who was on his roof for three days with two 73-year-old women. What did they have? No food, but plenty of filthy, dirty water.[104]

Approximately a minute and a half into the piece, a plucked string bass pedal point on G emerges underneath the strings, eliciting a sense of aural buildup and tension, plodding through the contrapuntal string tapestry. A few bars in, a trumpet solo emerges, piercing through the "rocking" strings in a plaintive cry rooted in G minor blues. This solo, performed by Blanchard himself, is an iteration of one of the prominent main themes utilized throughout the documentary. As the solo progresses, the strings snake chromatically underneath—descending, ascending, and making dissonant jumps of both augmented and diminished intervals; they maintain a constant, cycling tension beneath the bluesy cries, much as the swirling, cycling waters of the floods provoked continued anxiety among those crying for help. Blanchard's scoops, lip bends, and other blues inflections sonically depict the thousands of people wailing and crying for help, for food, for water, for safety, and for acknowledgment.

These pitch-bending techniques are characteristic of blues performances and are recognized for the ways in which they express the unique musicianship and authentic "voice" of the performer. As David Evans claims,

Blues players and singers tended to improvise and vary their melodic lines, instrumental parts and lyrics, and to experiment with sound quality, using growling, screaming, wailing, and falsetto singing and the muffling, snapping, sliding, and bending of notes. This spontaneous quality created the impression that the thoughts, feelings, and expressions of the moment were quite important, turning attention away from the song as product of a deliberate and often arduous process of composition, toward the performance itself and the personality and uniqueness of the performer.[105]

There is a long discursive history theorizing the blues as a medium of Black agency. Rooted in the idioms of field hollers and spirituals, it is strongly tied to expressions of individual emotion, (often) hardship, but also resilience. Pitch bending, blue notes, wailing utterances—these highly personal performative techniques reveal nuanced layers of emotional expression that exceed the meanings of the lyrics themselves. LeRoi Jones (Amiri Baraka) stated in his seminal work *Blues People*, "Blues-playing is the closest imitation of the human voice of any music I've heard."[106] This assertion resonates with Blanchard's choice to feature a bluesy trumpet as the "voiced" expression of human suffering. Ostensibly the melody was inspired by the story of a seventy-two-year-old trumpeter stuck on a roof with two elderly women while their neighborhood flooded beneath them; the blues-inflected solo represents their unanswered cries.[107] Through the aforementioned pitch bending, as well as rhythmic liberties and rubato phrasing, Blanchard successfully transformed "The Levees'" melody into an improvised, expressively articulated human story not unlike the stories riddling Lee's documentary.

Following a restatement of the primary "Levees" theme, Blanchard proceeds into an extensive blues-based improvisation. A bass/piano/drums vamp emerges with an implied 6/8 groove, while the trumpet voices its cries of reflection and longing through strained, sustained notes, conversational phrasing, and half-valved slurs and blue notes. As the trumpet solo ascends in pitch, the rhythm section simultaneously builds in dynamic and accentual fervor. The trumpet itself cracks and squeals, metaphorically screaming at the horror that has befallen the residents of New Orleans.

The calm gives way in the final vamp. The water and the cries, the strings and the trumpet, the deep menace and the pleas for help. The pleas asking, as I did, why did this happen?[108]

In this final vamp, the main theme eventually subsides, reintroducing another improvised solo from Blanchard, which becomes increasingly frenetic in terms of syncopation, range, and inflection. The pianist pounds out chords in a relentless 3 over 2 rhythm, and the drummer's hits and cymbal crashes become more sporadic and intense. After eight minutes, the track eventually fades into silence, with the ghost of the trumpet's high squeals faintly echoing in the listener's ears, suggesting the cries of those who continued to suffer.

In its entirety *A Tale of God's Will* is a sonic space for solace, reflection, communal mourning, political critique, and ultimately optimism and healing. Original pieces on the album reflect Blanchard's personal, political, and ideological investments in the devastating experience, its aftermath, and the spiritual will to overcome the adversity. A trio of specter-named compositions—"Ghost of Congo Square," "Ghost of Betsy," and "Ghost of 1927"—recall dark moments in New Orleans history that foreshadowed the devastation of both natural disaster and racial oppression in the Katrina events, actively critiquing treatment of African Americans in New Orleans, and challenging current administrators to work against such oppression both now and in the future. The closing tune, "Dear Mom," beautifully interweaves major and minor modalities to simultaneously mourn Blanchard's mother's loss of her home but celebrate her fortunate survival. The lush dialogue between the strings and Blanchard's elegiac trumpet melodies both condemns the disaster but celebrates the courage to move through it—an appropriate final track for this requiem album. Much like the jazz funerals so characteristic of New Orleans's African American culture, the requiem laments the loss but celebrates the life, spirit, and hope for the future.

A Tale of God's Will was released by Blue Note Records on August 14, 2006. It was very well received, garnering accolades such as Bill Milkowski's assertion that Blanchard "score[d] the aftermath of Hurricane Katrina with empathy and grace."[109] The album won Blanchard two Grammys—his firsts as a leader and for Best Large Jazz Ensemble Album. In addition, it was placed #2 on the *JazzTimes* list of the best albums of 2007. Arguably one of his most powerful works to date, *A Tale of God's Will*—like the *Malcolm X Jazz Suite*—illustrates how film soundtrack composition can be a powerful springboard for jazz artists' own artistic projects, and positions jazz's intersections with film as potentially dynamic, collaborative sites of personal, ideological, and creative expression.

CONCLUSIONS

Of all the artists examined throughout this book, Terence Blanchard is unquestioningly the one who maintains a committed dual career as both a full-time jazz artist and a film composer. He has stated on numerous occasions that he is first and foremost a jazz musician; yet his thirty-year tenure in the film industry is evidence of his legitimacy as a career film composer as well. His path to inclusion in the film industry's "inner circle" (reinforced through his recent Academy Award nomination for Best Score for *BlacKkKlansman*, 2019) began with his recognition (by Spike Lee) as a legitimate jazz musician. For Lee, Blanchard is the "real deal." As discussed throughout this chapter, Lee equates jazz with authentic Black creativity. Accordingly, he employs jazz as an integral component in his films: a sonic reflection (and assertion) of Black creativity and experience. Since Blanchard is an accomplished and renowned Black jazz musician as well as a composer, he is an ideal collaborator. Furthermore, both Lee and Blanchard view their respective mediums (i.e., film and music) as effective platforms for projecting awareness and criticism of racial injustice, as well as advocating for the recognition and support of Black culture, creativity, and social equity.

In chapter 2, I focused on examples of jazz/film collaborations that overturned conventional production methods, in which the films were effectively developed around the improvised soundtracks. Though Blanchard's work is more conventional from a production standpoint (i.e., he creates the scores during postproduction, after the films are mostly complete), it is his *content* that challenges conventional Hollywood approaches. What makes Blanchard's film work so unique is the manner in which he integrates and transforms jazz idioms into scores that both problematize the distinctions between classical, jazz, and popular music, as well as work against conventional "jazz soundtrack" typologies. For Blanchard, jazz is not a categorical style to sprinkle into films to suggest specific sensual, seedy, or sophisticated themes. Instead, it is an expressive style capable of reflecting variegated human emotion and experience with integrity and authenticity. As illustrated in the examples throughout this chapter, Blanchard blends jazz elements and techniques with a myriad of musical influences. In so doing, he generates soundtrack models that expand the possibilities of how jazz can intersect with and influence film and its meanings, as well as effectively engage with new cultural mediums. As Joe Henderson lauded, "He's showing that there are great possibilities out there for jazz musicians, particularly in film scoring. Just seeing Terence deal out those cards for people to pick up will influence the scene because it will get jazzers to think much broader in terms of their career goals. I mean, that's a pretty fair amount of power there."[110]

Chapter 4

"A FILM DIRECTOR'S DREAM"

DICK HYMAN PLAYS THE PERSONAL FOR WOODY ALLEN

It's Thanksgiving. A convivial crowd of family and friends is intimately gathered in a perhaps too-small sitting room, standing elbow-to-elbow amidst bursting bookshelves, family pictures in slightly crooked frames, and decorative potted plants. As the guests sip wine and sample hors d'oeuvres, their attention is focused on an older couple sitting at an upright piano, gazing into each other's eyes while singing "a wimpering, simpering child again . . . bewitched, bothered, and bewildered am I."

This scene from Woody Allen's 1986 film *Hannah and Her Sisters* is quintessential Allen. The romanticized and nostalgic depiction of a sophisticated, middle-class New York family celebrating the holidays is heightened through the on-screen performance of Richard Rodgers and Lorenz Hart's 1941 standard, "Bewitched, Bothered, and Bewildered"—a piece performed by Dick Hyman that is heard in various forms through the entire film, functioning as a "love theme" that reflects the romantic trials and tribulations of the main characters. The aforementioned scene is the first place we hear it: Evan (the patriarch of the family, played by Lloyd Nolan) sings it in heterophonic unison with his wife Norma (played by Maureen O'Sullivan), while accompanying himself on the piano. Neither Evan nor Norma sound like professional singers—they are slightly out of tune and out of sync with each other and Evan's piano accompaniment. Yet the amateurism of the performance enhances its charm. Here, the music functions as a representation of love and unity, bringing characters together in a bright moment of nostalgic reminiscence and hopeful optimism in the midst of emotional turbulence, dissatisfaction, and betrayal. As described by Lee (played by Barbara Hershey), one of Evan and Norma's daughters in the film, "Mom and Dad are floating down memory lane again."

Jazz, nostalgia, New York sophistication, complicated romance—these are the staples of Woody Allen's films. The opening monologue to his 1979 film

Manhattan evocatively and self-reflexively articulates these obsessions. Over a visual background of romanticized black-and-white images of Manhattan, coupled with the foregrounded soundtrack of George Gershwin's renowned *Rhapsody in Blue*, Allen's own disembodied voice narrates the following: "Chapter One. He adored New York City, and idealized it all out of proportion. No, make that, he *romanticized* it all out of proportion. . . . To him, no matter what the season was, this was still a town that existed in black and white, and pulsated to the great tunes of George Gershwin."[1]

Raised in New York City since childhood, Allen has an unequivocal love for the city, affirming that he doesn't think he "could live beyond a thirty-minute radius of the Russian Tea Room."[2] This unconditional love exists despite his frustrations with what he identifies as the city's deep-seated issues of crime, violence, and drugs. "I'm a big New York lover despite all its problems. The city has so much going for it. I enjoy the country only if I'm with nice people. Here you don't have to be with nice people to enjoy it. You can be with muggers."[3] He has claimed: "I love the city in an emotional, irrational way, like loving your mother or father even though they're drunk or a thief. I've loved the city my whole life—to me, it's like a great woman."[4]

Allen's "irrational" infatuation with New York City manifests in nostalgic romanticization, rooted in his perceptions of the city's "Golden Age"—the era of Cole Porter, of glamorous stars, of Park Avenue in the early twentieth century. As Allen himself has claimed, the New York he represents in his films is the way he would like it to be, not necessarily the way it is.[5] His on-screen geography pointedly reflects this idealism, primarily restricted to the affluent, sophisticated Upper East Side, Central Park, and Times Square.

> From the very first time I came here from Brooklyn with my father, I wanted to live in New York, and I wanted to live in the elegant, Cole Porter part of New York, which is why I live on the East Side. . . . I love Park Avenue, and Fifth Avenue. There is something wonderful about the way the streets feel here, it hasn't been ruined the way other parts of the city have.[6]

His claim that "it hasn't been ruined the way other parts of the city have" reveals his own biases. He protects his almost exclusively white, middle-class characters from the inconveniences of urban poverty, crime, violence, and racial conflict, avoiding commentary on the sociological and political underpinnings of such phenomena. His "peculiar geography" (as Joe Klein calls it)[7] ends where Harlem begins, also excluding the boroughs of Brooklyn, Queens, Staten Island, and the Bronx, with little acknowledgment of the people, cultures, and experiences beyond his preferred area of Manhattan (where he also, notably, happens to live).

Allen has received criticism for the lack of diverse representation in his films. His movies predominantly feature all-white casts, with a few exceptions (e.g., Hazelle Goodman in *Deconstructing Harry*, Chiwetel Ejiofor in *Melinda and Melinda*, and Penélope Cruz and Javier Bardem in *Vicky Cristina Barcelona*). These critiques are long-standing, dating back to his early career. A few examples: in 1999 law professor Jerome McCristal Culp Jr. argued, "In the world described by Woody Allen's movies, there are no 'real' Black people [read: serious characters with primary roles]."[8] Compare this with recent criticism by actress Zoe Kravitz, who claimed in 2018: "I wouldn't work with Woody Allen, but I also don't think Woody Allen would want to have me in his films because he doesn't put people of color in his films, and they're all set in New York City. The melting pot of the world, and there's no Black people."[9] Recent criticisms come at a time when there has been significant outcry for increased Black, minority, and female representation in the film industry, as discussed in the previous chapter. Yet, despite the importance of such social movements, it is important not to "throw the baby out with the bathwater," so to speak, and let ideology limit our understanding of Allen's work.

As I hope to illustrate throughout this chapter, Allen's films are personal. They reflect what he knows, and what he is familiar with. It is no coincidence that his characters are white, middle-class artists/intellectuals who live on the Upper East Side, listen to jazz, and immerse themselves in Freud and Dostoevsky (sound familiar?). A self-identified introvert, Allen's interactions with others are often contained to his close-knit circle of family and friends, limiting his familiarity with the experiences of others who are not in his immediate purview. While identifying himself as a "typical liberal and sometimes maybe even radical" on the topic of advocacy for civil rights and Black equality, Allen has responded to diversity criticisms regarding his casting by stating: "While affirmative action can be a fine solution in many instances, it does not work when it comes to casting. I always cast the person who fits the part most believably in my mind's eye. . . . When it comes to casting, I do not go by politics but by what feels dramatically correct to me."[10] Hazelle Goodman, the only Black actress who has had a significant role in one of Allen's films, has supported Allen's right to make his own choices. In an interview with the *Hollywood Reporter*, she affirmed: "Any filmmaker has the right to create his vision. That's his vision. That's how he sees the world. And he has a right to that, just like if Spike Lee does a film, he puts a lot of black folk in it. Everyone is creating from their vision. If Woody sees the world that way, that's Woody's world. I don't trip about that."[11] For better or for worse, Allen's characters are his own.

Yet Allen's New York has not remained his own. Through his extensive film oeuvre—in which the vast majority of the settings are in New York[12]—he has shared his perceptions and romanticizations of the city with the world, tapping into both native New Yorkers' and potential tourists' aspirations as well as anxieties, igniting a collective nostalgia for an idealized metropolis of sophistication, romance, intellectualism, and art that "pulsated to the great tunes of George Gershwin." As Peter Biskind wrote in *Vanity Fair*, "Allen was the closest thing New York City ever had to a poet laureate." It is worth considering how his representations of the city, as well as its people, images, and sounds (including jazz), have shaped audience perceptions and expectations over time.

Allen's body of work as a filmmaker is extensive. To date, he has directed over fifty films, roughly one per year since he started filmmaking in the late 1960s. While he may be most notably recognized for his (romantic) comedies—consistent with his background as a comedy sketch writer and stand-up comedian in New York City during his young adulthood—his works also include poignant dramas (e.g., *Interiors* [1978], *September* [1987], *Another Woman* [1988], *Blue Jasmine* [2013]), comedy/drama blends (e.g., *Crimes and Misdemeanors* [1989], *Husbands and Wives* [1992], thrillers (e.g., *Match Point* [2005]), and even musicals (e.g., *Everyone Says I Love You* [1996]). This versatility reflects Allen's interests in creative experimentation, and his desire to continually try new creative approaches to filmmaking, despite the risks. He claimed: "I'd like to keep growing in my work. I'd like to do more serious comical films and do different types of films, maybe write and direct a drama. And take chances—I would like to fail a little for the public. . . . What I want to do is go on to areas that I'm insecure about and not so good at."[13]

Similar to the other directors discussed in this book, Allen is recognized for having a distinct authorial signature, having been described as "an auteur among auteurs."[14] *New York Times* critic Vincent Canby claimed—after comparing Allen with the likes of Bergman, Truffaut, and Fellini—"I can't think of any filmmaker of Mr. Allen's generation with whom he can be compared. . . . The entire Allen canon . . . represents a kind of personal cinema for which there is no precedent in modern American movies."[15] While describing him as an auteur can run the risk of diminishing the contributions of others who have participated in the creation of his films (and the usage of such terminology must be treated carefully as such), there is no question that each of his films bears a unique Woody Allen "stamp." Beyond the consistent aesthetic features that characterize his movies (e.g., the quintessential black background/white text credits, neurotic intellectual characters, themes of love and death), his direct involvement in and influence over his films is in some ways unparalleled. Naturally Allen directs his films, but he also writes the scripts, produces the films, and in many cases plays a lead character (particularly in his early films from the 1970s through the 1990s). Allen himself claimed:

> I think that for all their flaws and immaturities, you can say that [my movies] weren't factory-made films. They were not the usual Hollywood product. I think those films will always be playing around, even fifty years from now, because they represent a certain kind of filmmaking. They're not great, but they're not machine made either. . . . I do have a certain kind of style, it's my own. . . . It's a one-man thing—it's not that one guy wrote the script, and another guy edited it. For better or worse, you can recognize it as my picture.[16]

Allen's level of involvement in the creation and production of his films amounts to what he himself describes as "total control:" "I have total control over [my films], final cut. No one approves the script. I have everything going for me."[17] This creative freedom is facilitated through two primary circumstances: one, his willingness to "take risks" and produce on limited budgets in order to avoid production company involvement; and two, a handful of generous, "no-strings attached" patrons who have financially supported his work and artistic vision over the decades (perhaps most notably Arthur Krim, the former head of United Artists and cofounder of Orion Pictures). Interestingly, despite these assertions of "total control," Allen is not known as a particularly involved or authoritative director. He often gives very little direction/guidance to actors, leaving them to interpret characters as they see fit (even if he does not always agree), and generally accepting scenes after very few takes. While positive responses to this approach have led to him being dubbed an "actor's director," Allen himself has attributed this approach to his own lack of motivation: "I'm lazy and an imperfectionist. . . . Steven Spielberg and Martin Scorsese will work on the details until midnight and sweat it out, whereas for me, come 6 o'clock, I want to go home, I want to have dinner, I want to watch the ballgame. Filmmaking is not [the] end-all be-all of my existence."[18] Such directorial indifference might also be influenced by Allen's social aloofness and insecurity in articulating what he is looking for. Yet, regardless of how (non-) authoritatively he wields his directorial power, it remains true that Allen is not beholden to any "final approval" but his own.

It is precisely this aspect of "total control" that leads audiences to interpret Woody Allen's films as "Woody Allen's films"—or, in other words, films *about* Woody Allen. The fact that he has often played lead characters in his films reinforces this conflation, sometimes even to Allen's own detriment. For example, Allen received much criticism in response to his film *Stardust Memories* (1980), in which he played a popular film director (Sandy Bates) disillusioned with sycophantic fans who preferred his "earlier, funnier films" to his more recent artistic aspirations. Fans criticized Allen, interpreting the film as autobiographical, and believing that Sandy's views about his audiences reflected Allen's own. Allen has denied the correlation and expresses regret that audiences interpreted the film in that manner, describing *Stardust Memories*—which he views as one of his finest films—as one of his most misunderstood. As he expressed in an interview with Charles Champlin for the *Philadelphia Inquirer* shortly after *Stardust Memories*' release: "From the time of *Annie Hall*, people regard anything I do as autobiographical, so I guess they look at *Stardust Memories* and say, 'Is that what you think of us?' I can't always sit with people and tell them to think of it as a fictional film about a filmmaker going through a crisis in his life. It's hard for them to dissociate him from me."[19]

I would also be remiss to overlook how Allen's romantic scandal in the 1990s—details of which have since resurfaced with the rise of the #MeToo movement—influenced how audiences perceived him and his films. Without fully rehashing what was a tabloid feeding frenzy in 1992, Allen became the object of much derision when his girlfriend and regular costar at the time, Mia Farrow, discovered that he was having an affair with her adopted daughter Soon-Yi Previn, who is thirty-five years his junior. What commenced was a bitter emotional and legal battle for custody of Farrow's and Allen's children: Moses, Dylan, and Satchel. Farrow claimed that Allen had molested their seven-year old daughter, Dylan, launching criminal investigations. The courts found no conclusive evidence that molestation had occurred; however, Allen was stigmatized as a result of months of tabloid headlines portraying him as a child molester. Audiences began surveying his movies with new bias, looking for potential revelatory clues in the case. Under particular scrutiny was his role in *Manhattan*, in which he plays a middle-aged man who is in a relationship with a seventeen-year old girl (played by Mariel Hemingway). Consider the following opinion by A. O. Scott, part of his *New York Times* article entitled "My Woody Allen Problem": "The Woody Allen figure in a Woody Allen movie is almost always in transit from one woman to another, impelled by a dialectic of enchantment, disappointment and reawakened desire. The rejected women appear shrewish, needy, shallow or boring. Their replacements, at least temporarily, are earnest, sensuous, generous and, more often than not, younger and less worldly than their predecessors."[20] Scott confesses his belief in Allen's guilt, drawing evidence for his assessment on the content and characters in Allen's films. There is certainly inherent fallacy in such an approach, reinforcing the question of at what point we separate the art from the artist. The fact that audiences struggle to divorce Allen's characters and themes from himself has unquestionably contributed to his condemnation—a condemnation that has resurfaced with the recent molestation allegations leveled by his adopted daughter Dylan, and amidst the rise of the #MeToo and #TimesUp movements.[21] Within the last five years, the Allen-Farrow imbroglio has manifested in media attacks, lawsuits, and a "he said, she said" battle played out in high-profile publications/media productions such as Allen's 2020 memoir, *Apropos of Nothing*, and Amy Ziering's and Kirby Dick's four-part documentary series *Allen v. Farrow*, which premiered on HBO in February 2021. Allen has not been criminally charged, but—innocent or not—the continued controversy has effectively condemned him regardless. Many of his previous star collaborators, including Michael Caine, Greta Gerwig, Kate Winslet, Rebecca Hall, and Timothée Chalamet, have publicly distanced themselves from him (though others such as Diane Keaton, Alec Baldwin, and Scarlett Johansson have unequivocally stood by him),[22] and his last two films (*A Rainy Day in New York* [2019] and *Rifkin's Festival* [2020]) failed to secure theatrical distributors in the United States.

I found continued evidence for the proliferation of the belief that Allen is (or is like) his on-screen characters in my review of the numerous interviews he has given over the years. In many cases interviewers are surprised that Allen does not appear in person as he does in his films; rather than projecting over-the-top anxiety and rapid intellectual banter, he is quiet, thoughtful, and serious. Kathleen Carroll, for example, suggested the following: "What surprises most people is that Woody is so serious when he talks about his work. There is no suggestion of the zany neurotic he plays on the screen. He is very much the straight man."[23] Accordingly, Allen has made a point to draw attention to the distinction between his characters and his actual self, stating, "I'm not that iconic figure at all. I'm very different from that."[24]

It would be naive to suggest that Allen's own life does not somehow inform the characters that he writes and then portrays on-screen. In fact, the crux of my argument in this chapter is that it does. He has admitted that his films are "autobiographical in the large, overall sense," while the specific details are largely invented.[25] I argue that rather than looking primarily at Allen's *characters* for insight into his personality and ideologies (characters that are largely exaggerated/caricatured, in deference to his background in comedy), audiences should look deeper at the specific *themes* that undergird his body of work. Love, sex, death, psychoanalysis, existentialism, conflict between idealism and reality—these themes not only shape the narratives but pointedly pervade the characters' dialogue. Here are a few one-liners from his works that give a sense of these themes (while also giving a sense of his sarcastic sense of humor):

- "Only human beings are divided into mind and body. The mind embraces all the nobler aspirations, like poetry and philosophy, but the body has all the fun." (from the film *Love and Death*)
- "It's not that I'm afraid to die. I just don't want to be there when it happens." (from *Death*, a one-act play)
- "All people know the same truth. Our lives consist of how we choose to distort it." (from the film *Deconstructing Harry*)
- "To you, I'm an atheist; to God, I'm the loyal opposition." (from the film *Stardust Memories*)

There is another pervasive theme in Allen's films that has gone largely unaddressed. In some ways it is hidden in plain sight. His use of jazz recordings as the sonic framework of his movies is one of the most quintessentially unique aspects of his work. It is also, as I argue here, very personal—a reflection of the "authentic" Woody Allen.

WOODY ALLEN'S JAZZ

Watch almost any Woody Allen film, and within minutes you will be listening to the likes of Cole Porter, Sidney Bechet, Harry James, or Duke Ellington. Jazz permeates Allen's movies. As Adam Harvey thoroughly documented in *The Soundtracks of Woody Allen: A Complete Guide to the Songs and Music in Every Film, 1969–2005*, you would be hard-pressed to find a single film that doesn't extensively use jazz recordings in its soundtrack. The music undergirds opening and closing credits, appears as nondiegetic underscoring, provides sonic transitions between scenes, and is also featured diegetically in on-screen performances.

Notably, unlike the other soundtracks discussed in this book, Allen's are primarily compilation soundtracks of licensed original recordings. While the films do feature original scoring (primarily by Dick Hyman, who I discuss below), they are most recognizable for their prominent featuring of renowned jazz recordings from the early twentieth century—particularly the 1920s through 1940s. Some of the most significant tunes include Louis Armstrong's "Stardust," the Glenn Miller Orchestra's "In the Mood," the Duke Ellington Orchestra's "Take the 'A' Train," and the Harry James Orchestra's "I've Heard That Song Before," among many others. In fact, Allen's soundtracks have inspired a variety of compilation albums featuring his most prominently used recordings, such as *Woody Allen's Movie Music* (Disconforme SL, 2001), *Songs That Made Woody Allen Movies Great* (Varèse Sarabande, 2009), *Swing in the Films of Woody Allen* (Jackpot, 2012), and *Music from the Films of Woody Allen* (Triangle Music, 2013). One only need watch the numerous song credits scrolling by at the end of his films to get a sense of the prominence of the music.

His selection of these tunes is intentional. Jazz—early jazz especially— holds personal meaning for Allen. He fell in love with the music as a teenager: "I started to listen to jazz in my teens.... When I was fourteen, maybe, I heard Sidney Bechet. On record. And I was very, very taken with it. And this gradually introduced me to more jazz recordings.... And I got very, very interested in jazz. I loved it."[26] Allen's fascination with the music was so strong that he began learning how to play it. He recalls in his recent memoir, *Apropos of Nothing*:

[Sidney Bechet's music] was the first New Orleans jazz I heard. Why it clicked so deeply I'll never know. Here I was, a Brooklyn Jew, never out of New York, with kind of a cosmopolitan taste, a great appreciation for Gershwin, Porter, Kern, very sophisticated popular composers, and here were these African-Americans in the Deep South, having nothing in common with me and yet they quickly became an obsession, and soon I was a wannabe African-American jazz musician. I bought a soprano sax, I learned to play it; I bought a clarinet and learned to play it. I bought a Victrola. That I could play with no lessons. I bought records, books on the birth of jazz, the life of Louis Armstrong.... [My friends and I] sat at our record players playing jazz music hour after hour, day after day. We listened to all kinds of jazz, but our favorites were the primitive New Orleans records. Bunk Johnson, Jelly Roll Morton, Louis Armstrong, and of course Sidney Bechet, whom I worshipped and modeled my playing after.... I sat in my bedroom alone playing along to Bechet and later George Lewis recordings. He was another idol of mine; with him and Johnny Dodds, yet another clarinet genius, I felt I had finally found myself. The pleasure was so intense I decided I would devote my life to jazz.[27]

Certainly, Allen's assertion that he was a "wannabe African-American jazz musician" is fraught with privilege; he does not acknowledge the music's social and racial history, or contextualize what he seems to identify as the distinctions between his experience and those of Black jazz musicians in the Deep South, who often faced extensive racial discrimination and violence. Instead, he acknowledges the music's roots in Black culture while glossing over its historical complexity, espousing a fascination with what he calls the "primitive New Orleans records"[28] in a manner reminiscent of white audiences' perceptions and descriptions of Black music during the 1920s (strongly rooted in the legacy of minstrelsy[29]). Problematically, his juxtaposition of Black, New Orleans-style jazz with the "sophisticated," cosmopolitan jazz of white composers such as Gershwin, Porter, and Kern reifies the dichotomies of Black vs. white, rural vs. urban, and primitive vs. sophisticated.

Yet despite these troublesome articulations, Allen's reverence for the music—and the artists who created it—seems to be genuine. Upon further analysis of his discussions of New Orleans jazz, his problematic description of its "primitiveness" might be better understood if described as "structural simplicity." He describes soloists such as Bechet, Armstrong, and Dodds as "musical geniuses" who uniquely expressed themselves, transcending the seemingly limiting structures of blues and ragtime form: "Within the parameters of New Orleans jazz, they had something truly magical inside them that oozed out of every note they blew."[30] Again, Allen's word choice, this time "magical," risks intimating historical white perceptions that ascribed innate musicality to Black musicians, believing their talent to be (or at least describing it as) primitive, natural inclination while often dismissing musical literacy and technical training, reifying the dichotomies between Black and white, body and mind, emotion and intellect. Yet, for Allen, the term "magic" has personal meaning. As I discuss in more detail below, magic, comedy, and music have been his means of escaping reality, his sources of psychological and emotional comfort. It is this perception of "magic"—of artistic beauty that transcends the limits of reality and transports both performers and audiences—that drives Allen's musical interests.

Allen's devotion to playing jazz has thrived since his youth. Soon after taking up the clarinet as a teenager, he studied with Gene Sedric, a renowned jazz clarinetist known for his work with Fats Waller, Mezz Mezzrow, and Don Redman. Allen began playing with groups around New York City, performing regularly on Monday nights at the local Michael's Pub until it closed in the 1990s. Today, he performs regularly with the Eddy Davis Jazz Band in residency at the Carlyle Hotel in Manhattan and has toured professionally throughout the United States and Europe (as depicted in Barbara Kopple's documentary of his 1997 European tour, *Wild Man Blues*). The music is straight out of 1920s New Orleans—featuring tunes popularized by many of Allen's musical heroes, including Louis Armstrong, George Lewis, and Sidney Bechet.

Allen has claimed that his primary aspiration is to be a great musician. As he contended in an interview with Douglas McGrath, "If I could just hope to have a major talent, then I would rather have it in music, than in any other field. . . . If you said, 'Would you rather be the best film director in the world or the best painter in the world or a great musician?' then I'd rather be a great musician."[31] Although one could argue that Allen's dreams of "making it" as a professional jazz musician have been fulfilled, given his regular performance gig and sold-out concert tours, he maintains humility about his abilities and certainly does not compare himself to his musical idols such as Bechet and Dodds. In his recognizable self-deprecating style, he criticizes his own skills, while crediting his fame as a movie director for facilitating his performance opportunities: "I [do] not have that genius, [and I am] destined, for all my enthusiasm and love of the music; to never amount to more than a musical nonentity who would be listened to and tolerated on the basis of a movie career and not for anything worth a damn as far as jazz is concerned."[32]

It is true that Allen's technical proficiency is not as advanced as the clarinetists that he idolizes. His knowledge of the New Orleans jazz idiom seems clear, as he navigates through the pieces with fidelity to the harmonic changes, an idiomatic solo style rooted in the blues, and an effective ability to collectively improvise. His timbre is quite raw, often straining in the higher and lower registers of the instrument with cracked notes (the seeming result of limited breath support). His embouchure is tight, often resulting in clipped tones and phrases. He has a solid sense of pulse, yet his rhythmic approach is decidedly punctuated and staccato, more abrupt in phrasing than lyrical. The element of his performance style that most clearly reveals the influence of artists like Bechet is his pronounced, warm vibrato. I concur with jazz critic John Fordham's assessment that his playing style occasionally provides glimpses of Johnny Dodds and George Lewis, while it is, "for the most part, apparent that his clarinet playing was closer to the superior-amateur than the awful-dreadfulness [as Allen himself described it] class."[33]

What Allen may lack in technical skill, he makes up for in dedication. He prides himself on never missing his rehearsals or performances, a fact that became newsworthy when he skipped the 1978 Academy Awards (for which his film *Annie Hall* had multiple nominations and ended up winning four, including Best Picture) so as not to miss his regular Monday-night gig.[34] He practices daily, often playing along with recordings of his musical idols like Bechet and Dodds. He stated, "I play with all the great players without having to meet them. To me, it's like real. It's transporting. It's like being bathed in honey."[35]

It is in his films that Allen has perhaps most successfully paid homage to the jazz he loves. One of the most poignant examples is the opening scene to his popular 2011 film *Midnight in Paris*. The first three minutes are a cinematic love letter to the eponymous city, a glamorous visual montage of quintessential Parisian locations—from the Louvre, to quaint outdoor cafés, to riverboats floating along the Seine, to the Eiffel Tower, brilliantly ablaze in gold against the night sky. Yet perhaps just as evocative as the vibrant images on-screen is the foregrounded music. The images correspond to the full length of "Si tu vois ma mère," a 1953 recording performed by the expatriate, Paris-loving jazz artist himself Sidney Bechet (who, as we know, was one of Allen's biggest musical idols). There are no voiceovers in this scene, unlike in *Manhattan* (a similar filmic love letter to New York, backed by Gershwin's *Rhapsody in Blue*); the focus is entirely on the romance between the iconic visuals and the music itself.

Holistically, Allen's stories are permeated with jazz—regardless of setting, time period, or plot. In an interview with Fred Kaplan for the *Boston Globe*, he stated: "The putting in of music "[is] the highest form of pleasure I get in making a film. . . . I get to go through my record collection and select anything, from Beethoven to Monk to Erroll Garner. It's so much better than hiring someone to write a score."[36] In a separate interview with Michel Ciment and Yann Tobin for *Positif*, he affirmed: "When I've finished the editing [of a film], I have lots of records around. I think that such and such a piece could work, I try it and it's good, if not I try another one. In two days maximum, I have the score of the whole film."[37] It is true that his soundtracks may appear to read more as a catalog of his favorite hits than as having anything to do with the films' narratives (take, for example, the rather incongruous "alien" scene in *Stardust Memories* where, after Sandy's [Allen's] humorous yet philosophical exchange with extraterrestrials about life's meanings, the aliens float away in hot-air balloons to the strains of Glenn Miller's "Moonlight Serenade"). Yet I argue that his specific musical choices, rather than functioning in traditional manners (per Claudia Gorbman's taxonomy of film music's principle functions), reveal much deeper relationships between Allen's views of jazz and his philosophies on reality, human relationships, life's meanings, and his own personal psyche.

For Allen, jazz is freedom. It represents an escape from the violence and disappointment of reality—a theme that permeates many of his films. In *The Purple Rose of Cairo*, for instance, a Depression era young woman (played by

Mia Farrow) escapes her daily disillusionment and abusive, loveless marriage by going to the theatre to watch films, eventually engaging in a fantastical romance with one of the on-screen characters (played by Jeff Daniels). Addressing this premise, Allen maintained: "Clearly I do believe that reality is dreadful and that you are forced to choose it in the end or go crazy, but that it kills you."[38] This pessimistic view shapes his philosophies on life, love, death, and art, while also greatly influencing his own interests and means of self-expression. As Allen himself has detailed in numerous interviews, as well as in his recently published memoir, the few positive experiences that he recalls from his childhood were going to the movies, listening to the radio, doing magic tricks, watching comedy acts, and (later) listening to and playing along with jazz records. Cole Porter records, *Your Hit Parade*, Bob Hope, Fred and Ginger films, magic books—these were his means of escapism. "I've never felt Truth was Beauty. Never. I've always felt that people can't take too much reality. I like being in Ingmar Bergman's world. Or in Louis Armstrong's world. . . . I'm always fighting against reality."[39]

Therefore, for Allen, jazz represents freedom from that reality. New Orleans jazz of the 1920s, Tin Pan Alley songbook standards, swing—these styles exude joy, optimism, and rhythmic drive. Their emergence during the early twentieth century reflected the milieu of America: the 1920s was an era bursting with technological progress, modernism, and optimism; Gershwin and Porter wrote songs that corresponded to the burgeoning developments in musical theater and film; throughout the 1930s and 1940s, swing dominated the radio airwaves and provided hope and escapism in the midst of economic depression and war. In Allen's films the music appears in direct contrast to his espoused views of reality. Juxtaposed against the bleak, often nihilistic discussions that his onscreen characters have about life, romance, philosophy, and death, Allen's jazz functions as a remedy to life's disappointments, a glimmer of hope, a necessity of psychic survival.

Nostalgia permeates Allen's approach to filmmaking. As mentioned previously, he identifies music, movies, and Manhattan as the few bright spots of his childhood. Cole Porter, Irving Berlin, Billie Holiday—these were the pop stars of his youth. He found escape and magic in the movie theater, contrasted with mundane reality: "So now the double feature is over, and I leave the comfortable, dark magic of the movie house and reenter Coney Island Avenue, the sun, the traffic, back to the wretched apartment on Avenue K. Back into the clutches of my archenemy, reality."[40] In returning to these "bright spots"—particularly through the music of that era—Allen attempts to, at least temporarily, escape the disappointments of the present, returning to an idealized past.

Allen is certainly aware of his propensity for nostalgic longing; he acknowledges his obsession with the idealized "champagne world"[41] of 1940s Hollywood and the "larger than life, the superficial, the falsely glamorous."[42] Yet he is also quick to say: "But I do not regret a frame of it."[43] While he describes nostalgia as a "trap" that is rooted in the "Golden Age fallacy" of believing that oneself would be happier in another time, he also believes that such nostalgic escapism allows people to (at least temporarily) escape the disappointments and frustrations of reality.[44] Two of his films in particular are directly based on the concept of nostalgia. *Radio Days* (1987), strongly inspired by Allen's own love of radio as a child, portrays a series of vignettes built around memories associated with specific songs and radio shows during the 1940s. The protagonist of the film—a young boy who appears to represent a young Woody Allen (and whose recollections are articulated in narrative voiceovers by Allen himself)—is shown in charming, nostalgic childhood scenes with his family, backed by such tunes as Glenn Miller's "In the Mood," the Mills Brothers' "Paper Doll," and Frank Sinatra's "If You Are But a Dream."

More recently, *Midnight in Paris* (2011) portrays the experiences of Hollywood director Gil Pender (played by Owen Wilson), who travels to Paris to find inspiration for his book (appropriately about a nostalgia-shop owner) and ends up fantastically traveling back in time to the "golden age" of 1920s Paris. There he meets several of his artistic idols, including Ernest Hemingway, Cole Porter, F. Scott Fitzgerald, and Gertrude Stein, also engaging in a passionate romance with the captivating Adriana (played by Marion Cotillard). As he revels with these figures of the past, he becomes increasingly dissatisfied with his current reality (and his incompatible fiancée, played by Rachel McAdams). Yet, while Gil loves his experiences in the 1920s, he realizes through Adriana—who, as a contemporary of the 1920s, is instead nostalgic for "the Belle Epoque"—that nostalgia is a fallacy, and that people ultimately have to come to terms with their own realities, no matter how potentially unsatisfying.

So, what is the relationship between Allen's nostalgic approach and the notion of "authenticity"—one of the primary themes of this book? In many ways these concepts seem to be in opposition to one another; one represents wistful longing for an idealized place or time, while the other represents something genuine, uncompromised or untainted. How can something be "authentic" if it is romanticized and idealized "all out of proportion" (as Allen narrates in *Manhattan's* opening scene)? The connection, I argue, is that nostalgia *feels real*. Our experiences of nostalgia are rooted so strongly in personal emotion that they are real to us, despite the fact that "authenticity" and the idealized objects of our nostalgia are not. Allen recognizes the inherent fallacies of nostalgia but at the same time acknowledges the genuine human emotions and psychological needs that lead to its manifestation. Authenticity lies not in nostalgia itself but in the genuine human need to employ nostalgia as a method of emotionally coping with (or temporarily escaping) reality.

The emotional connections between nostalgia and perceived authenticity have been perhaps most purposefully studied in the field of marketing. Consider the titles of the following business articles featured in *Forbes* within the last five years: "What Was Old Is New Again –The Power of Nostalgia Marketing," "Why Nostalgia Marketing Works So Well with Millennials, and How Your Brand Can Benefit," and "Use Nostalgia to Improve your Marketing Results."[45] The past is seductive. It has familiarity and comfort, with the added advantage of temporal distance, allowing us to foreground its most exhilarating and glamorous aspects, while glossing over its less positive moments. The act of remembering is strongly emotional and is effectively triggered by the senses—imagery, taste, smell, sound. How many of us have heard a song on the radio that seems to immediately "take us back" to a moment in time, instigating a cascade of nostalgic reminiscences? Herein lies the power of nostalgia in marketing. As CMO Jenna Gross argues, "By sharing a compelling blast from the past, you can reach your audience on an emotional level, linking your brand message with familiar concepts to evoke feelings of security, comfort and trust. It can signify to your customers that you are worthy of attention because you are associated with something they already love. And those sentimental feelings make people increasingly willing to spend money on consumer goods and services."[46] Nostalgic longing is a full-body experience: psychological recollection, emotion, and physical sensation grounded in an encounter with a specific triggering "object." Susan Stewart's seminal work *On Longing* provides a valuable framework for thinking about the ways such objects of nostalgic desire (e.g., souvenirs, collections) function in humans' quests for "authentic" experience and connection.[47] It is not surprising, therefore, that we ascribe "authenticity" or genuineness to things that trigger our sentimental longings, whether it be a souvenir playbill from a trip to Broadway or a recording of the Frank Sinatra song you danced to at your wedding.

Allen's nostalgia is his vehicle of escape from reality, yet it is also indicative of his personal grappling with life and its meanings. The nostalgic elements of his films—whether depictions of the Manhattan skyline in black and white or Billie Holiday's emotion-laden rendition of "I'll Be Seeing You"—give us insight into the "authentic" Woody Allen himself, who defends his own psyche against the challenges and disappointments of reality by creatively reshaping it with the filigree of a bygone age. To be clear, Allen's representations of the past, though glamorous, are laced with irony. The idealized facades of his talented, smart, beautiful, champagne-sipping characters are stripped away to reveal neurotic, dysfunctional, anxious figures struggling with their own realities and relationships. Picture-perfect romances ultimately end in betrayal, dissatisfaction, or lack of resolution. Reality is never as elegant as it seems and consistently disappoints. Yet the characters themselves find solace in reminiscence, and with it—the strength to move on. What is particularly striking in Allen's films is that these moments of nostalgic reminiscence are triggered by specific musical pieces; for example, Norma and Evan (in *Hannah and Her Sisters*) "floating down memory lane" while singing "Bewitched, Bothered, and Bewildered," Sandy Bates (in *Stardust Memories*) fondly remembering the "best moment of his life" while watching his ex-girlfriend Dorrie and listening to Louis Armstrong's "Stardust," and Alvy Singer (in *Annie Hall*) wistfully recalling romantic moments with his lost love, Annie Hall, montaged over a poignant rendition of the nostalgic ballad "Seems like Old Times" (sung by Diane Keaton). Nostalgia—particularly musically induced nostalgia—is a driving force in Allen's art, as well as his psychic survival.

SCORING ALLEN'S FILMS

So far, I have primarily been discussing Allen's compilation scores, comprising original licensed recordings that he himself has selected from his own record collection. But what about original underscoring, featuring music that is composed specifically for the film? Early in his filmmaking career, Allen hired a young Marvin Hamlisch to compose scores for his films *Take the Money and Run* (1969) and *Bananas* (1971).[48] Despite Hamlisch's skills as a composer, Allen was disappointed in the scores, feeling that they didn't meet his expectations. He recalls:

> For my first films, I had a composer, Marvin Hamlisch. He sat down and played the piano—excellently—while watching the films, but that wasn't quite what I wanted. He was disappointed when I told him I didn't like it very much. He answered, "But I worked all night long on it! It's beautiful!" We had it recorded by an orchestra, and I still didn't like it; we didn't use it.[49]

By the time Allen made his 1973 film *Sleeper*, he had determined to no longer hire a film composer; instead, the *Sleeper* soundtrack consisted of all New

Orleans–style jazz pieces recorded by the Preservation Hall Jazz Band and the New Orleans Funeral and Ragtime Orchestra, featuring Allen on clarinet.

Allen's frustrations with his early film scores were perhaps in part due to his own inexperience as a director, lacking clear ideas about what he wanted the score to sound like. He was new to filmmaking, and grappling with developing his own approach to directing, filming, and editing. He knew what he didn't want, but not necessarily what he wanted. In hindsight he claimed that Hamlisch's scores—and traditional film scoring approaches in general—were not ideal for his films, as they relied heavily on film scoring conventions, seeming too contrived and heavily dependent on concrete film scenes. Given Allen's propensity for reshooting scenes and allowing for organic improvisation during filming,[50] he discovered that he needed film music that allowed for such flexibility.

It was at this point—early in his filmmaking career—that Allen adopted the approach of using selected jazz recordings for his soundtracks. It is very likely that his inspiration came during his work on *Take the Money and Run*. Amid his disappointment with Hamlisch's score, as well as a less-than-successful test screening for Palomar (the production company), Allen brought in Ralph Rosenblum for consultation on editing. He recalls:

> Enter Rosenblum, a sardonic, highly gifted editor who turned my movie from a failure to a success, and here's how. . . . First thing he did was take all the funny stuff I had cut out and put it back in. . . . He stuck in some Eubie Blake jazz in place of Hamlisch's lovely but sad background music, and the mere switch from slower music or no music to lively jazz transformed it, or should I say transmogrified it because the change was magical.[51]

From *Sleeper* onward Allen has used early jazz recordings (occasionally sprinkled with classical music) as the sonic basis of his films. He explains, "This way, I don't bother myself with anyone. I take George Gershwin or Beethoven, I edit it into the film and it works perfectly."[52] It would not be until years later that he would again entertain the notion of working with a film composer.

DICK HYMAN: "A FILM DIRECTOR'S DREAM"

For close to seventy years, pianist Dick Hyman has maintained a prolific career as a performer, recording artist, and composer. Since the 1970s he has largely been recognized for his performances of early jazz piano music of the

1920s and 1930s, including ragtime, stride, and the early swing piano styles of such artists as Scott Joplin, James P. Johnson, Eubie Blake, Fats Waller, Zez Confrey, and Duke Ellington. He has also recorded tributes to the music of several Tin Pan Alley composers, including Harold Arlen, Irving Berlin, Cole Porter, and George Gershwin. Yet Hyman's jazz performance capabilities well exceed the styles of the early twentieth century. The most effective illustration of his command of a range of jazz styles is his *Century of Jazz Piano* (released on Arbor Records in 2009), which includes over 120 solo piano recordings highlighting Hyman's pianistic virtuosity—from ragtime to free improvisation.

Throughout his extensive career, Hyman has performed with a number of renowned jazz artists, including Teddy Wilson (whom he took lessons from), Benny Goodman, Charlie Parker, and Dizzy Gillespie, as well as recurrently performing and recording with contemporaries Ruby Braff, Ken Peplowski, Milt Hinton, Randy Sandke, Bucky Pizzarelli, and Howard Alden. Hyman has also been highly involved in jazz festivals and concert series. In the 1970s he acted as musical director for George Wein's New York Jazz Repertory Company, organizing jazz concert seasons at Carnegie Hall that featured the works of early jazz pianists. In 1984 he founded the Jazz in July concert series at the 92nd Street Y in New York City and served as its artistic director for twenty years, until handing over the position to fellow jazz pianist Bill Charlap. This impressive résumé supports his recognition as one of the most historically knowledgeable jazz pianists of our time. His wide diversity of performances has been characterized as masterfully accurate and stylistically "authentic" on numerous occasions. Consider this enthusiastic description by William Zinsser, for the *Atlantic*:

> For almost fifty years it has been common knowledge in the entertainment business that the person to call for whatever kind of music you need is the pianist-arranger-composer-organist Dick Hyman. Computerized in Hyman's brain, instantly transferable to his fingers is every popular piano and organ style that has ever been played in America, historically correct to the year when it was in vogue. He can also replicate, note for note, the style of all the American giants of jazz piano in this century, from the intricate rags of Eubie Blake and the galloping stride of James P. Johnson to the jagged bebop of Bud Powell and the introspective lyricism of Bill Evans.[53]

So how did Hyman develop a relationship with Woody Allen? In the mid-twentieth century, Hyman became very active in the New York studio circuit, establishing his reputation as a performer and making connections with many New York-based artists at the time. He informed me, "I was part of a few hundred people who were making the records and playing in bands for every possible circumstance around New York at that time, and I met a lot of people, and I often met producers, and that's how I did it. I did not have an agent, I just was there."[54] During this period he became acquainted with Allen, who was just beginning to make movies at the time.

It is therefore unsurprising that Allen and Hyman—two contemporary, active New York artists devoted to performing 1920s and '30s jazz and popular music—established a relationship. Allen first hired Hyman as a pianist/keyboardist (suggested by composer/jazz guitarist Mundell Lowe) on the soundtrack for *Everything You Always Wanted to Know about Sex** *(*But Were Afraid to Ask)* (1972). For thirty years Hyman remained highly involved in many of Allen's soundtracks, acting as an original score composer, arranger, music supervisor, performer, and even an on-screen performer in a few short cameos.[55] He ultimately contributed to the soundtracks of fourteen of Allen's films, spanning from 1972 to 2004 (see Table 4.1 below). Allen has remarked, "[Dick] is a film director's dream. He looks at the scenes and knows what works. He can do whatever you want. He can be Erroll Garner, or Bud Powell, or Fats Waller. He has a mastery of the tunes of Jelly Roll Morton and Bix Beiderbecke and the New Orleans style that I love. I'm amazed at the scenes with music he has given us."[56]

What did Hyman have, in Allen's eyes, that Hamlisch did not? It is here that I want to get back to the concept of "authenticity." For Allen, Hyman is a direct connection to the music that he loves. He is well versed in an immense diversity of jazz idioms, with comprehensive technical performance knowledge, as well as the rare ability to comfortably compose (as well as improvise) in a variety of historically informed styles. "[Dick] . . . knows all the kinds of songs that I like. When I need the kind of songs that Cole Porter would write or the kind of jazz arrangements that Paul Whiteman or Jelly Roll Morton would do, Dick Hyman knows that code."[57] The value of such an artist for a filmmaker who consistently wants to feature early jazz in his soundtracks is clear. With Hyman, if Allen wanted to include original scoring that is reminiscent of jazz from the 1930s, he could have it. If the licensing of original jazz recordings was cost-prohibitive, he could avoid purchasing rights by having Hyman record jazz tunes himself. Last but certainly not least, he could commission Hyman to write "new" pieces in old styles, which could be used as part of the film narrative. Allen employed Hyman in all these capacities.

Let's look at a few specific examples. *Zelig* (1983) is arguably one of Allen's most creative and technically intricate comedies to date. This

Table 4.1. Dick Hyman's film soundtracks for Woody Allen's films	
Film	**Year**
Everything You Always Wanted to Know about Sex* (*But Were Afraid to Ask)	1972
Manhattan	1979
Stardust Memories	1980
Zelig	1983
Broadway Danny Rose	1984
The Purple Rose of Cairo	1985
Hannah and Her Sisters	1986
Radio Days	1987
Bullets over Broadway	1994
Mighty Aphrodite	1995
Everyone Says I Love You	1996
Sweet and Lowdown	1999
The Curse of the Jade Scorpion	2001
Melinda and Melinda	2004

"mockumentary" documents the (mis)adventures of Leonard Zelig, a "social quick-change artist whose neurotic insecurity forces him to mimic—mentally and physically—whomever he's with."[58] The film documents Zelig's life during the period of the 1920s and 1930s, convincingly achieved through Gordon Willis's magnificent cinematography, replete with vintage newsreels, black-and-white reenactments of actual historical events, and superimpositions of Zelig (played by Allen) and his psychiatrist Eudora Fletcher (played by Mia Farrow) into archival footage. The "documentary" aesthetic of the film is further enhanced through the employment of voiceovers (in the style of 1920s newsreels), and interviews with contemporary "talking heads" (e.g., Nat Hentoff, Susan Sontag, and fictional historians and scholars), discussing Zelig's popularity and influence in society.

If the cinematography and documentary-style interviews are not enough to make you question whether Zelig actually existed, Hyman's music fully transports you back into the 1920s. What is particularly unique about this soundtrack is that Hyman wrote "new" pieces in an "old" 1920s style, creating what I call *historically informed compositions* (HICs). Allen commissioned Hyman to write these pieces because they aided the story. The character of Zelig—referred to as a "human chameleon" in the film—becomes an overnight sensation/celebrity. Suddenly people go wild for all things Zelig—toys,

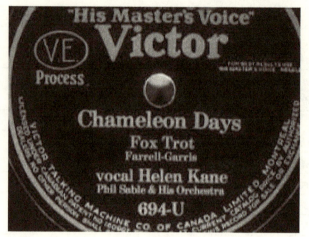

Figure 4.1. Screenshot of "Chameleon Days" record, as shown in the film *Zelig*.

watches, dolls, and of course, hit songs. Hyman wrote several Zelig-related pieces that sound straight out of the 1920s pop catalogs (aided through vintage recording equipment), including "Leonard the Lizard," "Reptile Eyes," "Doin' the Chameleon," and "Chameleon Days," among others.

For a closer look, let us consider "Chameleon Days" in detail. The song deliberately parodies Helen Kane, a popular American singer during the 1920s, whose signature cutesy voice and "boop-a-doop" licks inspired the Fleischer Studios cartoon character Betty Boop. The connection to Helen Kane is overtly affirmed on-screen; as "Chameleon Days" plays in the background, an image parade of popular Zelig paraphernalia (and footage of fans using it) culminates in a close-up image of a seemingly authentic-looking Victor record entitled "Chameleon Days," featuring Phil Sable and His Orchestra, with Helen Kane on vocals (see Figure 4.1). A more subtle but significant connection is the fact that "Chameleon Days" is sung by Mae Questel, a vocalist best known for providing the original voice of Betty Boop (as well as Olive Oyl in *Popeye*) in the 1930s; appropriately, she inserts a quick "boop-boop-be-doop" homage toward the end of the song. Musically, Hyman's "Chameleon Days" captures the sound of the era. From the punctuated stop-time, to the thirty-two-bar popular song form, to the twenties jazz band instrumentation (including banjo), to Questel's recognizable voice, this recording may have jazz aficionados double-checking Victor's 1920s catalogs just to make sure the Zelig craze was a fabrication.

Beyond writing original historically informed pieces for *Zelig*, Hyman also arranged and performed actual pieces from the era, including the famed "Charleston" (James P. Johnson, 1923), and "Chicago (That Toddlin' Town)"

(Fred Fischer, 1922). As mentioned previously, Hyman's ability to "authentically" capture the style of an era—whether through performances of standards or composition of new tunes—is what made him such an asset to Allen. Whether he was performing "Bewitched, Bothered, and Bewildered" on solo piano in *Hannah and Her Sisters* (as discussed at the opening of this chapter), arranging Django Reinhardt's "I'll See You in My Dreams" for the jazz mockumentary *Sweet and Lowdown* (featuring guitarist Howard Alden), or appearing to play (and conduct) a romantic arrangement of "How High the Moon" in an on-screen cameo in *The Curse of the Jade Scorpion*, he helped Allen bring early jazz into his films without the necessity of licensing recordings, while opening up the possibilities for the ways the music could appear in and contribute to the film, both diegetically and nondiegetically.

I'd like to take a moment to briefly discuss the relationships between improvisation, historically informed performance (HIP), and authenticity. Historically informed performance practice is born out of musicians' and scholars' desires to authentically recreate the music of the past. The height of criticism and scholarship in the traditional-HIP performance practice movement during the 1960s–1990s reflected a growing investment in identifying and establishing conventions for appropriately performing early Western art music—from medieval chant through the early twentieth-century pieces of composers such as Stravinsky and Elgar.[59] Jazz historicists—including "neo-classicists" such as Wynton Marsalis, revivalists such as Vince Giordano, and repertory ensembles such as the Preservation Hall Jazz Band and the Smithsonian Jazz Masterworks Orchestra, among numerous others—have similarly placed a large investment in achieving period-appropriate performance styles, inflections, and perceptibly "authentic" fidelity to the original pieces or idioms in question. These performers' contentions and decisions about what constitutes authentic performance can be varied, and questions arise concerning what and how performance techniques should be employed.[60] Yet the big questions all focus on one large overarching query—how much fidelity to the original works is expected, and what does that fidelity constitute? Instrumentation? Performance style/inflection? Rhythmic approach? And how does improvisation fit into these expectations?

There are two primary elements of musical performance—the "facts" of the performance (e.g., the notes, instruments, dynamics) and the "experience" of the performance (by performers and audience members alike). The first focuses on appropriately replicating the "facts" of history—written scores, instrumentation, and commonly accepted performance practice as evidenced through contemporary theoretical literature, criticism, and (in the case of twentieth-century works) recordings. The second seeks to replicate the more

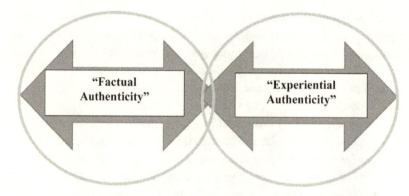

Figure 4.2. Potential interactions of dual spheres of authenticity in historically informed performance.

abstract and ephemeral qualities of performance—the "experience" as it was perceived by those who witnessed the performance at the time.

I argue that these two elements manifest in two overarching perceptions of performance authenticity that encompass all other dimensional definitions of the term—nominal/factual authenticity, and expressive/experiential authenticity.[61] I refer to these primary elements as the interactive components of "*dual authenticity*." To fully re-create a given performance, one would ideally need to replicate *all* the elements that constitute these dual spheres. This is of course impossible, which is why no two performances—despite consistency in personnel, scores, etc.—are ever exactly the same. This does not, however, discourage HIP practitioners from attempting such recreation. Whether for scholarly interests, nostalgia, or commissions that request "authentic" historically informed performances (such as film soundtrack projects), many artists still attempt to approximate original performances as "accurately" as possible.

In engaging elements of both factual and experiential authenticity, HIP artists come closer to approximating the experience of the performance in its original period setting. Now, I am not arguing that one approach is inherently "better" than another. Rather, I am contending that those artists who draw on elements of perceived authenticity in both historical content and experience will come the closest to attaining a re-creation of the original event. Denis Dutton has expressed a similar viewpoint, arguing, "The best attitude towards authenticity in music performance is that in which careful attention is paid to the historic conventions and limitations of a composer's age, but where one also tries to determine the larger artistic potential of a musical work, including implicit meanings that go beyond the understanding that the composer's age might have derived from it."[62]

I argue that "determining the larger artistic potential" of a musical work need not only include efforts to find new ways of interpreting the work but may also include performing the work in ways that make its contemporary musical meanings relevant for present-day audiences. This can certainly be challenging in situations where the cultural contexts of the original music are far removed from our present-day culture—such as in the case of medieval or Renaissance idioms. For more recent twentieth-century genres such as jazz, achieving expressive and experiential authenticity is less complicated, as the styles still retain similarities to contemporary practices. It is for this reason that jazz-HIP offers particularly interesting readings of dual authenticity in historically informed performance in general—a larger project worth considering in the future.

Early jazz was an interactive music—not for quiet listening but for dancing and audience participation. Throughout the 1920s and '30s, jazz styles such as stride, New Orleans style, and the blues dominated the city streets, apartment and house parties, speakeasies/clubs, and dance halls. As an improvised and interpretive idiom, early jazz was not highly regulated by written-out scores but instead utilized lead sheets or head arrangements as interpretive frameworks for musicians' performances. Jazz HIP, therefore, emphasizes interactive experience. The similarity of early jazz reception to today's pop music reception gives jazz-HIP artists a culturally relevant framework for attempting to approximate experiential authenticity in their performances. The "facts" of the original performances—often accessed through recordings (and in some cases, written scores)—provide textual references that practitioners may choose to re-create, with varying levels of fidelity. I argue that the majority of successful jazz HIP artists utilize these textual elements in conjunction with efforts to draw modern-day audiences into the excitement and interactive experiences that characterized the original 1920s and '30s performances.

This dual-authenticity deftness is what makes Dick Hyman such an invaluable asset for Woody Allen. His encyclopedic knowledge of historic jazz styles allows him to project "factual authenticity" by employing historically accurate performance techniques, rhythmic style, idiomatic phrasing, articulation, etc. But his ability to effectively extemporize and improvise in those styles allows for more "experiential authenticity," in which audiences may perceive them as "live," more spontaneous, and thus more interactive.[63] Hyman claimed in an interview for the *Wall Street Journal*, "On some [early music performances/recordings] I'm perfectly authentic [read: adhering to original scores/recordings]; on others, more interpretive."[64] Either way, Hyman's unique aptitude as a HIP jazz pianist positions him as an ideal film collaborator for Woody Allen, resulting in poignant visual and sonic tapestries that reflect Allen's personal, complex, nostalgia-laden worldviews.

CLOSING THOUGHTS

The concept of "authenticity" as a facilitating factor in integrative jazz/film collaborations has been a thematic thread of this book. In each case study, the directors have their own conceptions of what authenticity means, and how jazz functions as a sonic representation of it. For Iñárritu, improvised jazz percussion evinced lived experience and gritty reality. For Rudolph, jazz represented raw, human emotion: love, lust, betrayal, and disillusionment. For Lee, the music functioned as a sonic representation of authentic Black creativity and culture. And for Allen, his jazz soundtracks reflected personal authenticity: projecting his emotional and psychological relationships to the music through the lenses of nostalgia, romanticism, escapism, irony, and idealism.

At initial glance, it may seem that Allen conventionally utilizes jazz as a period place-marker or indicator of romance. But it signifies more. For him, jazz represents many things. It represents freedom, improvisation, and, perhaps most pointedly—the New York that he idealizes and wishes existed (while recognizing that it doesn't). It represents his most treasured pastime. It represents emotion and personal expressivity. The work that jazz does in his films goes beyond the films themselves; it helps us connect with him personally.

In the bigger picture, Allen's films represent jazz as a relevant part of everyday life. Armstrong, Ellington, and Porter are timeless in his view; their music dominates his soundtracks, regardless of whether they are set in the 2000s or the 1920s. While his usage of New Orleans–style jazz in *Sleeper*— a futuristic sci-fi comedy set two hundred years in the future—may come across as jarringly anachronistic, the entirety of his body of film work normalizes its presence, while also suggesting that Allen believes jazz will (or should) continue to be valuable in the future. The music also permeates his films as a regular, if subtle, subject. Many of his movies feature "live" diegetic scenes of jazz performances—some understated in the background (e.g., *Curse of the Jade Scorpion, Manhattan, Blue Jasmine*) and others more pronounced and foregrounded in the narrative (e.g., *Annie Hall, Sweet and Lowdown*). Through these diegetic representations, Allen illustrates that jazz constitutes the sonic fabric of his characters' worlds.[65]

Allen's usage of jazz in his film soundtracks—as well as his collaborations with Dick Hyman—uniquely contribute to this book's broader discussion about jazz/film integrations that challenge the ways we think about movie music and its potential meanings. In developing compilation soundtracks that are essentially "greatest hits" playlists of his personal favorite jazz tunes, Allen challenges the conventional approach that subjugates the soundtrack to the narrative, instead using his films as a vehicle for sharing his love of jazz with his audiences. Hyman's role in the film productions is less about composing original works that enhance the overall emotion/mood of the visual scenes, and more about injecting further "authenticity" into the soundtrack through high-level, idiomatic jazz performance. Accordingly, Allen and Hyman's unique collaborations provide a model for potential ways that filmmakers can use their films as musical platforms, structuring the narratives to highlight musical pieces that are revelatory of their own personal ideologies and preferences.

Conclusion

MILES AHEAD

A NEW WAY OF MAKING MOVIE MUSIC?

Within the last decade, there has been a noticeable uptick in jazz-related films. Beyond Damien Chazelle's particularly successful *Whiplash* (2014) and *La La Land* (2016), a number of jazz biopics have also emerged, including *Bessie* (2015), *Miles Ahead* (2015), *Born to Be Blue* (2015), and *Bolden* (2019). Though these films certainly vary in their subject matter (as well as in their representations of jazz/jazz artists), the simultaneity of their emergence seems to suggest an interest in jazz as a narrative subject—a topic that hasn't been popular in film since the 1950s and 1960s (despite a seemingly brief resurgence in the 1980s with films like *The Cotton Club* [1984], *Round Midnight* [1986], and *Bird* [1988]).

So why this recent resurgence? I have a few theories. The first could simply be that reaching jazz's centennial has launched a renewed historical interest in the idiom. Films like *Bessie* and *Bolden* affirm this theory, as they focus on seminal jazz figures from the early twentieth century. These movies' directors (and scriptwriters), Dee Rees (*Bessie*) and Daniel Pritzker (*Bolden*), were both drawn to their projects after listening to early jazz and learning about the artists' lives. Rees grew up listening to Bessie Smith with her grandmother and also cites Vernel Bagneris's revue "One Mo' Time" (which features characters based on figures like Smith) as a source of inspiration for her understanding of early twentieth-century Black vaudeville. Pritzker, an amateur musician who claims he has "loved New Orleans music since [he] was a kid,"[1] began writing the script in the late 1990s after learning about Buddy Bolden and his mythological status in jazz history.[2] Baz Luhrmann's remake of *The Great Gatsby* (2013)—despite a soundtrack featuring hip-hop rather than jazz[3]—further suggests the appeal of the 1920s to modern-day audiences. The recent proliferation of Gatsby- or 1920s-themed New Year's Eve parties, murder mysteries, escape rooms, and "speakeasy" bars affirms contemporary fascination with the era—however temporary that fascination might be.

Yet interest in the early twentieth century cannot be the sole reason for this increase in jazz-related films, particularly since several of them focus on later twentieth-century jazz artists (e.g., Miles Davis, Chet Baker) and/or modern-day settings (as in *Whiplash* and *La La Land*). Therefore, my second theory is that jazz (or more specifically, jazz musicians) makes for good drama. Consider the subjects of the aforementioned films: Buddy Bolden, Bessie Smith, Miles Davis, and Chet Baker. These larger-than-life figures have been mythologized in jazz history, presented as enigmatic yet brilliant artists embroiled in drugs, tumultuous relationships, violence, mystery, and tragedy (affirming the long-held Hollywood associations between jazz and vice). They are recognized as rebels, seeming to challenge conventions and institutions at every turn. Now, further consider Damien Chazelle's fictionalized jazz characters in *La La Land* and *Whiplash*. In the former, struggling jazz pianist Sebastian Wilder (played by Ryan Gosling) portrays a snobbish, skeptical, eccentric (staunchly traditionalist), yet charmingly passionate artist, a romantic rebel whose obsessive zeal is reserved only for the things he loves: Mia (his love interest, played by Emma Stone) and his music. In *Whiplash*, the tyrannical and psychologically abusive jazz bandleader/professor Dr. Terence Fletcher (played by J. K. Simmons) leaves a trail of humiliation, violence, and destruction in his quest to find "the next Charlie Parker." For better or for worse, these are the types of characters that sell movie tickets.

You might ask, then, why haven't there been more jazz films if they make for good drama? In short, I think that filmmakers have only recently (re)recognized this. In the 1950s and early 1960s, films about jazz musicians abounded: *Young Man with a Horn, Pete Kelly's Blues, The Glenn Miller Story, The Benny Goodman Story, The Five Pennies, The Man with the Golden Arm, Paris Blues*, etc. Jazz was prominent in popular culture, and drama-laden stories about jazz musicians were highly alluring. However, from the late 1960s into the new millennium, jazz's popularity waned, overtaken by numerous subgenres of rock/pop, and later, hip-hop. No longer prominent in the popular sphere, its presence in film (either as subject or soundtrack) became sparser, while rock/pop/hip-hop compilation soundtracks or neo-Romantic symphonic film scores dominated the cinema. Only recently have jazz stories returned to the limelight, often initiated as pet projects by jazz-loving filmmakers (as discussed above). My belief is that these films' successes have reignited some filmmakers' interests (and commercial confidence) in making movies about jazz—or at least, jazz subjects. Even as I complete my last round of editing on this book, three new jazz-based films have been released to significant critical acclaim: George C. Wolfe's *Ma Rainey's Black Bottom* (2020), based on the August Wilson 1982 play of the same name;

Disney-Pixar's animated feature *Soul* (2020); and Lee Daniels's *The United States vs. Billie Holiday* (2021). (It is notable that these films also reflect initiatives in the film and television industries to promote stories about Black figures and Black culture.) As long as such jazz biopics/dramas continue to be successful, I anticipate we will continue to see more of them.

My final theory is that jazz represents something bigger than itself; it is imbued with meaning that filmmakers believe is relevant to contemporary audiences. These meanings vary, but they are rooted in the history of jazz's representations in popular culture over the last one hundred years. As we have seen, jazz can represent freedom, rebellion, Blackness, urbanity, sophistication, sexuality, anxiety, intellectualism . . . the list goes on. So, you may ask, if there is such an abundance of potential meanings that are already well established in popular culture, what is it about the last ten years that has sparked a renewed interest in jazz as a film subject?

I argue that a significant factor in this resurgence is the current ideological milieu. There are many parallels between the 2010s and the beginning of the twentieth century, when jazz first emerged. Technology proliferates, continually adapting and influencing nearly all aspects of society, including manufacturing, work, education, transportation, consumption, and connectivity (including globalization). It is a time of experimentation and continual social change. The "you do you" ethos of the millennial generation in many ways parallels the self-indulgent narcissism and individualism that characterized youth culture during the Roaring Twenties. Jazz—an idiom strongly associated with individual excellence, experimentation, and improvisation—significantly resonates with these ideologies that are permeating contemporary culture.

And while one might argue that jazz's low sales and download rankings are a harbinger of the genre's demise, rather than revitalization, I believe these ratings are more reflective of the limitations of consumption statistics than of the vitality of the art form itself. Jazz is continually transforming, appearing in hybridized forms and mediums (such as film soundtracks!) that defy singular categorization. It is also a music that is often fully experienced *live*, in real time (which may account for why its record sales and downloads are not particularly high). Regardless of what the industry statistics say, I believe that the music's relevance is strong in contemporary culture; it is the methods of preferred consumption, not jazz's relevance, that have transformed. In a society characterized by continuous, interactive engagement with visual and social media and "real-time" streaming, perhaps the notion of recording sales itself as an indicator of consumption is becoming outdated. Jazz's intersections with such contemporary media may very well be the future of the genre.

I do not believe any single one of the aforementioned theories accounts for the recent reemergence of jazz films; rather, I believe they all do to some extent. The filmmakers of these productions have expressed varying motivations for making the movies they did. Damien Chazelle's inspirations stemmed from his own love of jazz (instilled by his father), rooted in his experience as a jazz drummer in his youth.[4] Whereas *Whiplash* presents jazz's potential dark side—not-so-loosely based on Chazelle's own experience with an overbearing jazz bandleader in high school—*La La Land* is a love letter to jazz (and classic Hollywood musicals), paying reverence to the idiom through Sebastian's ardent defense of and commitment to studying, performing, and promoting it, regardless of the obstacles. Don Cheadle's *Miles Ahead*—which garnered mixed critical reception for its unconventionality as a biopic that was more fiction than fact—was inspired by Cheadle's own respect for Davis's music (particularly his propensity for improvisation and experimentation) and understanding of his complex, mercurial personality. The film is fragmented, jumping between the 1970s (during Davis's musical hiatus) and flashbacks of his life during the 1960s, replete with love affairs, car chases, an unlikely Butch-and-Sundance relationship with a white *Rolling Stone* reporter (played by Ewan McGregor),[5] and of course, Davis's music. In an interview with *Rolling Stone*, Cheadle described how he pitched his vision for the film in the following way:

> I said, "I think we've got to make a movie about this dude as a gangster"—'cause that's how I feel about Miles Davis. He's a G. All those apocryphal stories about how bold and dynamic he was, the gangster shit he'd do . . . you could fit all that into a biopic, I guess. But I just thought, let's do a movie that Miles Davis would say, 'I want to be the star of that movie. Not the one about me. The one where I'm the fucker running it, and I tell everybody what happens.'" Take the music he made in 1950 and put it over scenes set in 1978, or take his 1965 album and drop it into 1945. Just do it without the constraints of any rules. Make some mistakes, go crazy, crash into a wall—anything but something fucking cookie-cutter.[6]

These directors' motivations are personal. All love jazz, and are drawn to it for personal reasons. Some are musicians. Some are fascinated by the dramatic histories and/or mythologies surrounding the jazz figures they depict. Some pay homage to the music itself; others use the music as a framework for understanding the musicians and their psyches. Some utilize aspects of jazz culture or jazz musicians' personal lives to provide commentary on modern-day art and society. Ultimately, the point that I am trying to make is that each of these filmmakers recognizes jazz/jazz musicians as a topic worthy of a film narrative, and (ideally) relevant to contemporary audiences. The implications are that perhaps we will continue to see films that focus on jazz subjects in the coming years.

However, I want to move beyond the limitations of jazz-as-subject when considering the contemporary intersections between jazz and film. As illustrated throughout this book, some of the most significant films featuring jazz soundtracks (e.g., *Birdman*, *Afterglow*, *Malcolm X*, the majority of Woody Allen's films) have nothing to do with jazz at all. Accordingly, they provide the strongest support for my third theory—that jazz represents something bigger than itself to filmmakers and consuming audiences.

As I have argued, for filmmakers Iñárritu, Lee, Rudolph, and Allen, jazz represents "authenticity." The jazz soundtracks featured in their films fundamentally shaped the fabric and meanings of the movies themselves. Through the "behind the scenes" examinations in the previous chapters, I have illustrated that these specific jazz/film collaborations are not conventional. While the soundtracks do operate in some "traditional" ways (e.g., signifying emotion, providing narrative cuing, providing continuity), they also represent the filmmakers' larger commitment to jazz as a source of authentic meaning (be it liveness, emotion, Blackness, or personal nostalgia). Accordingly, the relationships between the films and their soundtracks—as well as the filmmakers and the composers—are uniquely more collaborative than in conventional filmmaking. These examples illustrate how jazz's function in film can exceed the technicalities (and even emotional effects) of the music, representing larger ideas that are integral to the messages of the films themselves.

I have subtitled this chapter "A New Way of Making Movie Music?" My intention is not to suggest that the unique works discussed in the previous chapters will suddenly inspire similar jazz soundtracks in the future. In fact, the distinctive production of each of those jazz/film collaborations was dependent on numerous factors that were unique to each specific film, and the people involved in its creation. In other words, what made these films unique is also what makes (or should make) them inimitable. Rather, I suggest that these films offer a general model of film soundtrack production that challenges conventional production methods, experimenting with the possibilities of interactive collaboration between the visual and sonic aspects of cinema.

There certainly has been an increase in experimental (read: nontraditional) soundtracks within the last ten to fifteen years. Consider recent scores by Radiohead's Jonny Greenwood (*There Will Be Blood* [2007], *The Master*

[2012], *Phantom Thread* [2018]), Nine Inch Nails' Trent Reznor and Atticus Ross (*The Social Network* [2010], *The Girl with the Dragon Tattoo* [2011], *Gone Girl* [2014], and HBO's *Watchmen* [2019]), Portishead's Geoff Barrow (*Ex Machina* [2014], *Annihilation* [2018]), Mica Levi (*Under the Skin* [2013], *Jackie* [2016]), and avant-garde saxophonist Colin Stetson (*Outlaws and Angels* [2016], *Hereditary* [2018], *Color out of Space* [2019]). Each score is undoubtedly unique, pushing the boundaries of dissonance, atonality, texture, and timbre while often experimenting with the possibilities of electronic instruments and technology. For example, Greenwood's ominous, string-heavy score for Paul Thomas Anderson's *There Will Be Blood* dramatically utilizes dissonance, silence, sinister-sounding rhythmic pulsing, and harsh string articulations to convey oil tycoon Daniel Plainview's (played by Daniel Day-Lewis) sinisterness and ruthlessness. Reznor and Ross's Oscar-winning score for *The Social Network* undergirds Mark Zuckerberg's (played by Jesse Eisenberg) dark anxiety, obsessiveness, and social alienation alongside the Facebook revolution, reflected in an experimental soundtrack of industrial rock, alternative, ambient electronic music, and buzzing/scratching/squeaking noises which—as Drew Litowitz describes them—"carr[y] an agonizing sense of dread and restlessness."[7] Levi's debut film score for Jonathan Glazer's alien thriller *Under the Skin* conveys the dark horror of a predatory alien disguised as a human female (played by Scarlett Johansson), captured through harsh dissonances, distortions, and haunting, unfamiliar timbres (achieved through altering instrument tunings, speed distortion, and clashing microphones).[8]

It is perhaps fitting that the majority of these scores appear in three primary film genres: sci-fi, horror, and psychological thrillers. Films in these genres are designed to keep audiences on the edges of their seats, driven by constant tension, suspense, emotional anxiety, and anticipation. Such is the ideal medium for sonic experimentation, disrupting expectations and generating aural anxiety through lack of resolution, harsh dissonance, and unfamiliar instrumental sounds. The "alien-ness" of the soundtracks serves to reinforce the aspects of fear, anxiety, and horror in the films themselves. Accordingly, recent movies in these genres have become playgrounds for avant-garde musicians and composers; their propensity for experimentation and risk-taking making them particularly well suited for such projects.

That said, even "established" film composers have been pushing their compositional styles in new directions. Prominently, Hans Zimmer—a film music icon with over one hundred original score credits ranging from the sweepingly epic (*Gladiator* [2000], *The Last Samurai* [2003], *Pirates of the Caribbean: At World's End* [2007], *12 Years a Slave* [2013]) to the quirkily playful (*Madagascar* [2005], *Sherlock Holmes* [2009], *Rango* [2011])—has produced some of his most experimental work to date in his recent collaborations with director Christopher Nolan: *The Dark Knight* (2008), *Inception* (2010), *Interstellar* (2014), and *Dunkirk* (2017). For example, *Dunkirk*, a stressfully intense drama about the Allied troops' rescue on the eponymous French beach during World War II, features a powerfully tense ninety-minute score characterized by a continuous, seemingly unresolving rise in pitch (based on the illusory Shepard Tone audio technique[9]) and a relentless rhythmic propulsion sonically embodied in a synthesized pocket-watch "ticking" sound. This Oscar-nominated score was an intricate fusion between the visuals and the soundtrack, driven by the allied rhythm of the visual shots, the sound effects (e.g., gunfire, crashing waves, boat motors), and the score. Zimmer described this as his "most intimate work" with Nolan: "This was the closest collaboration that I ever had with a director where even though he would never ever play a note, he somehow played every note that was in that score."[10] It is worth noting that this collaborative relationship parallels the close-knit partnerships between the directors and composers considered in the previous chapters; due to Zimmer's "inner circle" status with Nolan, their work together is significantly more collaborative, "risky," and experimental than conventional film score productions.

There are likely multiple reasons for this proliferation of experimental film scoring. One is the simultaneous artistic and commercial demands of film production. For film composers to successfully set themselves apart within the industry (thereby gaining more commissions/work), they often must do something new, carving out new creative territory. Film music giants like John Williams, Howard Shore, James Horner, Hans Zimmer, and Danny Elfman have already cornered the soundtrack market with their unique brands of neoromantic film scores. These figures—along with more recent film composers Alexandre Desplat and Thomas Newman—have dominated the Academy Award nominations for Best Original Score for decades. Therefore, it is not surprising that newer composers on the scene have been experimenting with new sonic approaches to movie music.

Another reason is certainly the continued development of technology. As evidenced throughout the history of music culture, musical works and trends adapt to reflect contemporary technological capabilities. Throughout the twentieth century, developments in recording technology/formats (e.g., phonograph, electrical recording, magnetic tape, digital MP3s), amplification (e.g., microphones, loudspeakers), and digital workstations/instruments (e.g., computers, electronic synthesizers, audio editing programs) continually influenced the emergence and production of new musical styles and approaches.[11] The electric microphone was an essential catalyst in shifting popular-music singing styles from theatrical belting to the more intimate "crooning" style popularized by singers such as Gene Austin and Bing Crosby in the late 1920s and 1930s (as Allison McCracken addresses in her valuable work *Real Men Don't Sing: Crooning in American Culture*).[12] Beginning in the mid-twentieth century, the electric guitar played a significant aesthetic and cultural role in shaping popular music—particularly rock and roll—as deftly considered by Steve Waksman in his *Instruments of Desire: The Electric Guitar and the Shaping of Musical Experience*.[13] The art of digital sampling was foundational in the emergence and development of hip-hop and rap in late 1970s and the 1980s,[14] and has since become increasingly influential in pop and electronic genres as well.

Since the start of the twenty-first century, the proliferation of accessible electronic instruments such as keyboards and synthesizers and MIDI technology, as well as digital audio workstations that enable an immense diversity of music-editing capabilities (e.g., cutting, looping, sampling, auto-tuning, digital composition) has greatly influenced contemporary popular music trends. Technology-based genres such as hip-hop and electronic dance music (EDM) thrive, while the Top 40 pop hits reveal a healthy dose of auto-tune and digital editing/manipulation. Our contemporary fascination with (and dependence on) computers, digital technology, and electronic media is just as evident in our music as it is in our daily lives.

Therefore, it is not surprising that contemporary film composers draw inspiration from these technological developments. These diverse technologies afford a wealth of opportunities for artistic experimentation. Furthermore, they provide potential financial advantages. It is significantly less expensive to hire a composer who is able to produce a soundtrack electronically with limited personnel than it is to hire a full orchestra to record an entire score. Guy Michelmore—a prolific film composer who has scored for Marvel, Disney, Dreamworks, and many other companies—claims that a "reasonable average" to record a sixty-to-ninety- minute orchestral film score in Los Angeles or London is around $100,000 (ranging anywhere from $30,000 to over $1,000,000).[15] When the soundtrack is produced entirely by the composer using digital technology, filmmakers can potentially save thousands of dollars on their bottom line. This can be a very attractive option—particularly when a filmmaker believes that a synthesized score is more fitting than a live, orchestral sound for the film's overall aesthetic (e.g., in a sci-fi or thriller film).

Perhaps the most significant reason for the proliferation of experimental soundtracks is the augmented appreciation for interdisciplinary production and inter-arts collaboration in contemporary culture. Educational institutions are enthusiastically promoting liberal arts approaches, cross-departmental collaboration, and interdisciplinary study—a trend that began in higher education in the late 1970s and 1980s.[16] Universities and K–12 schools across the United States strategically tout their curricula as preparing their students with "twenty-first-century skills," ideally positioning them to successfully participate and innovate in an increasingly globalized and technological world. Accordingly, these institutions actively facilitate interdisciplinary, collaborative learning and communication, emphasizing engaged, integrative approaches to education that blur disciplinary boundaries and experiment with new structures and modalities. It is in this milieu that inter-arts collaborations have flourished. Among millennials and Gen Zers, developing visual memes, gifs, and videos has been an outlet for political and social commentary.[17] Visual, literary, and performing arts permeate health-care programs and institutions throughout the world.[18] Improvisation has even served as a framework for inculcating leadership and business management skills, emphasizing creativity, innovation, and flexible collaboration within organized structures.[19]

Because media is such a pervasive aspect of human society today (particularly in the aftermath of the COVID-19 pandemic), artists and musicians recognize the value of collaborating with film, television, video game, and advertising producers. Media production—filmmaking, for our purposes—has always been collaborative. Yet the examples examined in this book illustrate the potential of complicating these production hierarchies, positioning musical scores on more collaborative footing with the visual narratives. It is this type of mutual, creative collaboration and experimentation between diverse disciplines that is championed by proponents of the integrative arts and is, as I argue, the key to jazz's longevity in the modern era.

LARGER IMPLICATIONS FOR JAZZ

So far in this concluding chapter, I have been discussing how the case studies in this book illustrate, *in general*, the possibilities of collaborative, experimental approaches to filmmaking shaped by unconventional soundtrack production. But what are the implications of these examples for jazz, specifically?

In one regard, these case studies reveal what possible integrative jazz/film collaborations might look like. Certainly, the examples are diverse. However, the consistent essential component in all these projects is the presence of a self-sufficient director/producer who *values jazz* (and/or its perceived meanings) *as an essential part of the film itself,* facilitating opportunities for the music and the film to collaboratively shape each other. In several of the explored cases—particularly *Birdman* and Woody Allen's films—the soundtracks have received just as much recognition as (if not more than) the films themselves. This parallels how some of the most significant jazz soundtracks to date—including Miles Davis's *Elevator to the Gallows,* Duke Ellington's *Anatomy of a Murder,* and Henry Mancini's *The Pink Panther*—have received significantly more historical attention than the films they underscored. This problematizes the assumption that films are the territory of the director alone. If we think "Ellington" more quickly than "Preminger" when someone mentions *Anatomy of a Murder,* or if we link "Antonio Sánchez" with "Alejandro Gonzalez Iñárritu" when discussing *Birdman,* we recognize the essentiality of the soundtrack in the film's production and reception. The larger implication is that when film directors give (jazz) musicians the creative space to develop soundtracks that they (the directors) conceive to be an essential component of the movie's meaning (rather than ancillary underscoring), the music's (and the musicians') significance in shaping the overall film is transformed. The film is not just a movie that has jazz music in it; it is a collaborative project representing an integrative jazz/film project.

Additionally, the examples examined in these chapters are illustrative of the ways that the jazz idiom may be continually explored and/or transformed through collaboration with film/media production. We have already seen the ways that jazz artists such as Antonio Sánchez, Mark Isham, Terence Blanchard, and Dick Hyman have adapted their compositional/performance approaches for film. Whether improvising to a verbalized script and hand signals (Sánchez), creating a score through a structured "jam session" featuring extensive improvisation (Isham), blending elements of classic film scores with blues and jazz idioms (Blanchard), or composing new "period" pieces for a mockumentary set in the 1920s (Hyman), these artists have integrated their experience as professional jazz musicians with new modalities and structures, thereby expanding the possibilities of what jazz is and what jazz does.

Improvising to film has also become more prominent within the last decade. Beyond Antonio Sánchez's continued live *Birdman*-accompanying performances, other jazz artists have engaged in improvising scores for silent and experimental film screenings. For example, guitarist Marc Ribot has performed live scores for such silent film productions as Charlie Chaplin's *The Kid* (1921), and Josef von Sternberg's *The Docks of New York* (1928), employing his idiosyncratic, genre-blending free improvisational style with "the language of film scoring," providing an emotional catalyst for connecting

154 CONCLUSION

contemporary audiences with the drama on-screen.[20] Certainly, the practice of improvising scores for silent film has been around for many years (effectively since film's inception). That said, jazz musicians' recent involvements in these live performances introduces new possibilities for the ways that these artists can uniquely integrate jazz expression with intimate knowledge of a film, generating new and ever-changing artistic productions that engage directly with audiences' expectations and emotions.

Finally, it is essential to acknowledge the inherent value of jazz's presence in film/media in influencing its continued recognition and reception. The Hollywood industry is a multibillion-dollar industry. Streaming services like Netflix, Hulu, and Disney+ have over 269 million subscribers, collectively.[21] Now especially—in the era of the COVID-19 virus, when people throughout the world are under governmental stay-at-home orders—film, television, and other forms of visual media dominate a significant portion of people's free time. As of April 2020, Nielsen reported a 50–60 percent increase in media streaming across markets, strongly correlated to shelter-in-place mandates.[22] According to a highly publicized poll of two thousand Americans conducted by streaming service Tubi (via OnePoll), consumers have been averaging eight hours of streaming per day.[23] In response to these results, a Tubi spokesperson claimed, "The findings of the survey illuminate just how much people are turning to streaming as a way to stay entertained and cope with social isolation."[24] Alexia Quadrani, head of U.S. Media Equity Research at J. P. Morgan, believes this trend will continue: "We think the ongoing spread of COVID-19 will lead to higher engagement and better subscriber growth for streaming services around the world near-term."[25]

It is true that the COVID era has hit two of America's largest media industries—film and music—hard. Movie theaters have closed their doors, film premieres (even much-anticipated blockbusters such as *James Bond: No Time to Die*, *Black Widow*, and Disney's live-action *Mulan*) have been postponed or cancelled, and production companies have been feeling extreme pressure to release films for at-home access. The global box office has experienced a sharp decline in admissions (approximately 25 percent), with predictions that the pandemic could cause over five billion dollars in collective losses.[26] Film festivals and awards ceremonies (e.g., Cannes, Venice, Telluride) have been cancelled, postponed, or downsized,[27] while in-process film and television projects have postponed production due to the manifold challenges of health concerns, travel restrictions, stay-at-home mandates, and financial loss.[28]

The music industry has not fared much better. Physical album sales have sharply declined (down by approximately 30 percent), correlated to the closing of retail stores.[29] Music venues from Carnegie Hall, to the Sydney Opera

House, to countless local clubs and theaters have shut down, crippling the livelihoods of artists, crews, venue staff, and promoters. Live performances—which make up approximately 50 percent of the total revenue of the global music industry—are at a record low due to health and safety concerns.[30] Concerts, tours, music events, and large-scale festivals such as Coachella, CMA Fest, Firefly Music Festival, Jazz Fest, and SXSW (among numerous others) have been cancelled,[31] dramatically decreasing (or effectively eliminating) ticket sale revenue, while also having a significant negative impact on artist/album promotion, merchandise sales, and sponsorship. The most significant casualties have been the musicians themselves, who generate approximately 75 percent of their income from their live performances.[32] Consider these comments by Caleb Caudle—an independent singer-songwriter who had planned a tour to promote the release of his new album, *Better Hurry Up*, when the pandemic hit:

> If my tour goes away, it's like a farmer losing their crops. Anyone who is not a huge superstar, the time right before you go on an album release tour—that's famine right there. That's when things are the tightest. All your funds are allocated to press, radio, and merch. We just placed a huge merch order for the album release tour. All that stuff is already paid for. You've got everything out there, and the tour is like the tide coming back in. We're completely reliant on merch sales and live shows. That's how this career is set up. Without that, we wouldn't be able to do this.[33]

These economic circumstances are particularly bleak for the jazz world. Jazz is a social, interactive idiom, predicated on the success of live performance (not to mention performance that has historically taken place in small, intimate venues with close proximity between performers and audience members). In a new century that increasingly promotes digital music streaming—a format in which jazz's ratings have been abysmally low[34]—jazz musicians strive to grow and maintain their audiences through the appeal of live experience. It is this draw of "authenticity"—of musicians improvising, collaborating, and creating new music in front of our eyes—that has attracted audiences to jazz since its inception. Live performance is how most jazz musicians maintain their relevance in this digital age; it is also how they pay the bills. Many of these musicians are freelance artists without steady paychecks, employer-paid health insurance, sick leave, and so forth, making them particularly vulnerable to the economic repercussions of COVID-related venue closures and event cancellations. Chicago jazz guitarist Andy

Brown reported: "I never quite saw something like this, where in one 48-to-72 hour period all the gigs ended. It's like somebody dropped an atom bomb on the town, and all the power went out."[35] As we now head into the fifth month of the pandemic (as of August 2020)—which has already claimed the lives of such renowned jazz leaders as Ellis Marsalis, Lee Konitz, Wallace Roney, and Bucky Pizzarelli[36]—jazz musicians across the globe fear for their livelihoods as well as their lives.

Yet necessity is the mother of invention, to borrow the adage. Jazz musicians (as well as musicians from all genres) have transitioned to offering livestream performances, collecting online payment or "virtual tips" through Venmo or PayPal. Vocalist Cécile McLorin Salvant has launched a "patreon"—a membership platform through her website that requires a five-dollar monthly subscription for fans to access her livestreamed performances.[37] Pianist/vocalist Norah Jones has offered free daily recitals from her living room through Facebook Live, promoting her latest albums and engaging directly with followers as they chat/respond to her performances. Numerous independent jazz artists who do not have Salvant's and Jones's established fan bases have also taken to Facebook Live, Instagram, and YouTube to share and promote their music directly with fans, hoping to benefit from exposure and donations/tips. Renowned jazz institutions have also converted to a livestream format, including Jazz at Lincoln Center, the Village Vanguard, SFJazz Center, Blues Alley, and the Monterey Jazz Festival. What is clear is that jazz artists need to be creative and willing to adapt in order to survive the current circumstances. As Shabaka Hutchings, British saxophonist and leader of Sons of Kemet stated in an interview with NPR: "There is no magic solution, but I think this is really the time to become creative about survival. Because that's what it is. . . . We have to make the best of the situation, or the situation will just be tragic. And all situations have the potential to be tragic, or the potential to be tragic and transformative."[38]

It is this notion of "transformation" that connects strongly with the premise of this book. In all honesty, when I submitted this book proposal to the University Press of Mississippi, the coronavirus pandemic had not happened yet, nor had the previously discussed repercussions for the film and music industries. Yet these developments have augmented the significance of my contention that the aforementioned jazz/film projects provide models for new—and necessary—integrative collaborations between media and music. The filmmakers and composers in the previous pages experimented with unprecedented ways of integrating jazz soundtracks with film, adapting their techniques and approaches accordingly. I believe that such adaptability and willingness to experiment with new platforms/media/creative modalities is going to be essential for jazz musicians (and musicians of all genres) in the coming years.

As Stefan Hall of the World Economic Forum has posited: "The [COVID] crisis is likely to accelerate underlying trends in the music industry, based on the importance of streaming, which has grown from 9% to 47% of total industry revenues in just six years."[39] With the growing dominance of digital media across the entertainment industry, musicians would do well to think about how they can utilize these modalities to share and promote their own work. An interesting recent example was rapper/producer Travis Scott's cross-industry collaboration with the popular video game platform Fortnite. In April 2020—in the midst of the pandemic—Scott held a concert as an avatar *within the game itself*, leading gamers through a fusillade of vibrant visual graphics (e.g., underwater and outer space scenes) while also premiering his new single "The Scotts," set to hit streaming services shortly after the performance.[40] Attendance was "astronomical" (pun intended); 12.3 million concurrent players participated in the concert,[41] and as of a few months later, over 83 million viewers had watched the performance on YouTube.[42] This is just one significant example of the ways that contemporary musical artists are adapting to the media technology and audience consumption patterns of the times. Independent artists across genres have engaged in other "do-it-yourself" methods of promoting and disseminating their work, including developing interactive app-albums, homemade music videos, and free download netlabels, while self-promoting through personal websites, YouTube, and social media outlets.[43]

Jazz's presence in popular culture is essential for its continued growth and longevity. Exposure is necessary for anything to flourish, be it arts, business, or ideas. Without question, media is one of the strongest and most pervasive formats for such exposure, particularly in an era when physical movement and interaction is significantly limited. Jazz's own historical successes tied to its inextricability from the technological revolutions of the early twentieth-century entertainment industry—including synchronized-sound film, radio broadcasting, printed media music criticism, liner notes, and visual iconography—justify this claim. Musicologists Haftor Medbøe and José Dias have thoughtfully argued that jazz's recent struggles for maintaining and growing its audience base are the result of its reticence in keeping up with technological transformations and methods of consumption in the digital age. They claim:

> The jazz community currently treads an uncomfortable path on one side of which is the face-to-face interaction of the gig and the

outmoded industry that created its canon, and on the other the seemingly limitless and ever mutating resources and opportunities provided by the Internet. Perhaps due in no small part to the genre's basis in, and reverence for, tradition, the jazz community continues to organize itself around conventional models of relationship with music and is often seen to struggle in effectively embracing new technologies of creation and transmission.[44]

As jazz's "traditional" listenership ages, musicians should consider ways of engaging modern-day audiences through the technologies, modalities, and cultural ideologies of the twenty-first century. As Medbøe and Dias suggest, "We stand on the edge of a new cultural landscape, with untested value chains, where innovative and creative strategies and reappraisals of identity are key to the health and sustainability of jazz in this new millennium."[45] It is my contention that the unique jazz-film collaborations examined in the previous chapters represent some of these "innovative and creative strategies" that can reposition jazz at the cutting edge of the media revolutions of our time. (It is worth noting that in addition to film, video games are a ripe medium for featuring jazz. Games such as *Cuphead*—whose 1930s jazz-inspired soundtrack topped Billboard's Jazz Album charts in 2019—illustrate the possibilities of jazz's intersections with this type of visual media. The fact that video game music is so often foregrounded [as it is integral to driving the player's interactive experience] also makes it a rich potential medium for interactive jazz-media collaboration. This is a certainly a topic worth pursuing in a future work.)

Jazz's collaborations with film (and other media) also provide the opportunities to challenge (or reinforce) long-held jazz mythologies and conventional stereotypes. They create spaces for new voices and ideas to flourish. The filmmakers in the preceding pages utilized jazz as a sonic signifier of authenticity, establishing and reinforcing the connections between jazz and lived experience, improvisation, Black creativity, nostalgia, freedom, and more. The soundtracks in these films did not just function "conventionally" but served as essential components in the films' fabrics, contributing integral ideas and meanings that shaped audiences' experiences and understanding of the movies' messages alongside the music. Furthermore, the composers/musicians utilized these projects as creative spaces to hone and develop their own crafts as collaborative jazz artists, as well as platforms to express their own ideologies and understandings of jazz's meanings and significance in contemporary culture.

While I do not expect there to be a sudden overtaking of jazz or jazz-influenced film soundtracks, these examples provide a model for new, collaborative ways of creating movie music that recognize the music as an integral ingredient that shapes the film itself, as well as its meanings. Jazz—a style rooted in improvisation and experimentation, which has throughout its lengthy history continually transformed in response to cultural, social, technological, artistic, and personal changes—is ideally suited to help transform film, and twenty-first-century collaborative media, as well.

NOTES

INTRODUCTION: JAZZ GOES TO THE MOVIES: FROM "AUTHENTICITY" TO INNER CIRCLE

1. Several scholarly works have extensively examined Ellington's score through a representational lens: Mervyn Cooke's "Anatomy of a Movie: Duke Ellington and 1950s Film Scoring," in *Thriving on a Riff: Jazz and Blues Influence in African American Literature and Film*, ed. Graham Lock and David Murray (New York: Oxford University Press, 2009); Krin Gabbard's *Jammin' at the Margins: Jazz and the American Cinema* (Chicago: University of Chicago Press, 1996); and Jans B. Wager's *Jazz and Cocktails: Rethinking Race and the Sound of Film Noir* (Austin: University of Texas Press, 2017).

2. Duke Ellington, *Music Is My Mistress* (New York: Da Capo Press, 1973), 194.

3. Quoted in Mark Tucker, ed., *The Duke Ellington Reader* (New York: Oxford University Press, 1993), 313.

4. Klaus Stratemann, *Duke Ellington, Day by Day and Film by Film* (Copenhagen: Jazz Media, 1992), 407.

5. Tom Piazza, "Black and Tan Fantasy," *New Republic*, July 1988, 39.

6. Quoted in Tucker, *Duke Ellington Reader*, 442.

7. Wynton Marsalis, "Music by Duke Ellington," liner notes for *Anatomy of a Murder Soundtrack* (Columbia, 1999).

8. Anthony Magro, *Contemporary Cat: Terence Blanchard with Special Guests* (Lanham, MD: Scarecrow, 2002), 141.

9. Gabbard, *Jammin' at the Margins*, 190.

10. Cooke, "Anatomy of a Movie."

11. Wager, *Jazz and Cocktails*, 96, 110.

12. Nicolas Pillai, *Jazz as Visual Language: Film, Television, and the Dissonant Image* (London: I. B. Tauris, 2017), 6.

13. Pillai, *Jazz as Visual Language*, 6.

14. Pillai, *Jazz as Visual Language*, 3.

15. Ellington's brief comments regarding *Anatomy* mention the commission in passing, focusing primarily on the lodgings and the food in his Sunset Boulevard penthouse provided by Preminger during production. Ellington says very little about the production process (other than that the majority of the writing happened within a very short time frame—approximately forty-eight hours) and only dismissively addresses his thoughts on the final product: "It turned out all right, too, because we won awards for it." Ellington, *Music Is My Mistress*, 193–94.

16. The compilation score maintains a stronghold in the industry, replacing commissioned compositions with licensed commercial recordings of popular music. Such "pop scoring" has

become economically valuable in the Hollywood industry in multiple ways—including its commercial accessibility for paying audiences, its functions as a source of extradiegetic allusion/association that supports the movie's dramatic narrative, and its potential for synergistic cross-promotion with record companies and the film industry alike. For more information on this topic, see Jeff Smith, *The Sounds of Commerce: Marketing Popular Film Music* (New York: Columbia University Press, 1998).

17. One obvious absence is Herbie Hancock. In a future study, I would like to examine his experiences working in film as well.

18. Mark Isham is the only one of these artists who is not still involved in a full-time jazz performance career (i.e., playing regular gigs, recording albums, etc.). While he still practices regularly and plays gigs on occasion, he dedicates the majority of his time to film composition.

19. Here, I draw inspiration from sociologist Howard Becker's theorization of "art worlds." See Howard Becker, *Art Worlds* (Berkeley: University of California Press, 1982).

20. Paul Lopes, *The Rise of a Jazz Art World* (New York: Cambridge University Press, 2002), 173.

21. See K. J. Donnelley, *Film Music: Critical Approaches* (Edinburgh: Edinburgh University Press, 2001), for a discussion of this phenomenon. As Donnelley contends, "Music scholarship has persisted in the prejudice that film music is somehow below the standard of absolute [or autonomous] music" (1).

22. For more examples, see composers' quotations in Robert Faulkner, *Music on Demand: Composers and Careers in the Hollywood Film Industry* (New Brunswick, NJ: Transaction Books, 1983), 89–100.

23. David Meeker, *Jazz in the Movies: A Guide to Jazz Musicians, 1917–1977* (New Rochelle, NY: Arlington House, 1977).

24. David Ake, Charles Hiroshi Garrett, and Daniel Goldmark, eds., *Jazz/Not Jazz: The Music and Its Boundaries* (Berkeley: University of California Press, 2012), 1.

25. Ake, et al. *Jazz/Not Jazz*; Larry Kart, *Jazz in Search of Itself* (New Haven: Yale University Press, 2004); and Eric Porter, *What Is This Thing Called Jazz? African American Musicians as Artists, Critics, and Activists* (Berkeley: University of California Press, 2002).

26. For key works that formatively influenced the emergence of New Jazz Studies criticism, see Scott DeVeaux, "Constructing the Jazz Tradition: Jazz Historiography," *Black American Literature Forum* 25, no. 3 (1991): 65–78; Krin Gabbard, "Introduction: The Canon and Its Consequences," in *Jazz among the Discourses*, ed. Krin Gabbard (Durham, NC: Duke University Press, 1995). Also see more recent texts Robert G. O'Meally, Brent Hayes Edwards, and Farah Jasmine Griffin, eds., *Uptown Conversation: The New Jazz Studies* (New York: Columbia University Press, 2004); and Sherrie Tucker, "Deconstructing the Jazz Tradition: The 'Subjectless Subject' of New Jazz Studies," in Ake et al., *Jazz/Not Jazz*.

27. Scott DeVeaux, "Core and Boundaries," *Jazz Research Journal* 2, no. 1 (2005): 15–30.

28. I use the pronoun "he" here, drawing attention to the history of gender discrepancy among film industry directors (and executives in general). Gendered discourse permeates theories of auteurism, directorial power, and creativity—contributing to film directing being a highly male-dominated field. My own case studies represent this phenomenon—in which all of the pertinent directors discussed are men. For two texts that address how specific female filmmakers negotiate their own careers and identities within the gendered structures

of filmmaking and the patriarchal model of auteurism, see Julia Dobson, *Negotiating the Auteur: Dominique Cabrera, Noémie Lvovksy, Laetitia Masson and Marion Vernoux* (New York: Manchester University Press, 2012); and Sandy Flitterman-Lewis, *To Desire Differently: Feminism and the French Cinema* (New York: Columbia University Press, 1996). For a broader look at gendered discourses of creativity and "genius," see Christine Battersby, *Gender and Genius: Toward a Feminist Aesthetics* (London: Women's Press, 1989).

29. See Andrew Sarris, "Notes on Auteur Theory in 1962," in *Film Theory and Criticism: Introductory Readings*, ed. Leo Braudy and Marshall Cohen (New York: Oxford University Press, 2009); also Sarris, *The American Cinema: Directors and Directions, 1929–1968* (New York: Da Capo Press, 1996).

30. Roland Barthes, "The Death of the Author," in *Image-Music-Text*, trans. Stephen Heath (London: Fontana Press, 1977).

31. Pauline Kael, "Raising Kane—Parts I and II," *New Yorker*, February 20 and 27, 1971.

32. Examples of literature that feature these criticisms include Aljean Harmetz, *Round Up the Usual Suspects: The Making of Casablanca: Bogart, Bergman, and World War II* (New York: Hyperion, 1992); and David Kipen, *The Schreiber Theory: A Radical Rewrite of American Film History* (Hoboken, NJ: Melville House, 2006)—among others.

33. Becker, *Art Worlds*, 16.

34. For an interesting ethnographic study of contemporary American independent film production, see Sherry B. Ortner, *Not Hollywood: Independent Film at the Twilight of the American Dream* (Durham, NC: Duke University Press, 2013).

35. Denis Dutton, "Authenticity in Art," in *The Oxford Handbook of Aesthetics*, ed. Jerrold Levinson, 258–74 (New York: Oxford University Press, 2003), 258.

36. Peter Kivy, *Authenticities: Philosophical Reflections on Musical Performance* (Ithaca: Cornell University Press, 1995), 3.

37. For valuable reading on these controversies, see Bernard Gendron, "Moldy Figs and Modernists: Jazz at War (1942–1946), *Discourse* 15, no. 3 (Spring 1993): 130–57; and DeVeaux, "Constructing the Jazz Tradition."

38. Frank A. Salamone, *The Culture of Jazz* (Lanham, MD: University Press of America, 2009), 29.

39. DeVeaux, "Constructing the Jazz Tradition," 529.

40. US Congress, House, A Concurrent Resolution Expressing the Sense of Congress Respecting the Designation of Jazz as a Rare and Valuable National American Treasure, H. R. Res 57, 100th Congress, introduced in House March 3, 1987, https://www.congress.gov/bill/100th-congress/house-concurrent-resolution/57.

41. Jason Robinson, "The Challenge of the Changing Same: The Jazz Avant-Garde of the 1960s, the Black Aesthetic, and the Black Arts Movement," *Critical Studies in Improvisation* September 2005, https://www.criticalimprov.com/index.php/csieci/article/download/17/47?inline=1.

42. Gene Lees, *Cats of Any Color: Jazz, Black and White* (New York: Oxford University Press, 1995); and Randall Sandke, *Where the Dark and the Light Folks Meet: Race and the Mythology, Politics, and Business of Jazz* (Lanham, MD: Scarecrow Press, 2010).

43. Dominic Lees, "Cinema and Authenticity: Anxieties in the Making of Historical Film, *Journal of Media Practice* 17, no. 2–3 (October 2016): 1–14.

44. See James Naremore, *Acting in the Cinema* (Berkeley: University of California Press, 1988), for a more in-depth historical overview and problematization of Method Acting.

45. Quoted in Gabbard, *Jammin'*, 282.

46. Recommended literature on this topic includes: John Caldwell, *Production Culture: Industrial Reflexivity and Critical Practice in Film and Media* (Durham, NC: Duke University Press, 2008); Vicki Mayer, Miranda J. Banks, and John Caldwell, eds., *Production Studies: Cultural Studies of Media Industries* (New York: Routledge, 2009); and Petr Szczerpanik and Patrick Vonderau, eds., *Behind the Screen: Inside European Production Cultures* (New York: Palgrave Macmillan, 2013).

47. Much scholarship on jazz and film has addressed these associations. For a few key examples, see Krin Gabbard's *Representing Jazz* (1995) and *Jammin' at the Margins* (1996); Andrew Clark, ed., *Riffs and Choruses: A New Jazz Anthology* (2001); David Butler's *Jazz Noir* (2002); and Peter Stanfield's *Body and Soul* (2005). Katharine Kalinak also addresses jazz's associations with transgressive "other-ness"—particularly in reference to gender and race—in *Settling the Score: Music and the Classical Hollywood Film* (Madison: University of Wisconsin Press, 1992). Race is critical to these discussions, as jazz's recognitions as a historically Black music have greatly shaped its reception and representations in American culture.

48. Simon Frith, *Performing Rites: Evaluating Popular Music* (Cambridge: Harvard University Press, 1996), 120. Another useful scholarly work on the semiotic dimensions of conventional (or "classical") Hollywood film scores is Anahid Kassabian's *Hearing Film: Tracking Identifications in Contemporary Hollywood Film Music* (New York: Routledge, 2001).

49. Bill Kirchner, interview with the author, October 29, 2015.

50. Marx delineates his theories of worker alienation in detail in *The Economic and Philosophic Manuscripts of 1844*, ed. Dirk J. Struik, trans. Martin Milligan (New York: International, 1964).

51. Robert Blauner, *Alienation and Freedom: The Factory Worker and His Industry* (Chicago: University of Chicago Press, 1964).

52. Faulkner, *Music on Demand*, 97.

53. David Hesmondhalgh and Sarah Baker, *Creative Labor: Media Work in Three Cultural Industries* (New York: Routledge, 2011).

54. Jason Toynbee, *Making Popular Music: Musicians, Creativity, and Institutions* (New York: Oxford University Press, 2000).

55. Toynbee, *Making Popular Music*, 46.

56. Matt Stahl, *Unfree Masters: Recording Artists and the Politics of Work* (Durham, NC: Duke University Press, 2013).

CHAPTER I: WHEN STRANGERS MEET: STRUCTURES, TENSIONS, AND NEGOTIATIONS IN JAZZ/FILM COLLABORATIONS

1. Becker, *Art Worlds*, xxiv.

2. "Mid-Year Report: U.S. 2019," *Nielsen Music*, https://www.nielsen.com/wp-content/uploads/sites/3/2019/06/nielsen-us-music-mid-year-report-2019.pdf.

3. David Hesmondhalgh, *The Cultural Industries*, 2nd ed. (London: Sage, 2007), 199.

4. For a thorough investigation of the balance of autonomy and alienated labor in pop recording artists' careers, see Stahl, *Unfree Masters.*

5. Directors Guild of America. http://www.dga.org/Contracts/Creative-Rights/Summary .aspx.

6. Fred Karlin and Rayburn Wright, *On the Track: A Guide to Contemporary Film Scoring* (New York: Routledge, 2004), 12.

7. Mark Lopeman, interview with the author, October 11, 2014.

8. Vince Giordano, interview with the author, September 29, 2014.

9. Stewart Lerman, interview with the author, November 21, 2014.

10. Robert Faulkner, *Hollywood Studio Musicians: Their Work and Careers in the Recording Industry* (Chicago: Aldine-Atherton, 1971), 44.

11. Mark Isham, interview with the author, December 15, 2014.

12. Bob Noble, "Interview with Phil Ek," Hit Quarters, May 25, 2009, http://www.hitquarters .com/index.php3?page=intrview/opar/intrview_Phil_Ek_Interview.html.

13. The "temp track"—short for temporary track—is existing music that is temporarily utilized in film production during the editing phase. It functions as a sonic "place holder" that approximates the mood that the director wants for a given scene. Temp tracks are often later replaced with an original score prior to the film's release.

14. Karlin and Wright, *On the Track*, 10–11.

15. Terence Blanchard, interview with the author, August 25, 2015.

16. Vince Giordano, interview with the author, September 29, 2014.

17. For more information, see Karlin and Wright, *On the Track*, 124–25, or The Auricle's website, http://www.auricle.com/.

18. While distributers and patrons play a role in the art world as well, I am considering solely those involved in the production process.

19. Faulkner, *Music on Demand*, 31.

20. Faulkner, *Music on Demand*, 66.

21. Faulkner, *Music on Demand*, 115.

22. Faulkner, *Music on Demand*, 117.

23. Faulkner, *Hollywood Studio Musicians*, 97.

24. UCLA College Social Sciences, "Hollywood Diversity Report 2019: Old Story, New Beginning," https://socialsciences.ucla.edu/wp-content/uploads/2019/02/UCLA-Hollywood -Diversity-Report-2019-2-21-2019.pdf.

25. Zack Sharf, "Ava DuVernay Fires Back at Men Who Aren't Happy She Hires Female 'Queen Sugar' Directors: 'Sue Me,'" *Indie Wire*, May 4, 2018, https://www.indiewire.com /2018/05/ava-duvernay-men-unhappy-women-queen-sugar-directors-1201960610/.

26. Reggie Ugwu, "The Hashtag That Changed the Oscars: An Oral History," *New York Times*, February 6, 2020, https://www.nytimes.com/2020/02/06/movies/oscarssowhite-history .html.

27. UCLA College Social Sciences, "Hollywood Diversity Report 2019."

28. Maureen McCollum, "Behind 'La La Land,' a Long Relationship between a Director and a Composer," NPR (February 18, 2017), https://www.npr.org/2017/02/18/515848371/ the-long-relationship-of-the-director-and-composer-from-la-la-land.

29. Faulkner, *Music on Demand*, 89.

NOTES 165

30. Paul Hirsch, "Processing Fads and Fashions: An Organization-Set Analysis of Cultural Industry Systems," *American Journal of Sociology* 77 (1972): 642.

31. Faulkner, *Hollywood Studio Musicians*, 88.

32. Mark Isham, interview with the author, December 15, 2014.

33. Herbert Gans, "Popular Culture in America: Social Problems in a Mass Society or Social Asset in Pluralistic Society?" in *Social Problems: A Modern Approach*, ed. Howard Becker (New York: Wiley, 1966).

34. Quoted in David Morgan, *Knowing the Score: Film Composers Talk about the Art, Craft, Blood, Sweat, and Tears of Writing Music for Cinema* (New York: Harper Entertainment, 2000), 140.

35. Eric Porter, *What Is This Thing Called Jazz? African American Musicians as Artists, Critics, and Activists* (Berkeley: University of California Press, 2002), 48.

36. Faulkner, *Music on Demand*, 37–38.

37. Gergely Hubai, *Torn Music: Rejected Film Scores, a Selected History* (Los Angeles: Silman-James Press, 2012).

38. See Karlin and Wright, *On the Track*, 51–52.

39. For details, see chapter 24, "Licensing Recordings for Motion Pictures," in M. William Krasilovksy and Sidney Shemel, *This Business of Music: The Definitive Guide to the Music Industry*, 10th ed. (New York: Billboard Books, 2007), 269–73.

40. Dick Hyman, interview with the author, March 10, 2015.

41. Karlin and Wright, *On the Track*, 59.

42. Karlin and Wright, *On the Track*, 59.

43. Karlin and Wright, *On the Track*, 60.

44. Vince Giordano, interview with the author, September 29. 2014.

45. Terence Blanchard, interview with the author, August 25, 2015.

46. Terence Blanchard, interview with the author, August 25, 2015.

47. Karlin and Wright, *On the Track*, 359.

48. Quoted in Morgan, *Knowing the Score*, 50.

49. Henry Mancini, "Did They Mention the Music? (1989)," in *The Hollywood Film Music Reader*, ed. Mervyn Cooke (New York: Oxford University Press, 2010), 207.

50. Mark Lopeman, interview with the author, October 11, 2014.

51. For more detailed information on work-for-hire, see Krasilovsky and Shemel, *This Business of Music*, 260.

52. Stahl, *Unfree Masters*, 21.

53. Vince Giordano, interview with the author, September 29, 2014.

54. Vince Giordano, interview with the author, March 26, 2016.

55. For more details, see Krasilovsky and Shemel, *This Business of Music*, 264–65.

56. Faulkner, *Music on Demand*, 96.

CHAPTER 2: "NOT A LOT OF PEOPLE WOULD GO FOR THAT": RISK AND EXPERIMENTATION IN THE IMPROVISED SOUNDTRACKS OF *BIRDMAN* AND *AFTERGLOW*

This chapter contains information previously published in my works "Risk, Creative Labor, and the Integrative Jazz-Film: Producing the Improvised Soundtracks of *Birdman* and *Afterglow*,"

Jazz and Culture 2 (2019): 27–58, and "Antonio Sanchez, *Birdman (or the Unexpected Virtue of Ignorance) Original Motion Picture Soundtrack,*" *Journal of the Society for American Music* 10, no. 2 (May 2016): 229–33.

1. Specifically, I am referring to synchronized-sound film scores that are predominantly created in an improvised format, not scores that feature improvised passages over primarily prewritten arrangements. Aside from the case studies considered in this article, the few examples of predominantly improvised scores within the last fifty years include Bill Kirchner and Marc Copeland's improvised score for Marlyn Mason's short film *The Right Regrets* (2013), Mattias Bärjed and Jonas Kullhammar's score for Swedish filmmakers Klas Ostergren and Mikael Marcimain's *Gentlemen* (2014), (arguably) Howard Shore and Ornette Coleman's score for David Cronenberg's *Naked Lunch* (1991), and several of guitarist Marc Ribot's silent film and experimental film soundtracks.

2. *Ascenseur pour l'échafaud,* dir. Louis Malle (1957; Irvington, NY: The Criterion Collection, 2006), DVD.

3. For comprehensive scholarly texts addressing the French New Wave film movement, see Richard Neupert, *A History of the French New Wave Cinema,* 2nd ed. (Madison: University of Wisconsin Press, 2007); and Michel Marie, *The French New Wave: An Artistic School,* trans. Richard Neupert (Oxford: Blackwell, 2003). Also see Peter Graham, ed., *The New Wave: Critical Landmarks* (New York: Doubleday, 1968), for a collection of seminal film criticism texts written by prominent New Wave filmmakers such as André Bazin, François Truffaut, Claude Chabrol, and Jean-Luc Godard.

4. Neupert, *A History*; Marie, *French New Wave*; and Graham, *New Wave*.

5. For an insightful study on how jazz improvisation in *The Baker Boys'* film soundtrack functions in relation to Jack's character development, see Adam Biggs, "Jazz as Individual Expression: An Analysis of the Fabulous Baker Boys Soundtrack," *Soundtrack* 6, no. 1–2 (2014): 21–32. Biggs theorizes, "As well as a portrayal of sibling rivalry, the film is a study of the working jazz musicians and the suppression and expression of individual identity. . . . Dave Grusin uses jazz standards and original thematic compositions that . . . provide improvisatory contexts for the main character's emerging individuality and his relationships with the other characters" (21).

6. Gabbard, *Jammin' at the Margins*, 135.

7. For two useful resources on risk and risk management in the film industry, see Mette Hjort, ed. *Film and Risk* (Detroit: Wayne State University Press, 2012); and John Sedgwick and Michael Pokorny, eds. *An Economic History of Film* (New York: Routledge, 2005).

8. Dick Hyman, interview with the author, March 10, 2015, Venice, Florida.

9. This term originally defined unbranded calves who strayed from the herd (named for Texas pioneer Samuel A. Maverick, known for leaving his cows unbranded) and has since been used to describe people who are considered to be unorthodox, original, individualist, nonconformist, and/or free-spirited (or, more pejoratively, loose cannons). Throughout the twentieth and twenty-first centuries, the term has designated a family of card sharks in the 1950s television series *Maverick* (and a 1994 film adaptation of the same name); a 1960s–'70s stylish, youth-oriented Ford vehicle; Tom Cruise's egotistical, hypermasculine Navy fighter pilot character in the film *Top Gun* (1986); an NBA basketball team; and Senator John McCain during his presidential bid in the late 2000s.

10. Becker, *Art Worlds*, 232.

11. Geoff Andrew, *Stranger than Paradise: Maverick Film-Makers in Recent American Cinema* (New York: Limelight, 1999), 6.

12. *Babel* (2006), *Birdman* (won in 2015), and *The Revenant* (2016) were all nominated for Best Picture, while *Amores Perros* (2000) and *Biutiful* (2010) were nominated for Best Foreign Language Film.

13. Lorraine Ali, "Alejandro G. Iñárritu on Directing His Own Career," *Los Angeles Times*, February 3, 2015, http://www.latimes.com/entertainment/movies/moviesnow/la-et-mn -alejandro-gonzalez-inarritu-retrospective-20150203-story.html.

14. As an illustration, Iñárritu's recent film *The Revenant* was ultimately granted a production budget of $135 million, which ballooned from its initial $60 million budget projection. New Regency production company covered a significant portion of the costs, which were supplemented with funds from RatPac, Alpha Pictures, and Empyre. For more information, see Mike Fleming Jr., "No. 19 *The Revenant*—2015 Most Valuable Movie Blockbuster Tournament," *Deadline Hollywood*, March 18, 2016, http://deadline.com/2016/03/the-revenant-profit-box -office-2015-1201721740/; and Kim Masters, "How Leonardo DiCaprio's *The Revenant* Shoot Became 'A Living Hell,'" *Hollywood Reporter*, July 22, 2015, http://www.hollywoodreporter .com/news/how-leonardo-dicaprios-revenant-shoot-810290.

15. Elvis Mitchell, "Alejandro González Iñárritu," *Interview*, October 8, 2014, https://www .interviewmagazine.com/film/alejandro-gonzalez-inarritu.

16. The *Birdman* soundtrack was deemed ineligible for an Academy Award nomination for Best Original Score, with the Academy arguing that the ratio of original music to precomposed music was not sufficient to be considered (requiring that a minimum of 60 percent of the total music of the film be original). The justification was further based on Rule 15 Section II-E of the Academy guidebook, which states, "Scores diluted by the use of tracked themes or other preexisting music, diminished in impact by the predominant use of songs or assembled from the music of more than one composer shall not be eligible." Purposefully vague, this rule has been applied arbitrarily throughout the years. *Birdman's* dismissal is ripe for consideration through the lens of the Academy's musical conservatism and risk-reluctance. Perhaps Academy members were unfavorable toward a percussion score, rather than a score driven by melody. Perhaps the avant-garde, improvised quality of the score did not meet with Academy favor. We will never know for sure, but the snub is worth considering—particularly given the fact that Iñárritu submitted an appeal to the Academy for consideration and was rejected again. Regardless, Sánchez's soundtrack has still received much critical acclaim, including a nomination from the Golden Globes and the Grammy Award for Best Score Soundtrack for Visual Media. Pete Hammond, "*Birdman* Score Drummed Out of Oscars as Academy Rejects Filmmakers' Appeal," *Deadline Hollywood*, December 22, 2014, http://deadline.com/2014/12/birdman-out-oscars-academy-rejects-appeal-1201332029/.

17. The term "Chilango" is slang for a resident of Mexico City. Iñárritu's and Sánchez's racial and cultural affiliation is worth considering in more detail, particularly with regard to collaboration and opportunity within the highly Euro-dominated film industry.

18. Alejandro González Iñárritu, liner notes for *Birdman: or (The Unexpected Virtue of Ignorance): Original Motion Picture Soundtrack*, Milan M2–36689 (2014), CD.

19. Quoted in Lorraine Ali, "Antonio Sánchez's Soaring Beat Takes Flight in *Birdman*," *Los Angeles Times*, December 9, 2014, http://www.latimes.com/entertainment/envelope/la-et-mn-birdman-antonio-sanchez-20141209-story.html.

20. Michael Keaton's own roster of film roles contributed to Riggan's intertextuality. Keaton's acting career began with several miniseries and comedies (e.g., *Mr. Mom* [1983], *Beetlejuice* [1988]), followed by his eponymous role as *Batman* (1989), after which he acted in a series of "tough guy" roles (e.g., *One Good Cop* [1991], *Jackie Brown* [1997]), and finally to a mix of comedies, children's movies, and action thrillers. He was therefore an ideal figure to portray an intense, anxious actor struggling to move beyond his commercial background and establish a new reputation as an artist.

21. Quoted in Ali, "Antonio Sánchez's Soaring Beat Takes Flight."narrative and visual structures,viations. film or should it be filmmaker' use of a term but deleted them thereafter to adhere toánchez's Soaring Beat."

22. There are cases where film composers work closely with filmmakers from the inception of the project—including John Williams with Stephen Spielberg, Terence Blanchard with Spike Lee, and Ennio Morricone with Sergio Leone. In some of these cases, the music is prepared for scenes prior to filming. However, such circumstances remain rare and are generally in cases where the director and composer have an ongoing and successful working relationship. See Garrett Tiedemann, "Which Comes First, the Movie or the Music?" Classical MPR, April 5, 2015, https://www.classicalmpr.org/story/2014/11/05/film-score-picture.

23. See Faulkner, *Music on Demand*, and Fred Karlin and Rayburn Wright, *On the Track*, for excellent resources on conventional film-music production methods and expectations.

24. Iñárritu, liner notes, *Birdman*.

25. "Emmanuel Lubezki ASC, AMC on *Birdman*," *ARRI News*, accessed October 2017, http://www.arri.com/news/news/emmanuel-lubezki-asc-amc-on-birdman/.

26. Lesley Mahoney, "Antonio Sánchez '97: The Making of the *Birdman* Score," Berklee, November 5, 2014, https://www.berklee.edu/news/antonio-sanchez-97-making-birdman-score.

27. Quoted in Janowitz, "Drumming Out."

28. Ivan Radford, "*Birdman*, *Whiplash*, and the Sound of Drums," Den of Geek, February 23, 2015, http://www.denofgeek.com/us/movies/whiplash/243978/birdman-whiplash-and-the-sound-of-drums.

29. Janowitz, "Drumming Out."

30. Kristopher Tapley, "Oscar-winning Cinematographer Emmanuel Lubezki Details the 'Dance' of Filming Birdman," HitFix, December 20, 2014, http://uproxx.com/hitfix/oscar-winning-cinematographer-emmanuel-lubezki-details-the-dance-of-filming-birdman/.

31. Emmanuel Lubezki was the award-winning cinematographer responsible for executing this innovative filming approach. He has received three Academy Awards for Best Cinematography within the last five years, for *Gravity* (2013), *Birdman* (2014), and *The Revenant* (2015).

32. This performance is identified in both the film credits and film soundtrack as "Dirty Walk." It appears in *Birdman: Or (The Unexpected Virtue of Ignorance)*, directed by, Alejandro González Iñárritu (2014; Beverly Hills, CA: 20th Century Fox Home Entertainment, 2015), DVD.

33. Matt Collar, "Birdman (Original Motion Picture Soundtrack)," *AllMusic*, October 14, 2014, http://www.allmusic.com/album/birdman-original-motion-picture-soundtrack-mw0002796520.

34. Jonathan Godsall, "Birdman, Musical Materiality, and Embodied Cognition," paper presented for the British Audio-Visual Research Network Virtual Colloquium, May 13, 2021. Referenced works include Arnie Cox, "The Mimetic Hypothesis and Embodied Musical Meaning," *Musicae Scientiae* 5, no. 2 (2001): 195–212; and Miguel Mera, "Materializing Film Music," in *Cambridge Companion to Film Music*, ed. Mervyn Cooke and Fiona Ford, 157–72 (Cambridge: Cambridge University Press, 2016).

35. Emile Wennekes, "Out of Tune? Jazz, Film, and the Diegesis," in *Cinema Changes: Incorporations of Jazz in the Film Soundtrack*, ed. Emile Wennekes and Emilio Audissino (Turnhout, Belgium: Brepols, 2019): 11.

36. The filmmakers wanted to actually film Sánchez performing (through mimicry) his own improvisations for these scenes. However—due to a conflict with Sánchez's tour schedule—they hired a contemporary of Sánchez's, Nate Smith, to mimic the recordings on-screen.

37. For valuable ethnographic works on improvisation's centrality to jazz performance, see Ingrid Monson, *Saying Something: Jazz Improvisation and Interaction* (Chicago: University of Chicago Press, 1996); and Paul Berliner, *Thinking in Jazz, the Infinite Art of Improvisation* (Chicago: University of Chicago Press, 1994). See also Scott DeVeaux's sociological treatment of improvisation in bebop in *Bebop: A Social and Musical History* (Berkeley: University of California Press, 1997).

38. For studies on jazz's semiotic significations in film, see Krin Gabbard, *Jammin' at the Margins: Jazz and the American Cinema* (Chicago: University of Chicago Press, 1996); Krin Gabbard, *Black Magic: White Hollywood and African American Culture* (New Brunswick, NJ: Rutgers University Press, 2004); and Peter Stanfield, *Body and Soul: Jazz and Blues in American Film, 1927–63* (Urbana: University of Illinois Press, 2005). For considerations of jazz's semiotic dimensions in advertising, see Mark Laver, *Jazz Sells: Music, Marketing, and Meaning* (New York: Routledge, 2015).

39. Simon Frith, *Performing Rites: Evaluating Popular Music* (Cambridge: Harvard University Press, 1996), 120. Another useful scholarly work on the semiotic dimensions of conventional (or "classical") Hollywood film scores is Anahid Kassabian's *Hearing Film: Tracking Identifications in Contemporary Hollywood Film Music* (New York: Routledge, 2001).

40. David Butler, *Jazz Noir: Listening to Music from "Phantom Lady" to "The Last Seduction"* (Westport, CT: Praeger, 2002). Prior to *Streetcar*, jazz had primarily appeared in film as source music—not underscore. As source music, it appeared in association with moments of sexual promiscuity, aggression, erotic desire, and so on. North's "jazzy" underscore draws on these previous semiotic associations to reflect Blanche DuBois's internal mental state.

41. Butler, *Jazz Noir*.

42. Butler, *Jazz Noir*.

43. For a useful consideration of this topic, see Johannes Brusila, "Jungle Drums Striking the World Beat: Africa as an Image Factor in Popular Music, in *Encounter Images in the Meetings between Africa and Europe* (Nordic Africa Institute, 2001), 146–61. For a more specific look at these associations in early twentieth-century cartoons, see Daniel Goldmark, *Tunes for 'Toons: Music and the Hollywood Cartoon* (Berkeley: University of California Press, 2005).

NOTES

44. Steve Pond, "How *Birdman* Composer Improvised the Year's Most Audacious Film Score," *The Wrap*, October 19, 2014, http://www.thewrap.com/how-birdman-composer-improvised-the-years-most-audacious-film-score/.

45. Julie Miller, "How Jazz Drummer Antonio Sanchez Improvised the Birdman Score," *Vanity Fair Hollywood*, November 7, 2014, https://www.vanityfair.com/hollywood/2014/11/birdman-score-antonio-sanchez.

46. Mickey-Mousing is a film technique referring to synchronized, mirrored, or parallel scoring—in which the music is synced to directly accompany or mimic actions on screen. It was commonly used in early Walt Disney films, including Mickey Mouse films, hence its name.

47. Shaun Brady, "Chops: Marc Ribot and Antonio Sanchez on the Art of Improvising to Film," *JazzTimes*, June 2018, https://jazztimes.com/columns/chops/marc-ribot-antonio-sanchez-film/.

48. "Ed Norton on 'Birdman,' Wes Anderson, and Why $40 Makes Him Proud," NPR, October 21, 2014, https://www.npr.org/2014/10/21/357637203/ed-norton-on-birdman-wes-anderson-and-why-40-makes-him-proud.

49. John Patterson, "Alan Rudolph: 'People Just Don't Surrender to My Movies, Ever,'" *Guardian*, April 30, 2018, https://www.theguardian.com/film/2018/apr/30/alan-rudolph-film-robert-altman-interview.

50. Quoted in "Halves of a Dream: Making *Trouble in Mind*," directed by Greg Carson, in *Trouble in Mind*, 25th Anniversary Special Edition, directed by Alan Rudolph (1985; Los Angeles: Shout! Factory, 2010), DVD.

51. Quoted in Margaret Barton-Fumo, "Interview: Alan Rudolph," *Film Comment* (blog), May 2, 2018, https://www.filmcomment.com/blog/interview-alan-rudolph/.

52. Quoted in "Halves of a Dream."

53. Quoted in "Halves of a Dream."

54. Quoted in "Halves of a Dream."

55. Quoted in Barton-Fumo, "Interview."

56. Barton-Fumo, "Interview."

57. "Halves of a Dream."

58. "Halves of a Dream."

59. Mark Isham, interview with the author, December 17, 2014, Los Angeles, California.

60. Isham, interview with the author, December 17, 2014.

61. Isham, interview with the author, December 17, 2014.

62. Isham, interview with the author, December 17, 2014.

63. Isham, interview with the author, December 17, 2014.

64. Isham, interview with the author, December 17, 2014.

65. Isham, interview with the author, December 17, 2014.

66. Isham, interview with the author, December 17, 2014.

67. Isham, interview with the author, December 17, 2014.

68. Isham, interview with the author, December 17, 2014.

69. Quoted in Barton-Fumo, "Interview."

70. Altman (1925–2006) was considered a distinctive maverick director himself, receiving significant critical acclaim for his unique and influential filmmaking style. He was nominated five times for the Academy Award for Best Director. Altman expressed a love for jazz, which

manifested in his 1996 film *Kansas City*. This film exhibited visual and soundtrack recordings of improvised jam sessions featuring a number of contemporary jazz artists (e.g., Joshua Redman, Cyrus Chestnut, Ron Carter, Geri Allen), who portrayed historic jazz figures such as Lester Young, Basie, and so forth in the film itself. The *Kansas City* soundtrack has since become an iconic jazz film soundtrack as well. For more consideration of Altman's relationship to music in his films, see Gayle Sherwood Magee, *Robert Altman's Soundtracks: Film, Music, and Sound from "M*A*S*H" to "A Prairie Home Companion"* (New York: Oxford University Press, 2014). Also see Krin Gabbard, "Robert Altman's Jazz History Lesson," in *Black Magic*, 235–50.

71. Isham, interview with the author, December 17, 2014.

72. Gary Giddins and John Faddis, "Special Features," in Malle, *Ascenseur pour l'échafaud*, disc 2.

73. Don Cheadle's *Miles Ahead* (2016) may be worth considering in this discussion of jazz-film production. The film prominently features prerecorded jazz improvisation (primarily Miles Davis recordings), but it also experiments with narrative form. Don Cheadle, who produced, directed, and acted in the film, intentionally edited the scenes in a nonlinear manner, intending to make them visually "spontaneous" and "improvisational." Cheadle's reasoning for this production method was that Davis's life and art was "so mercurial and spontaneous and not dedicated to any sort of form that he had done before . . . [so] I thought it would really be totally anathema to him to do something that felt standard, so to speak." Quoted in Kervyn Cloete, "It's All about Improvisation in This First Trailer for Don Cheadle's *Miles Ahead*," *Critical Hit Entertainment*, February 5, 2016, https://www.criticalhit.net/entertainment/its-all-about-improvisation-in-this-first-trailer-for-don-cheadles-miles-ahead/.

CHAPTER 3: "HONEST, TRUE PORTRAYALS": TERENCE BLANCHARD, SPIKE LEE, AND THE RACIAL POLITICS OF JAZZ SCORING

1. Quoted in Henry Louis Gates Jr., "Just Whose 'Malcolm' Is It, Anyway? *New York Times* May 31, 1992, 16.

2. These nominations include an Emmy Award nomination for "Best Original Score for a TV Series" for miniseries *The Promised Land* (1995); Golden Globe, Sierra Award, and Central Ohio Film Critics Association (COFCA) nominations for Best Score for *The 25th Hour* (2002); and Black Reel nominations for Best Original Score for *She Hate Me* (2004) and *Inside Man* (2006).

3. Terence Blanchard, "Using Music to Underscore Three Words: I Can't Breathe," *Cuepoint*, June 25, 2015, https://medium.com/cuepoint/terence-blanchard-using-music-to-underscore-three-words-i-can-t-breathe-e956fca85731.

4. Michael Schelle, *The Score: Interviews with Film Composers* (Los Angeles: Silman-James Press 1999), 63.

5. His frustrations were particularly evident at the 2019 Academy Awards ceremony, where Lee, whose film *BlacKkKlansman* was nominated for Best Picture, attempted to storm out of the ceremony when the film *Green Book* was announced as the winner.

6. Key films include Melvin van Peebles's *Sweet Sweetback's Baadasssss Song* (1971), *Shaft* (1971), *Superfly* (1972), *Trouble Man* (1972), *Blacula* (1972), *Cleopatra Jones* (1973), and *Hell Up in Harlem* (1973), to name a few.

7. David Sterritt, *Spike Lee's America* (Cambridge, UK: Polity, 2013), 88.

8. Quoted in S. Torriano Berry and Venise T. Berry, *The Historical Dictionary of African American Cinema* (Lanham, MD: Scarecrow Press, 2007), xxiv.

9. See Vladimir Lenin, "Directives on the Film Business," in *Collected Works* vol. 42 (New York: International, 1934), 388–89.

10. Delroy Lindo, "Delroy Lindo on Spike Lee" in *Spike Lee: Interviews*, ed. Cynthia Fuchs (Jackson: University Press of Mississippi, 2002), 165.

11. I would argue that such two-dimensional representation of black characters is not as pronounced in contemporary films and television programs. There have been many mainstream motion pictures within the last twenty years that have depicted complex, relatable black characters, including *Save the Last Dance*, *Red Tails*, *Twelve Years a Slave*, *Selma*, *Concussion*, and hit television series such as *The Walking Dead*, *How to Get Away with Murder*, and *American Crime*—among others.

12. Spike Lee with Ralph Wiley, *By Any Means Necessary: The Trials and Tribulations of the Making of Malcolm X* (New York: Hyperion, 1992), 15.

13. Dan Flory, "*Bamboozled*: Philosophy through Blackface," in *The Philosophy of Spike Lee*, ed. Mark Conard (Lexington: University Press of Kentucky, 2011), 178.

14. Janice Mosier Richolson, "He's Gotta Have It: An Interview with Spike Lee," in Fuchs, *Spike Lee*, 26.

15. Spike Lee and Kaleem Aftab, *That's My Story and I'm Sticking to It* (London: W. W. Norton, 2005), 377.

16. Lee and Aftab, *That's My Story*, 377.

17. See bell hooks, "Whose Pussy Is This: A Feminist Comment"; Michele Wallace, "Spike Lee and Black Women"; and Wahneema Lubiano, "But Compared to What? Reading Realism, Representation, and Essentialism in *School Daze*, *Do the Right Thing*, and the Spike Lee Discourse"—all found in Paula Massood, ed., *The Spike Lee Reader* (Philadelphia: Temple University Press, 2007).

18. The few exceptions are the college girl who asks if she could help, and Muslims he is shown with in Mecca—but they are granted no agency and are entirely one-dimensional.

19. Amiri Baraka, "Spike Lee at the Movies," in *Black American Cinema*, ed. Manthia Diawara, 3–25 (New York: Routledge, 1993), 146.

20. Brandon Judell, "An Interview with Spike Lee, Director of *4 Little Girls*," in Fuchs, *Spike Lee*, 140.

21. Fuchs, *Spike Lee*, viii.

22. Steve Goldstein, "By Any Means Necessary: Spike Lee on Video's Viability," in Fuchs, *Spike Lee*, 186.

23. David Breskin, *Inner Views: Filmmakers in Conversation* (New York: Da Capo, 1997), 188.

24. Lee has claimed that he wants to counter notions that filmmaking is a magical, unattainable field—particularly for members of the African American community. He has stated that by "demystifying" the process—describing how one gets into film work, how films are actually made, how one can navigate and work with the industry executives, etc.—he is trying

to work against these mythologies and make the notion of filmmaking more accessible to those who might be interested in pursuing a career in film.

25. Paula Massood, ed., *The Spike Lee Reader* (Philadelphia: Temple University Press, 2007), xxiv.

26. Richolson, "He's Gotta Have It," in Fuchs, *Spike Lee*, 33.

27. Marlaine Glicksman, "Lee Way," in Fuchs, *Spike Lee*, 9.

28. Spike Lee with Lisa Jones, *Mo' Better Blues* (New York: Simon & Schuster, 1990), 161.

29. Mia Mask, ed. *Contemporary Black American Cinema: Race, Gender, and Sexuality at the Movies* (New York: Routledge, 2012), 11.

30. Mask, *Contemporary Black American Cinema*, 11.

31. This "signature shot" is a double-dolly technique that Lee has employed in several of his films, where he puts both the camera and the actor on a dolly and has the actor pushed toward the camera, while the camera is pushed away. This creates the cinematic illusion that the character is "floating" toward the camera/viewer. For a fascinating philosophical examination of Lee's usage of this technique, see Jerold J. Abrams, "Transcendence and Sublimity in Spike Lee's Signature Shot," in Conard, *Philosophy of Spike Lee*, 187–99.

32. Massood, *Spike Lee Reader*, xxii.

33. Henry Louis Gates, *The Signifying Monkey: A Theory of Afro-American Literary Criticism* (New York: Oxford University Press, 1989).

34. Glicksman, "Lee Way," in Fuchs, *Spike Lee*, 12.

35. Richolson, "He's Gotta Have It," in Fuchs, *Spike Lee*, 29.

36. Richolson, "He's Gotta Have It," in Fuchs, *Spike Lee*, 33.

37. Magro, *Contemporary Cat*, 105.

38. Lee, *Mo' Better Blues*, 155.

39. "Spike Lee on Gentrification, Jazz, and How He Got His Start in Film," NPR, February 15, 2019, https://www.npr.org/2019/02/15/694696224/spike-lee-on-gentrification-jazz-and-how-he-got-his-start-in-film.

40. Spike Lee, *Spike Lee's Gotta Have It: Inside Guerrilla Filmmaking* (New York: Simon & Schuster, 1997), 59.

41. Lee, *Mo' Better Blues*, 155.

42. African American jazz artists who have expressed such concerns include Wynton Marsalis, Branford Marsalis, Nicholas Payton, and Christian McBride. For a more comprehensive look at this discussion, see Magro, *Contemporary Cat*, 143–48.

43. Lee, *Spike Lee's Gotta Have It*, 21.

44. A tune that Blanchard composed, entitled "Swing Soweto," was used during the scene in which main character Bleek Gilliam is playing his trumpet solitarily on the Brooklyn Bridge. "Swing Soweto" was a piece that Blanchard had already composed in memory of the children who were killed in the Sharpeville Massacre in South Africa. Blanchard played the tune on the piano one day on set, and Lee liked it and asked him if they could use it in the film. The tune also later reemerged as a primary theme in Lee's soundtrack for *Jungle Fever* (1991).

45. Lee, *Mo' Better Blues*, 39.

46. Samuel G. Freedman, "Spike Lee and the 'Slavery' of the Blues," *New York Times*, July 29, 1990, 9.

47. Richolson, "He's Gotta Have It," in Fuchs, *Spike Lee*, 30.

48. These tropes of self-destruction are also evident in a number of recent musician biopics featuring both African American and non–African American figures—including *Ray* (2004), *Walk the Line* (2005), *La vie en rose* (2007), *Bessie* (2015), *Straight Outta Compton* (2015), *Born to Be Blue* (Robert Budreau's 2015 biopic of Chet Baker), and *Miles Ahead* (Don Cheadle's 2015 biopic of Miles Davis).

49. Freedman, *Spike Lee*, 9.

50. See Krin Gabbard, "Signifying the Phallus: Representations of the Jazz Trumpet," in *Jammin' at the Margins: Jazz and the American Cinema* (Chicago: University of Chicago Press, 1996), 138–59.

51. Lee, *Mo' Better Blues*, 39.

52. For insightful critical readings of Lee's treatment of Indigo and Clarke in this film, see Jason Vest, *Spike Lee: Finding the Story* (2014), 58–61.

53. Lee, *Mo' Better Blues*, 41.

54. Lee's rather silly names for the rhythm section members—"Bottom Hammer" (bass), "Left Hand Lacy" (piano), and "Rhythm Jones" (drums)—unfortunately make these characters seem more like caricatures than complex individuals. Their limited screen time (with the exception of Left Hand Lacy being continuously reprimanded for "breaking the rules" [e.g., being late, bringing his girlfriend into the dressing room, etc.]) does not allow for audiences to engage significantly with these characters.

55. Lee, *Mo' Better Blues*, 93.

56. Lee, *Mo' Better Blues*, 93.

57. These "parts" included both the primary tunes and all of the practice riffs and runs. Lee, *Mo' Better*, 158.

58. Lee, *Mo' Better Blues*, 187.

59. Lee, *Mo' Better Blues*, 158.

60. The personnel of this quartet included Bob Hirsch on bass, Jeff Watts on drums, Kenny Kirkland on piano, and Branford himself on tenor and soprano saxophone.

61. Initially, Lee wanted to use "A Love Supreme" as the title for the film, but—ostensibly due to the profanity exhibited in the screenplay—John's widow, Alice, would not grant him the rights to the title. She wanted the name of Coltrane's tune to stay associated with the purity and spirituality that its title was meant to evoke.

62. Lee, *Mo' Better Blues*, 162.

63. Jason Moore, "Melissa Harris-Perry Asks Terence Blanchard What Role Music Has in Social Activism; His Answer: Impeccable," *Atlanta Black Star*, June 3, 2015, http://atlantablackstar.com/2015/06/03/melissa-harris-perry-ask-terrence-roll-music-social-activism-answer-impeccable/.

64. Natalie Weiner, "Terence Blanchard on Ferguson vs. Waco, Spike Lee's 'Chiraq,' and His New Album 'Breathless,'" *Billboard*, May 27, 2015, http://www.billboard.com/articles/news/6576084/terence-blanchard-breathless-ferguson-chiraq-new-album.

65. Magro, *Contemporary Cat*, 114.

66. Schelle, *The Score*, 81.

67. Magro, *Contemporary Cat*, 141.

68. Schelle, *The Score*, 83.

69. It is worth noting that Blanchard's experimental opportunities were largely the product of the greater economic resources of the film industry; extensive budgets allow him to work with larger ensembles and a wider range of instrumentation than he would use for his usual jazz performances.

70. Terence Blanchard, interview with the author, August 25, 2015.

71. Schelle, *The Score*, 70.

72. Schelle, *The Score*, 72.

73. A particularly significant example of these extensive score manipulations occurred in Blanchard's work with director Matty Rich on *The Inkwell* (1994). Much of his score was cut and moved around to places it was not originally composed for. For a more detailed account of this experience, see Blanchard's interview in Schelle, *The Score*, 75–76.

74. Magro, *Contemporary Cat*, 108.

75. Terence Blanchard, interview with the author, August 25, 2015.

76. Vest, *Finding the Story*, 72.

77. Malcolm X and Alex Haley, *The Autobiography of Malcolm X* (New York: Grove Press, 1965). This text was a collaboration between Malcolm and journalist Alex Haley, and was one of the earliest comprehensive resources illustrating Malcolm's fascinating life. It was published soon after Malcolm's assassination.

78. Lee, *Spike Lee's Gotta Have It*, 253.

79. Lee, *By Any Means Necessary*, 11.

80. For more detail about these negotiations, see Anna Everett, "'Spike, Don't Mess Malcolm Up': Courting Controversy and Control in *Malcolm X*," in Massood, *Spike Lee Reader*, 73.

81. The film's production was not without complication. From the initial stages, Warner Bros. did not grant Lee the amount of money that he requested for the film ($33 million), and he very quickly ran over budget. Unwilling to compromise, the studio refused to grant him the extra funds that he wanted to complete the film, so he ended up using some of his own money, as well as requesting financial donations from wealthy members of the African American community (e.g., Michael Jordan, Oprah Winfrey, Janet Jackson, etc.). The film is also quite long—over three and a half hours—which caused problems with the studio, who wanted it to be closer to the traditional two-hour feature film length. Throughout production, he also received much concern from a variety of members of the African American community, believing he should represent Malcolm in certain ways, and urging him not to "mess Malcolm up."

82. Lee, *By Any Means Necessary*, xiv.

83. Lee, *By Any Means Necessary*, xiv.

84. Lee, *By Any Means Necessary*, 72.

85. Claudia Gorbman, *Unheard Melodies: Narrative Film Music* (Bloomington: Indiana University Press, 1987). Gorbman bases her "classic model" on film-scorer Max Steiner's compositional methods, "because of his voluminous presence and influence in the classical [film music] period" (73).

86. Gorbman, *Unheard Melodies*, 71.

87. Gorbman, *Unheard Melodies*, 73.

88. Gorbman, *Unheard Melodies*, 91.

89. The opening iteration of "Malcolm's Theme" is the only version that appears in C minor. All of the other versions throughout the film are performed in F minor (blues).

90. Beyond Blanchard's score, jazz plays a prominent role in the overall soundtrack. As mentioned previously, recordings of black jazz artists such as Louis Jordan, John Coltrane, and Ella Fitzgerald permeate the film. Jazz is also utilized diegetically in several club and party scenes. In one scene, Billie Holiday is represented performing in a local Harlem club, featuring Terence Blanchard himself in a cameo as her trumpet soloist.

91. Magro, *Contemporary Cat*, 168.

92. Magro, *Contemporary Cat*, 167.

93. Magro, *Contemporary Cat*, 157–58.

94. Geoffrey Himes, "'Malcolm X Suite': Blanchard Landmark," *Washington Post*, October 1, 1993, https://www.washingtonpost.com/archive/lifestyle/1993/10/01/malcolm -x-suite-blanchard-landmark/22a90c96-9936-46a8-ad1c-11a484e4ccfb/.

95. Scott Yanow, review, "Terence Blanchard: *The Malcolm X Jazz Suite*," AllMusic, http:// www.allmusic.com/album/the-malcolm-x-jazz-suite-mw0000618632.

96. The film received three Emmy Awards: Exceptional Merit in Nonfiction Filmmaking, Outstanding Directing for Nonfiction Programming, and Outstanding Picture Editing for Nonfiction Programming. It also received a 2006 Peabody Award from the University of Georgia, as well as the 2007 NAACP Image Award for Outstanding Television Movie, Mini-Series, or Dramatic Special.

97. "*When The Levees Broke: A Requiem in Four Acts*, Synopsis," HBO Documentaries, accessed December 5, 2013, http://www.hbo.com/documentaries/when-the-levees-broke-a -requiem-in-four-acts/synopsis.html.

98. A clip of this broadcast is shown in the documentary: Spike Lee, *When the Levees Broke: A Requiem in Four Acts*, DVD (Forty Acres and a Mule Filmworks, 2006).

99. Keith Spera, "Terence Blanchard Aimed for a Universal Feeling with 'A Tale of God's Will': Katrina and the Arts," *Times Picayune*, August 24, 2015, http://www.nola.com/katrina/ index.ssf/2015/08/terence_blanchard_katrina_a_ta.html.

100. Terence Blanchard, interview with the author, August 25, 2015.

101. Derrick Hodge (bass), Aaron Parks (piano), Kendrick Scott (drums), Brice Winston (saxophone), with Zak Harmon contributing on tabla.

102. The ensemble member contributions include Kendrick Scott's "Mantra," Derrick Hodge's "Over There," Brice Winston's "In Time of Need," and Aaron Parks's "Ashé."

103. Terence Blanchard, liner notes for *A Tale of God's Will: A Requiem for Katrina*, sound recording, CD (New York: Blue Note: 2007).

104. Blanchard, liner notes, *Tale of God's Will*.

105. David Evans, "The Development of the Blues," in *The Cambridge Companion to Blues and Gospel Music*, ed. Allan Moore (New York: Cambridge University Press, 2000), 23.

106. LeRoi Jones, *Blues People* (New York: Perennial, 2002), 28.

107. Keith Spera, *Groove, Interrupted: Loss, Renewal, and the Music of New Orleans* (New York: St. Martin's Press, 2011), 116–17.

108. Blanchard, liner notes, *Tale of God's Will*.

109. Bill Milkowski, "Tragic Symphony: Terence Blanchard Scores the Aftermath of Hurricane Katrina with Empathy and Grace," *JazzTimes* 37, no. 7 (September 2007): 52–56, 95.

110. Magro, *Contemporary Cat*, 143.

NOTES

CHAPTER 4: "A FILM DIRECTOR'S DREAM": DICK HYMAN PLAYS THE PERSONAL FOR WOODY ALLEN

1. Woody Allen, dir., *Manhattan* (Santa Barbara, CA: MGM, 1979), DVD.

2. Joe Klein, "Woody on the Town," *Gentlemen's Quarterly* 56, no. 2 (February 1986): 242–43, in *Woody Allen: Interviews*, ed. Robert E. Kapsis (Jackson: University Press of Mississippi, 2016), 83.

3. Kathleen Carroll, "Woody Allen Says Comedy Is No Laughing Matter, *New York Daily News* January 6, 1974, in *Woody Allen: Interviews*, ed. Kapsis, 23.

4. Douglas McGrath, "If You Knew Woody like I Knew Woody," *New York Magazine*, (October 17, 1994), 41–47, in *Woody Allen: Interviews*, ed. Robert E. Kapsis, 119.

5. Klein, "Woody on the Town," 89.

6. Klein, "Woody on the Town," 88.

7. Klein, "Woody on the Town," 86.

8. Jerome McCristal Culp Jr., "The Woody Allen Blues: Identity Politics, Race, and the Law," *Florida Law Review* 51 (1999): 511–28.

9. Charles Barfield, "Zoe Kravitz Says She'll Never Work with Woody Allen because 'He Doesn't Put People of Color in His Films,'" The Playlist, November 9, 2018, https://theplaylist .net/zoe-kravitz-woody-allen-johnny-depp-20181109/.

10. Woody Allen, *Apropos of Nothing* (New York: Arcade, 2020), 225.

11. Tatiana Siegel, "Only Featured Black Actress in a Woody Allen Film Defends His All-White Casts (Q&A), *Hollywood Reporter*, August 7, 2015, https://www.hollywoodreporter .com/news/hazelle-goodman-woody-allen-all-813921.

12. Allen has occasionally done on-location filming in Europe as well, including in London (*Match Point*, 2005), Barcelona (*Vicky Cristina Barcelona*, 2008), Paris (*Midnight in Paris*, 2011), and Rome (*To Rome with Love*, 2012).

13. Ken Kelley, "A Conversation with the Real Woody Allen," *Rolling Stone*, July 1976, 34–40, 85–89, in *Woody Allen: Interviews*, ed. Kapsis, 41–42.

14. Peter Biskind, "Reconstructing Woody," *Vanity Fair*, December 2005, 320–22, 326–27, 365, in *Woody Allen: Interviews*, ed. Kapsis, 163.

15. Vincent Canby, quoted in Peter Biskind, "Reconstructing Woody," *Vanity Fair*, December 2005, 320–22, 326–27, 365.

16. Robert Mundy and Stephen Mamber, "Woody Allen Interview," *Cinema* (Winter 1972/73): 14–21, in *Woody Allen: Interviews*, ed. Kapsis, 19.

17. Kapsis, *Woody Allen: Interviews*, xii.

18. Sam Fragoso, "At 79, Woody Allen Says There's Still Time to Do His Best Work," NPR interview, July 29, 2015.

19. Charles Champlin, "Allen Goes Back to the Woody of Yesteryears," *Philadelphia Inquirer*, February 15, 1981, in *Woody Allen: Interviews*, ed. Kapsis, 67.

20. A. O. Scott, "My Woody Allen Problem," *New York Times*, January 31, 2018, https:// www.nytimes.com/2018/01/31/movies/woody-allen.html.

21. The stigma surrounding Allen started to die down during the early 2000s. The courts had ruled no evidence for molestation, Allen and Previn got married (and remain married today), and no allegations of impropriety surfaced from any of the many women he had worked with over the years. Yet in 2013 Dylan—now an adult—publicly condemned Allen

for molesting her in an interview with *New York Times* columnist Nicholas Kristof, and has continued to speak out through open letters, op-eds, and television interviews. Her statements and allegations have garnered much support from advocates of the #MeToo and #TimesUp movements—initiatives that condemn sexual harassment and abuse, and grew in the aftermath of numerous sexual misconduct reports within the film industry, particularly against renowned film producer Harvey Weinstein.

22. Christopher Rosa, "These Are the Actors Who Now Regret Working with Woody Allen—and the Ones Who Don't," *Glamour*, September 11, 2020.

23. Carroll, "Woody Allen Says," 22.

24. John Lahr, "The Imperfectionist," *New Yorker*, December 8, 1996, 68–83, in *Woody Allen: Interviews*, ed. Kapsis, 132.

25. Robert F. Moss, "Creators on Creating: Woody Allen, *Saturday Review* 7 (November 1980): 40–44, in *Woody Allen: Interviews*, ed. Kapsis, 63.

26. Stig Björkman, *Woody Allen on Woody Allen* (New York: Grove Press, 1995), 37.

27. Allen, *Apropos*, 45.

28. Allen, *Apropos*, 45.

29. For a groundbreaking study that examines the dialectical complexity of white, working-class audiences' consumption and appropriation of Black culture through the medium of blackface minstrelsy, see Eric Lott, *Love and Theft: Blackface Minstrelsy and the American Working Class* (Oxford: Oxford University Press, 1993).

30. Allen, *Apropos*, 46.

31. Douglas McGrath, "Interview with Woody Allen," *Interview*, September 2008, 252–57, in *Woody Allen: Interviews*, ed. Kapsis, 201.

32. Allen, *Apropos*, 46.

33. John Fordham, "Woody Allen and His New Orleans Jazz Band—a Musician of 'Awful Dreadfulness?' Not at All," *The Guardian*, July 3, 2017, https://www.theguardian.com/music/2017/jul/03/woody-allen-his-new-orleans-jazz-band-review-royal-albert-hall-london.

34. Aljean Harmitz, "Annie Hall Wins 4 Academy Awards," *New York Times*, April 4, 1978, https://www.nytimes.com/1978/04/04/archives/annie-hall-wins-4-academy-awards-political-statement-under-a-50foot.html.

35. Lahr, "The Imperfectionist," in Kapsis, 150.

36. Fred Kaplan, "The Lowdown from Woody," *Boston Globe*, December 19, 1999,, N7, N11.

37. Michel Ciment and Yann Tobin, "Interview with Woody Allen: 'My Heroes Don't Come from Life, but from Their Mythology," *Positif*, no. 408 (February 1995): 26–32, in *Woody Allen: Interviews*, ed. Robert E. Kapsis, 129.

38. McGrath, "Interview with Woody Allen," 203.

39. Lahr, "The Imperfectionist," 133.

40. Allen, *Apropos*, 19–20.

41. Lahr, "The Imperfectionist," 150.

42. Allen, *Apropos*, 20.

43. Allen, *Apropos*, 20.

44. Scott Foundas, "Woody Allen Interview," *LA Weekly*, May 19, 2011, in *Woody Allen: Interviews*, ed. Kapsis, 233.

45. See: Steve Olenski, "What Was Old Is New Again—The Power of Nostalgia Marketing," *Forbes*, August 14, 2015, https://www.forbes.com/sites/steveolenski/2015/08/14/what-was-old-is-new-again-the-power-of-nostalgia-marketing/?sh=5a536f086881; Lauren Friedman, "Why Nostalgia Marketing Works So Well with Millennials, and How Your Brand Can Benefit," *Forbes*, August 2, 2016, https://www.forbes.com/sites/laurenfriedman/2016/08/02/why-nostalgia-marketing-works-so-well-with-millennials-and-how-your-brand-can-benefit/?sh=7e8603573636; and Jenna Gross, "Use Nostalgia to Improve Your Marketing Results," *Forbes*, May 24, 2018, https://www.forbes.com/sites/forbesagencycouncil/2018/05/24/use-nostalgia-to-improve-your-marketing-results/#1e63874a62b9.

46. Gross, "Use Nostalgia,".

47. Susan Stewart, *On Longing: Narratives of the Miniature, the Gigantic, the Souvenir, the Collection* (Durham, NC: Duke University Press, 1993).

48. Allen, *Apropos*, 169–70.

49. Ciment and Tobin, "Interview with Woody Allen," 129.

50. See interviews in Kapsis for details.

51. Allen, *Apropos*, 169–70.

52. Ciment and Tobin, "Interview with Woody Allen," 129.

53. William Zinsser, "Doin' the Chameleon," *The Atlantic*, October 1995, 98–108.

54. Dick Hyman, interview with the author, March 10, 2015.

55. Hyman had brief cameos in *Broadway Danny Rose* (1984) and *The Curse of the Jade Scorpion* (2001).

56. Quoted in John S. Wilson, "Allen Plans Year-Round Jazz Playing," *New York Times*, June 4, 1984, http://www.nytimes.com/1984/06/04/arts/allen-plans-year-round-jazz-playing.html?pagewanted=all.

57. Björkman, *Woody Allen on Woody Allen*, 142.

58. Taken from summary on back cover of *Zelig* (MGM, 1983), DVD (2001).

59. Thomas Forrest Kelly, *Early Music: A Very Short Introduction* (New York: Oxford University Press, 2011). Also see John Butt, *Playing with History: The Historical Approach to Musical Performance* (Cambridge: Cambridge University Press, 2002), for a comprehensive introduction to historically informed performance in music criticism.

60. See Chip Deffaa, *Traditionalists and Revivalists in Jazz* (Metuchen, NJ: Scarecrow Press, 1993), for an overview of the diverse practices and attitudes concerning "authenticity" espoused by a variety of jazz traditionalists and revivalists.

61. In distinguishing these terms, I draw on philosopher Denis Dutton's work in his article "Authenticity in Art." Dutton also distinguishes between two different types of authenticity in art in general, which he identifies as "nominal authenticity" and "expressive authenticity." The former encompasses accurate identification of the origins or provenance of a work of art (implying that the object is not fraudulent but "true"), or the perceivable fidelity of a performance to authorial intention or stylistic tradition. The second typology—expressive authenticity—pertains to self-expression, the notion that the work of art or performance possesses original authority through the genuineness and sincerity of its creator in performance. Nominal authenticity is empirical in nature, concerning fundamental, identifiable elements that inform claims that an object is authentic/inauthentic. Expressive authenticity, in

contrast, is more abstract, and can be accepted only if the artists' work is indeed accepted by the audience as being genuine, aligning with the artist's own personal expression and values.

62. Dutton, "Authenticity in Art."

63. When recording for film, he often experiments beforehand and writes down his ideas so that they can correspond with the timing necessities of the film. In live performance, he is much more likely to improvise in the moment.

64. John McDonough, "The Chameleon Days of Dick Hyman," *Wall Street Journal*, December 30, 2009, http://www.wsj.com/articles/SB10001424052748704107204574475193 134391938.

65. It is also worth noting that Allen's characters frequently, if subtly, make references to jazz figures and albums. While these moments are hardly pivotal to the films' narratives, they reinforce the notion that jazz exists as part of these characters' everyday lives.

CONCLUSION: MILES AHEAD: A NEW WAY OF MAKING MOVIE MUSIC?

1. Joe Bebco, "Director Daniel Pritzker Talks about His New Movie, 'Bolden,'" *Syncopated Times*, April 9, 2019, https://syncopatedtimes.com/director-daniel-pritzker-talks-about-bolden/.

2. It is worth noting that *Bolden*'s soundtrack features original music written, arranged, and performed by Wynton Marsalis.

3. For more information on Luhrmann's motivations for employing hip-hop instead of jazz, see "Baz Luhrmann—The Great Gatsby Interview," interview by Bonnie Laufer Krebs (Tribute Entertainment Media Group, 2013).

4. See "La La Land' Director Aimed to Make a Film Even Musical Skeptics Would Love," NPR, February 3, 2017, https://www.npr.org/2017/02/03/513235368/la-la-land-director-aimed-to -make-a-film-even-musical-skeptics-would-love; and A. A. Dowd, "Whiplash Maestro Damien Chazelle on Drumming, Directing, and J. K. Simmons," *AV Club*, October 15, 2014, https:// film.avclub.com/whiplash-maestro-damien-chazelle-on-drumming-directing-1798273033.

5. David Fear, "Don Cheadle: Why I Had to Make My Miles Davis Movie," *Rolling Stone*, March 14, 2016, https://www.rollingstone.com/music/music-news/don-cheadle-why-i-had- to-make-my-miles-davis-movie-53222/. In this interview, Cheadle revealed that including a white co-star was necessary to get the film funded: "To get this film financed, we needed a white co-star. And until Ewan came on, until we had cast the proper white co-star, there was no Miles Davis movie. . . . That's the reality."

6. Fear, "Don Cheadle."

7. Drew Litowitz, "Trent Reznor and Atticus Ross: The Social Network," Consequence of Sound.net, October 20, 2010, https://consequenceofsound.net/2010/10/album-review -trent-reznor-and-atticus-ross-the-social-network-7/.

8. Ryan Lattanzio, "Mica Levi on Why Composing 'Under the Skin' Was 'Really Mental,'" *Indie Wire*, November 10, 2014, https://www.indiewire.com/2014/11/mica-levi-on -why-composing-under-the-skin-was-really-mental-190232/.

9. Jason Guerrasio, "Christopher Nolan Explains the 'Audio Illusion' That Created the Unique Music in 'Dunkirk.'" *Business Insider*, July 24, 2017, https://www.businessinsider.com/ dunkirk-music-christopher-nolan-hans-zimmer-2017-7.

10. Melena Ryzick, "Ticking Watch. Boat Engine. Slowness. The Secrets of the 'Dunkirk' Score," *New York Times*, July 26, 2017, https://www.nytimes.com/2017/07/26/movies/the-secrets-of-the-dunkirk-score-christopher-nolan.html?auth=login-google.

11. Jonathan Kramer, "The Impact of Technology on the Musical Experience," College Music Society Symposium (1997), https://www.music.org/index.php?option=com_content&view=article&id=2675:the-impact-of-technology-on-the-musical-experience&catid=220&Itemid=3665.

12. Allison McCracken, *Real Men Don't Sing: Crooning in American Culture* (Durham, NC: Duke University Press, 2015).

13. *Steve Waksman, Instruments of Desire: The Electric Guitar and the Shaping of Musical Experience* (Cambridge: Harvard University Press, 1999).

14. See Justin A Williams, *Rhymin' and Stealin': Musical Borrowing in Hip-Hop* (Ann Arbor: University of Michigan Press, 2013).

15. Guy Michelmore, "A Producer's Guide to Working with Live Orchestra," Guy Michelmore.com, https://guymichelmore.com/2017/04/11/a-producers-guide-to-working-with-live-orchestra/#:~:text=How%20much%20does%20it%20does,and%20studio%20is%20around%20%24100%2C000.

16. See Frank John Messina and Mary Ann Stankiewicz, "A Critique of the Integrated Arts Experience: Its Relation to Learning Theory and Its Pedagogical Value (Abstract and Review), *Review of Research in Visual Arts Education* 6, no. 1 (Winter 1979): 45–50; Anna M. Kindler, "A Review of Rationales for Integrated Arts Programs," *Studies in Art Education* 29, no. 1 (Autumn 1987): 52–60; and William H. Newell and Julie Thompson Klein, "Interdisciplinary Studies into the 21st Century," *Journal of General Education*, 45, no. 2 (1996): 152–69.

17. Elia Rathore, "Living in the Age of Political Memes," *New York Times*, April 23, 2019, https://www.nytimes.com/2019/04/23/style/india-pakistan-political-memes.html.

18. For numerous current examples, see National Endowment for the Arts, "Examples of Arts in Healthcare Programs," https://www.arts.gov/accessibility/accessibility-resources/leadership-initiatives/arts-healthcare/arts-endowment-issues-0.

19. Nishith Anand, "From Performing Arts to Performing Organisations: A Typology for Improvisation in Creative Work Environments, *Samiksha* 3, no. 2 (July–December 2012): 30–39.

20. Shaun Brady, "Chops: Marc Ribot and Antonio Sanchez on the Art of Improvising to Film," *JazzTimes*, April 25, 2019, https://jazztimes.com/features/columns/marc-ribot-antonio-sanchez-film/.

21. As of spring 2020, Netflix had 182.8 million subscribers, Hulu had 32.1 million subscribers, and Disney+ had 54.5 million subscribers. See Gene Del Vecchio, "Disney Plus Has the Potential to Become a $30 Billion Giant in Only 5 Years," *Forbes*, May 11, 2020, https://www.forbes.com/sites/genedelvecchio/2020/05/11/disney-plus-has-the-potential-to-become-a-30-billion-giant-in-only-5-years/#11a962bd34a3; and Jessica Bursztynsky, "Disney Says It Now Has 54.5 million Disney+ Subscribers," CNBC, May 5, 2020), https://www.cnbc.com/2020/05/05/disney-reports-33point5-million-disney-plus-subscribers-at-end-of-q2.html.

22. Nielsen, "Streaming Consumption Rises in U.S. Markets with Early Stay-at-Home Orders during Covid-19," April 22, 2020, https://www.nielsen.com/us/en/insights/article/2020/

streaming-consumption-rises-in-u-s-markets-with-early-stay-at-home-orders-during
-covid-19/.

23. Allison Sadlier, "Americans Are Streaming 8 hours a Day during Coronavirus Lockdown," *New York Post*, April 14, 2020, https://nypost.com/2020/04/14/average-american
-streaming-content-8-hours-a-day-during-covid-19-according-to-new-research/.

24. Sadlier, "Streaming.".

25. J. P. Morgan, "Media Consumption in the Age of Covid-19," May 1, 2020, https://www
.jpmorgan.com/global/research/media-consumption.

26. J. P. Morgan, "Media Consumption."

27. Nate Jones, "How Each Major Film Festival Is Responding to the Coronavirus, *Vulture*, July 21, 2020, https://www.vulture.com/2020/07/how-film-festivals-are-handling-2020-amid
-the-coronavirus.html.

28. For a comprehensive listing, see Will Thorne and Kate Aurthur, "All the Shows and Movies Shut Down or Delayed Because of Coronavirus," *Variety*, March 12, 2020, https://
variety.com/2020/film/news/films-tv-delayed-coronavirus-canceled-1203532033/.

29. Stefan Hall, "This Is How Covid-19 Is Affecting the Music Industry," World Economic Forum, May 27, 2020, https://www.weforum.org/agenda/2020/05/this-is-how
-covid-19-is-affecting-the-music-industry/.

30. Hall, "This Is How Covid-19."

31. Angie Martoccio and Natalli Amato, "Coronavirus Cancellations: Festivals, Concerts, Tours, Films Affected by the Outbreak," *Rolling Stone*, March 10, 2020, https://www.rolling
stone.com/music/music-news/coronavirus-cancellations-music-fests-concerts-tours-964575/.

32. Hall, "This Is How Covid-19," 2020.

33. Joseph Hudak, "Coronavirus Could Decimate Touring Musicians' Livelihoods," *Rolling Stone*, March 11, 2020, https://www.rollingstone.com/music/music-country/
coronavirus-music-touring-cancellation-965380/.

34. See David Lowery, "Music Streaming Rates 2018: Per Stream Rates Drop and YouTube's Value Gap Is Very Real," All about Jazz, February 8, 2019, https://news.allaboutjazz.com/
music-streaming-rates-2018-per-stream-rates-drop-and-youtubes-value-gap-is-very-real;
and "Can Jazz Survive the Music Streaming Revolution?" *Jazzwise*, March 2, 2020, https://
www.jazzwise.com/features/article/can-jazz-survive-the-music-streaming-revolution.

35. Howard Reich, "With Little or No Safety Net, Jazz Musicians Watch Their Gigs Disappear as Coronavirus Spreads," *Chicago Tribune*, March 18, 2020, https://www.chicago
tribune.com/coronavirus/ct-ent-jazz-musicians-reich-coronavirus-0322-20200318-xme
g67zy5nbblpdj5flfd7oqfe-story.html.

36. Kyna Phillips and Deena Zaru, "Human Toll of Covid-19 Touches Every Corner of the Jazz World, ABC, June 12, 2020, https://abcnews.go.com/Entertainment/human
-toll-covid-19-touches-corner-jazz-world/story?id=71178081.

37. See website link here: https://www.patreon.com/CecileMcLorinSalvant.

38. Rachel Martin and Nate Chinen, "How the Coronavirus Fallout Could be Devastating to the Practice of Jazz," NPR, March 19, 2020, https://www.npr.org/2020/03/19/817342965/
how-the-coronavirus-fallout-could-be-devastating-to-the-practice-of-jazz.

39. Hall, "This Is How Covid-19," 2020.

40. William E. Ketchum III, "Fortnite's Travis Scott Concert Was Historic. But He's Not the Only Artist Getting Creative," Think, April 30, 2020, NBC, Newshttps://www.nbcnews.com/think/opinion/fortnite-s-travis-scott-concert-was-historic-he-s-not-ncna1195686.

41. Andrew Webster, "More Than 12 Million People Attended Travis Scott's Fortnite Concert," *The Verge*, April 23, 2020, https://www.theverge.com/2020/4/23/21233946/travis-scott-fortnite-concert-astronomical-record-breaking-player-count.

42. "Travis Scott and Fortnite Present: Astronomical," YouTube, April 26, 2020, https://www.youtube.com/watch?v=wYeFAlVC8qU.

43. Haftor Medbøe and José Dias, "Improvisation in the Digital Age: New Narratives in Jazz Promotion and Dissemination," *First Monday* 19, no. 10, October 6, 2014, https://firstmonday.org/ojs/index.php/fm/article/view/5553/4132.

44. Medbøe and Dias, "Improvisation in the Digital Age," 2014.

45. Medbøe and Dias, "Improvisation in the Digital Age," 2014.

BIBLIOGRAPHY

Abrams, Jerold J. "Transcendence and Sublimity in Spike Lee's Signature Shot." In *The Philosophy of Spike Lee*, edited by Mark Conard, 187–99. Lexington, KY: University Press of Kentucky, 2011.

Adorno, Theodor, and Hanns Eisler. *Composing for the Films*. Highlands, NJ: Athlone Press, 1994.

Ake, David, Charles Hiroshi Garrett, and Daniel Goldmark, eds. *Jazz/Not Jazz: The Music and Its Boundaries*. Berkeley: University of California Press, 2012.

Ali, Lorraine. "Antonio Sanchez's Soaring Beat Takes Flight in 'Birdman.'" *LA Times*, December 9, 2014. http://www.latimes.com/entertainment/envelope/la-et-mn-birdman-antonio-sanchez-20141209-story.html.

Allen, Woody. *Apropos of Nothing*. New York: Arcade, 2020.

Anand, Nishith. "From Performing Arts to Performing Organisations: A Typology for Improvisation in Creative Work Environments. *Samiksha* 3 no. 2 (July–December 2012): 30–39.

Andrew, Geoff. *Stranger than Paradise: Maverick Film-Makers in Recent American Cinema*. New York: Limelight, 1999.

Ashby, Arved, ed. *Popular Music and the New Auteur: Visionary Filmmakers after MTV*. New York: Oxford University Press, 2013.

Astruc, Alexandre. "The Birth of a New Avant-Garde: La Caméra-Stylo." In *The New Wave: Critical Landmarks*, edited by Peter Graham, 17–23. Garden City, NY: Doubleday, 1968.

Banks, Mark, Andy Lovatt, Justin O'Connor, and Carlo Raffo. "Risk and Trust in the Cultural Industries." *Geoforum* 31, no. 4 (2000): 453–64.

Baraka, Amiri. "Spike Lee at the Movies." In *Black American Cinema*, edited by Manthia Diawara, 3–25. New York: Routledge, 1993.

Barfield, Charles. "Zoe Kravitz Says She'll Never Work with Woody Allen because 'He Doesn't Put People of Color in His Films.'" The Playlist, November 9, 2018. https://theplaylist.net/zoe-kravitz-woody-allen-johnny-depp-20181109/.

Barrett, Margaret S., ed. *Collaborative Creative Thought and Practice in Music*. Burlington, VT: Ashgate, 2014.

Barthes, Roland. "The Death of the Author." In *Image-Music-Text*, translated by Stephen Heath London: Fontana Press, 1977.

Barton-Fumo, Margaret. "Interview: Alan Rudolph." *Film Comment* (blog), May 2, 2018. https://www.filmcomment.com/blog/interview-alan-rudolph/.

Battersby, Christine. *Gender and Genius: Toward a Feminist Aesthetics*. London: Women's Press, 1989.

Baumann, Shyon. "Intellectualization and Art World Development: Film in the United States." *American Sociological Review* (2001): 404–26.

BIBLIOGRAPHY

Baz Luhrmann (The Great Gatsby)—Interview. Bonnie Laufer Krebs, interviewer. Tribute Entertainment Media Group, 2013. https://www.google.com/url?q=https://www.tribute.ca/interviews/baz-luhrmann-the-great-gatsby/director/30553/&source=gmail&ust=1637194754631000&usg=AOvVaw3KycU9CbnBpGJlyeijKpub.

Bazin, André. "La politique des auteurs." In *The New Wave: Critical Landmarks*, edited by Peter Graham, 137–55 Garden City, NY: Doubleday, 1968.

Bebco, Joe. "Director Daniel Pritzker Talks about His New Movie, 'Bolden.'" *Syncopated Times*, April 9, 2019. https://syncopatedtimes.com/director-daniel-pritzker-talks-about-bolden/.

Becker, Howard S. "Art as Collective Action." *American Sociological Review* 39 (December 1974): 767–76.

Becker, Howard S. *Art Worlds.* 1982. Berkeley: University of California Press, 2008.

Benshoff, Harry M., and Sean Griffin. *America on Film: Representing Race, Class, Gender, and Sexuality at the Movies.* Malden, MA: Blackwell, 2004.

Berliner, Paul. *Thinking in Jazz: The Infinite Art of Improvisation.* Chicago: University of Chicago Press, 1994.

Berry, S. Torriano, and Venise T. Berry. *The Historical Dictionary of African American Cinema.* Lanham, MD: Scarecrow Press, 2007.

Biggs, Adam. "Jazz as Individual Expression: An Analysis of the *Fabulous Baker Boys* Soundtrack." *Soundtrack* 6, no. 1&2 (2014): 21–32.

Biskind, Peter. "Reconstructing Woody." *Vanity Fair*, December 2005, 320–22, 326–27, 365. In *Woody Allen: Interviews*, edited by Robert E. Kapsis, 161–75. Jackson: University Press of Mississippi, 2016.

Björkman, Stig. *Woody Allen on Woody Allen.* New York: Grove Press, 1995.

Blake, Richard. *Street Smart: The New York of Lumet, Allen, Scorsese and Lee.* Lexington: University Press of Kentucky, 2005.

Blanchard, Terence. "Using Music to Underscore Three Words: I Can't Breathe." *Cuepoint*, June 25, 2015. https://medium.com/cuepoint/terence-blanchard-using-music-to-underscore-three-words-i-can-t-breathe-e956fca85731.

Blauner, Robert. *Alienation and Freedom: The Factory Worker and His Industry.* Chicago: University of Chicago Press, 1964.

Blistein, John. "Great Gatsby Soundtrack Features Jay-Z, Andre 3000, Beyonce." *Rolling Stone.* April 4, 2013. http://www.rollingstone.com/music/news/great-gatsby-soundtrack-features-jay-z-andre-3000-beyonce-lana-del-rey-20130404.

Bourdieu, Pierre. *Distinction: A Social Critique of the Judgment of Taste.* Cambridge: Harvard University Press, 1984.

Bourdieu, Pierre. *The Field of Cultural Production: Essays on Art and Literature.* New York: Columbia University Press, 1993.

Bourdieu, Pierre. *The Logic of Practice.* Translated by Richard Nice. Cambridge, UK: Polity Press, 1990.

Bourdieu, Pierre. *Outline of a Theory of Practice.* Translated by Richard Nice. Cambridge, UK: Cambridge University Press, 1977.

Bourdieu, Pierre. *The Rules of Art: Genesis and Structure of the Literary Field.* Cambridge, UK: Polity Press, 1996.

Bowen, Jose A. "Finding the Music in Musicology: Performance History and Musical Works." In *Rethinking Music*, edited by Nicholas Cook and Mark Everist, 424–51. Oxford: Oxford University Press, 2001.

Brady, Shaun. "Chops: Marc Ribot and Antonio Sanchez on the Art of Improvising to Film." *JazzTimes*, June 2018. https://jazztimes.com/columns/chops/marc-ribot-antonio-sanchez film/.

Braudy, Leo, and Marshall Cohen, eds. *Film Theory and Criticism: Introductory Readings.* 7th ed. New York: Oxford University Press, 2009.

Breskin, David. *Inner Views: Filmmakers in Conversation.* New York: Da Capo Press, 1997.

Brunette, Peter, ed. *Martin Scorsese: Interviews.* Jackson: University Press of Mississippi, 1999.

Brusila, Johannes. "Jungle Drums Striking the World Beat: Africa as an Image Factor in Popular Music. In *Encounter Images in the Meetings between Africa and Europe*, 146–61. Nordic Africa Institute, 2001).

Bursztynsky, Jessica. "Disney Says It Now Has 54.5 Million Disney+ Subscribers." CNBC, May 5, 2020. https://www.cnbc.com/2020/05/05/disney-reports-33point5-million-disney-plus-subscribers-at-end-of-q2.html.

Butler, David. *Jazz Noir: Listening to Music from "Phantom Lady" to "The Last Seduction."* Westport, CT: Praeger, 2002.

Butt, John. *Playing with History: The Historical Approach to Musical Performance.* Cambridge: Cambridge University Press, 2002.

Caldwell, John. *Production Culture: Industrial Reflexivity and Critical Practice in Film and Media.* Durham, NC: Duke University Press, 2008.

"Can Jazz Survive the Music Streaming Revolution?" *Jazzwise*, March 2, 2020. https://www.jazzwise.com/features/article/can-jazz-survive-the-music-streaming-revolution.

Carlson, Gretchen. "Antonio Sanchez, *Birdman (or the Unexpected Virtue of Ignorance) Original Motion Picture Soundtrack.*" *Journal of the Society for American Music* 10, no. 2 (May 2016): 229–33.

Carlson, Gretchen. "Risk, Creative Labor, and the Integrative Jazz-Film: Producing the Improvised Soundtracks of *Birdman* and *Afterglow.*" *Jazz and Culture* 2 (2019): 27–58.

Carroll, Kathleen. "Woody Allen Says Comedy Is No Laughing Matter. *New York Daily News*, January 6, 1974. In *Woody Allen: Interviews*, edited by Robert E. Kapsis, 80–82. Jackson: University Press of Mississippi, 2016.

Chadwick-Shubat, Daniel. "Interview: Robert Budreau & *Born to Be Blue.*" GetReel, March 23, 2016). https://getreelmovies.com/interview-robert-budreau-born-to-be-blue.

Champlin, Charles. "Allen Goes Back to the Woody of Yesteryears." *Philadelphia Inquirer*, February 15, 1981. In *Woody Allen: Interviews*, edited by Robert E. Kapsis, 126–29. Jackson: University Press of Mississippi, 2016.

Chiu, David. "The Jazz Expert behind the *Boardwalk Empire* Soundtrack." *Brooklyn Based* (blog), November 20, 2013. http://brooklynbased.com/blog/2013/11/20/the-jazz-age -expert-behind- the-boardwalk-empire-soundtrack/.

Ciment, Michel, and Yann Tobin. "Interview with Woody Allen: 'My Heroes Don't Come from Life, but from Their Mythology.'" *Positif*, no. 408 (February 1995): 26–32. In *Woody Allen: Interviews*, edited by Robert E. Kapsis, 178–89. Jackson: University Press of Mississippi, 2016.

Clark, Andrew, ed. *Riffs and Choruses: A New Jazz Anthology.* New York: Continuum, 2001.

Cloete, Kervyn. "It's All about Improvisation in This First Trailer for Don Cheadle's *Miles Ahead.*" *Critical Hit Entertainment*, February 5, 2016. https://www.criticalhit.net/entertainment/its-all-about-improvisation-in-this-first-trailer-for-don-cheadles-miles-ahead/.

Collar, Matt. "*Birdman* (Original Motion Picture Soundtrack)." *AllMusic*, October 14, 2014. http://www.allmusic.com/album/birdman-original-motion-picture-soundtrack-mw0002796520.

Conard, Mark, ed. *The Philosophy of Spike Lee.* Lexington: University Press of Kentucky, 2011.

Cooke, Mervyn. "Anatomy of a Movie: Duke Ellington and 1950s Film Scoring. In *Thriving on a Riff: Jazz and Blues Influence in African American Literature and Film*, edited by Graham Lock and David Murray, 240–59. New York: Oxford University Press, 2009.

Cooke, Mervyn, ed. *The Hollywood Film Music Reader.* New York: Oxford University Press, 2010.

Corrigan, Timothy, Patricia White, and Meta Mazaj, eds. *Critical Visions in Film Theory: Classic and Contemporary Readings.* Boston: Bedford/St. Martin's, 2011.

Cox, Arnie. "The Mimetic Hypothesis and Embodied Musical Meaning." *Musicae Scientiae* 5, no. 2 (2001): 195–212

Crowdus, Gary, and Dan Georgakas. "Our Film Is Only a Starting Point: An Interview with Spike Lee." In *Spike Lee: Interviews*, edited by Cynthia Fuchs, 65–78. Jackson: University Press of Mississippi, 2002.

Culp, Jerome McCristal Jr. "The Woody Allen Blues: Identity Politics, Race, and the Law." *Florida Law Review* 51 (1999): 511–28.

Dan, Avi. "Will Marketers Revert to Nostalgia in the Coming Hard Times." *Forbes*, June 1, 2020. https://www.forbes.com/sites/avidan/2020/06/01/will-marketers-revert-to-nostalgia-in-the-coming-hard-times/#3c31586155e7.

Deffaa, Chip. *Traditionalists and Revivalists in Jazz.* Lanham, MD: Scarecrow Press, 1993.

Del Vecchio, Gene. "Disney Plus Has the Potential to Become a $30 Billion Giant in Only 5 Years." *Forbes*, May 11, 2020. https://www.forbes.com/sites/genedelvecchio/2020/05/11/disney-plus-has-the-potential-to-become-a-30-billion-giant-in-only-5-years/#11a962bd34a3.

DeVeaux, Scott. *The Birth of Bebop: A Social and Musical History.* Berkeley: University of California Press, 1997.

DeVeaux, Scott. "Constructing the Jazz Tradition: Jazz Historiography." *Black American Literature Forum* 25, no. 3 (1991): 65–78.

DeVeaux, Scott. "Core and Boundaries." *Jazz Research Journal* 2, no. 1 (2005): 15–30.

Dobson, Julia. *Negotiating the Auteur: Dominique Cabrera, Noémie Lvovksy, Laetitia Masson and Marion Vernoux.* New York: Manchester University Press, 2012.

Dohl, Frederick. "Creating Popular Music History: The Barbershop Harmony Revival in the United States around 1940." In *Popular History: Now and Then*, edited by Barbara Korte and Sylvia Paletschek, 169–83. New Brunswick, NJ: Transaction, 2012.

Donnelley, K. J. *Film Music: Critical Approaches.* Edinburgh: Edinburgh University Press, 2001.

Dowd, A. A. "Whiplas Maestro Damien Chazelle on Drumming, Directing, and J. K. Simmons." *AV Club.* October 15, 2014. https://film.avclub.com/whiplash-maestro-damien-chazelle-on-drumming-directing-1798273033.

Dreyfus, Laurence. "Early Music Defended against Its Devotees: A Theory of Historical Performance in the Twentieth Century." *Musical Quarterly* 69 (1983): 297–322.

Dutton, Denis. "Authenticity in Art." In *The Oxford Handbook of Aesthetics*, edited by Jerrold Levinson, 258–74. New York: Oxford University Press, 2003.

"Ed Norton on 'Birdman,' Wes Anderson, and Why $40 Makes Him Proud." NPR, October 21, 2014. https://www.npr.org/2014/10/21/357637203/ed-norton-on-birdman -wes-anderson-and-why-40-makes-him-proud.

Ellington, Duke. *Music Is My Mistress*. New York: Da Capo Press, 1973.

"Emmanuel Lubezki ASC, AMC on *Birdman*." ARRI News, October 2017. http://www.arri .com/news/news/emmanuel-lubezki-asc-amc-on-birdman/.

Evans, David. "The Development of the Blues." In *The Cambridge Companion to Blues and Gospel Music*, edited by Allan Moore, 20–43. New York: Cambridge University Press, 2000.

Everett, Anna. "'Spike, Don't Mess Malcolm Up': Courting Controversy and Control in *Malcolm X*." In *The Spike Lee Reader*, edited by Paula Massood, 91–114. Philadelphia: Temple University Press, 2007.

Faulkner, Robert. "Dilemmas in Commercial Work: Hollywood Film Composers and Their Clients." *Urban Life* 5, no. 1 (1976): 3–32.

Faulkner, Robert. *Hollywood Studio Musicians: Their Work and Careers in the Recording Industry*. Chicago: Aldine-Atherton, 1971.

Faulkner, Robert. *Music on Demand: Composers and Careers in the Hollywood Film Industry*. New Brunswick, NJ: Transaction Books, 1983.

Fear, David. "Don Cheadle: Why I Had to Make My Miles Davis Movie." *Rolling Stone*, March 14, 2016. https://www.rollingstone.com/music/music-news/don-cheadle-why -i-had-to-make-my-miles-davis-movie-53222/.

Finnegan, Ruth. *The Hidden Musicians: Music-Making in an English Town*. Cambridge: Cambridge University Press, 1989.

Fleming, Mike Jr. "No. 19 *The Revenant*—2015 Most Valuable Movie Blockbuster Tournament." *Deadline Hollywood*, March 18, 2016. http://deadline.com/2016/03/ the-revenant-profit-box-office-2015-1201721740/.

Flitterman-Lewis, Sandy. "Varda in Context, French Film Production in the Early Sixties— The New Wave." In *To Desire Differently: Feminism and the French Cinema*. New York: Columbia University Press, 1996.

Flory, Dan. "*Bamboozled*: Philosophy through Blackface." In *The Philosophy of Spike Lee*, edited by Mark Conard, 164–83. Lexington: University Press of Kentucky, 2011.

Fordham, John. "Woody Allen and His New Orleans Jazz Band—A Musician of 'Awful Dreadfulness?' Not at All." *Guardian*, July 3, 2017. https://www.theguardian.com/music/2017/ jul/03/woody-allen-his-new-orleans-jazz-band-review-royal-albert-hall-london.

Foundas, Scott. "Woody Allen Interview." *LA Weekly*, May 19, 2011. In *Woody Allen: Interviews*, edited by Robert E. Kapsis, 231–34. Jackson: University Press of Mississippi, 2016.

Fragoso, Sam. "At 79, Woody Allen Says There's Still Time to Do His Best Work." NPR, July 29, 2015.

Freedman, Samuel G. "Spike Lee and the 'Slavery' of the Blues." *New York* Times, July 29, 1990. http://www.nytimes.com/1990/07/29/movies/film-spike-lee-and-the-slavery-of - the-blues.html?pagewanted=all.

Friedman, Lauren. "Why Nostalgia Marketing Works So Well with Millennials, and How Your Brand Can Benefit." *Forbes*, August 2, 2016. https://www.forbes.com/sites/laurenfried man/2016/08/02/why-nostalgia-marketing-works-so-well-with-millennials-and-how -your-brand-can-benefit/?sh=7e8603573636.

Friedwald, Will. "Sound of an 'Empire': To Recreate '20s Music, HBO Series Went to an Authority." *Wall Street Journal*, October 16, 2010. http://www.wsj.com/articles/SB10001 424052748704361504575552893404047312.

Frith, Simon. *Performing Rites: Evaluating Popular Music*. Cambridge: Harvard University Press, 1996.

Fuchs, Cynthia, ed. *Spike Lee: Interviews*. Jackson: University Press of Mississippi, 2002.

Gabbard, Krin. *Black Magic: White Hollywood and African American Culture*. New Brunswick, NJ: Rutgers University Press, 2004.

Gabbard, Krin. "Introduction: The Canon and Its Consequences." In *Jazz among the Discourses*, edited by Krin Gabbard, 1–28. Durham, NC: Duke University Press, 1995.

Gabbard, Krin. *Jammin' at the Margins: Jazz and the American Cinema*. Chicago: University of Chicago Press, 1996.

Gabbard, Krin. "Race and Reappropriation: Spike Lee Meets Aaron Copland." *American Music* 18, no. 4 (Winter 2000): 370–90.

Gabbard, Krin. *Representing Jazz*. Durham, NC: Duke University Press, 1995.

Gabbard, Krin. "Signifying the Phallus: Representations of the Jazz Trumpet." In *Jammin' at the Margins: Jazz and the American Cinema*. Chicago: University of Chicago Press, 1996.

Gans, Herbert. "Popular Culture in America: Social Problems in a Mass Society or Social Asset in a Pluralist Society?" In *Social Problems: A Modern Approach*, edited by Howard Becker, 549–620. New York: Wiley, 1966.

Gates, Henry Louis Jr. "Just Whose 'Malcolm' Is It, Anyway? *New York Times*, May 31, 1992.

Gates, Henry Louis Jr. *The Signifying Monkey: A Theory of Afro-American Literary Criticism*. New York: Oxford University Press, 1989.

Gebhardt, Nicholas. "Do You Know What It Means to Miss New Orleans? Historical Metaphors and Mythical Realities in Spike Lee's *When the Levees Broke*." *Jazz Research Journal* 6, no. 2 (2012): 113–28.

Gendron, Bernard. "Moldy Figs and Modernists: Jazz at War (1942–1946)." *Discourse* 15, no. 3 (Spring 1993): 130–57.

Glicksman, Marlaine. "Lee Way." In *Spike Lee: Interviews*, edited by Cynthia Fuchs, 3–12. Jackson: University Press of Mississippi, 2002.

Godsall, Jonathan. "Birdman, Musical Materiality, and Embodied Cognition." Paper presented for the British Audio-Visual Research Network Virtual Colloquium, May 13, 2021.

Goehr, Lydia. *The Imaginary Museum of Musical Works: An Essay in the Philosophy of Music*. New York: Oxford University Press, 1992.

Goldmark, Daniel. *Tunes for 'Toons: Music and the Hollywood Cartoon*. Berkeley: University of California Press, 2005.

Goldstein, Steve. "By Any Means Necessary: Spike Lee on Video's Viability." In *Spike Lee: Interviews*, edited by Cynthia Fuchs, 184–86. Jackson: University Press of Mississippi, 2002.

Gopnik, Adam. "The Outside Game: How the Sociologist Howard Becker Studies the Conventions of the Unconventional." *New Yorker*, January 12, 2015. http://www.newyorker .com/magazine/2015/01/12/outside-game.

Gorbman, Claudia. *Unheard Melodies: Narrative Film Music.* Bloomington: Indiana University Press, 1987.

Grace, Helen. "Aesthetic Risk and Deficit Thinking: Some Profit and Loss Statements about Cinema and Thought." *LOLA* no. 2 (June 2012). http://www.lolajournal.com/2/aesthet ic_risk.html.

Graham, Peter, ed. *The New Wave: Critical Landmarks.* New York: Doubleday, 1968.

Gridley, Mark. *Jazz Styles: History and Analysis.* 5th ed. Englewood Cliffs, NJ: Prentice Hall, 1994.

Gross, Jenna. "Use Nostalgia to Improve Your Marketing Results." *Forbes,* May 24, 2018. https://www.forbes.com/sites/forbesagencycouncil/2018/05/24/use-nostalgia-to -improve-your-marketing-results/#1e63874a62b9.

Guerrasio, Jason. "Christopher Nolan Explains the 'Audio Illusion' That Created the Unique Music in 'Dunkirk.'" *Business Insider,* July 24, 2017. https://www.businessinsider.com/ dunkirk-music-christopher-nolan-hans-zimmer-2017-7.

Hall, Stefan. "This Is How Covid-19 Is Affecting the Music Industry." *World Economic Forum,* May 27, 2020. https://www.weforum.org/agenda/2020/05/this-is-how-covid -19-is-affecting-the-music-industry/.

Halves of a Dream: Making "Trouble in Mind." Directed by Greg Carson. In *Trouble in Mind,* 25th Anniversary Special Edition. Directed by Alan Rudolph. 1985. Los Angeles, CA: Shout! Factory, 2010.

Hammond, Pete. "*Birdman* Score Drummed out of Oscars as Academy Rejects Filmmakers' Appeal." *Deadline Hollywood,* December 22, 2014. http://deadline.com/2014/12/ birdman-out-oscars-academy-rejects-appeal-1201332029/.

Handel, Leo. *Hollywood Looks at Its Audience: A Report of Film Audience Research.* Urbana-Champaign: University of Illinois Press, 1950.

Harmitz, Aljean. "Annie Hall Wins 4 Academy Awards." *New York Times,* April 4, 1978. https:// www.nytimes.com/1978/04/04/archives/annie-hall-wins-4-academy-awards-political -statement-under-a-50foot.html.

Harmitz, Aljean. *Round Up the Usual Suspects: The Making of Casablanca: Bogart, Bergman, and World War II.* New York: Hyperion, 1992.

Harrison, Barbara Grizutti. "Spike Lee Hates Your Cracker Ass." *Esquire,* October 1992, 137.

Harrison, Max. "Ellington's Music for *Anatomy of a Murder.*" In *The Duke Ellington Reader,* edited by Mark Tucker, 313–15. New York: Oxford University Press, 1993.

Harvey, Adam. *The Soundtracks of Woody Allen: A Complete Guide to the Songs and Music in Every Film, 1969–2005.* Jefferson, NC: McFarland, 2007.

Haynes, Bruce. *The End of Early Music: A Period Performer's History of Music for the Twenty-First Century.* Oxford: Oxford University Press, 2007.

Hedling, Erik. "Music, Lust, and Modernity: Jazz in the Films of Ingmar Bergman." *Soundtrack* 4, no. 2 (October 2011): 89–99.

Heile, Björn, Peter Elson, and Jenny Doctor, eds. *Watching Jazz: Encounters with Jazz Performance on Screen.* New York: Oxford University Press, 2016.

Helmetag, Charles. "Recreating Edith Wharton's New York in Martin Scorsese's *The Age of Innocence.*" *Literature Film Quarterly* 26, no. 3 (1998): 162–65.

Hesmondhalgh, David. *The Cultural Industries.* 2nd ed. Los Angeles: Sage, 2007.

BIBLIOGRAPHY

Hesmondhalgh, David, and Sarah Baker. *Creative Labor: Media Work in Three Cultural Industries*. New York: Routledge, 2011.

Himes, Geoffrey. "'Malcolm X Suite': Blanchard Landmark." *Washington Post*, October 1, 1993. https://www.washingtonpost.com/archive/lifestyle/1993/10/01/malcolm-x-suite -blanchard-landmark/22a90c96-9936-46a8-ad1c-11a484e4ccfb/.

Hirsch, Paul. "Processing Fads and Fashions: An Organization-Set Analysis of Cultural Industry Systems." *American Journal of Sociology* 77 (1972): 639–59.

Hjort, Mette, ed. *Film and Risk*. Detroit: Wayne State University Press, 2012.

Hoad, Phil. "Hollywood and the New Abnormal: Why the Industry Is Scared of Risk." *Guardian*, October 31, 2013. http://www.theguardian.com/film/2013/oct/31/hollywood -new-abnormal-lynda-obst-scared-risk.

hooks, bell. *Outlaw Culture: Resisting Representations*. New York: Routledge, 1994.

hooks, bell. "Whose Pussy Is This: A Feminist Comment." In *The Spike Lee Reader*, edited by Paula Massood, 1-9. Philadelphia: Temple University Press, 2007.

Hubai, Gergely. *Torn Music: Rejected Film Scores, a Selected History*. Los Angeles: Silman-James Press, 2012.

Hudak, Joseph. "Coronavirus Could Decimate Touring Musicians' Livelihoods." *Rolling Stone*, March 11, 2020. https://www.rollingstone.com/music/music-country/coronavirus -music-touring-cancellation-965380/.

Jones, LeRoi. *Blues People: Negro Music in White America*. New York: Perennial, 2002.

Jones, Nate. "How Each Major Film Festival Is Responding to the Coronavirus." *Vulture*, July 21, 2020. https://www.vulture.com/2020/07/how-film-festivals-are-handling-2020-amid -the-coronavirus.html.

J. P. Morgan. "Media Consumption in the Age of Covid-19." May 1, 2020. https://www.jp morgan.com/global/research/media-consumption.

Judell, Brandon. "An Interview with Spike Lee, Director of *4 Little Girls*." In *Spike Lee: Interviews*, edited by Cynthia Fuchs, 139–43. Jackson: University Press of Mississippi, 2002

Kael, Pauline. "Circles and Squares." *Film Quarterly* 16, no. 3 (Spring 1963): 12–26.

Kael, Pauline. "Raising Kane—Parts I and II." *New Yorker*, February 20 and 27, 1971.

Kalinak, Katharine. *Settling the Score: Music and the Classical Hollywood Film*. Madison: University of Wisconsin Press, 1992.

Kaplan, Fred. "The Lowdown from Woody." *Boston Globe*, December 19, 1999, N7, N11.

Kapsis, Robert E., ed. *Woody Allen: Interviews*. Jackson: University Press of Mississippi, 2016.

Karlin, Fred, and Rayburn Wright. *On the Track: A Guide to Contemporary Film Scoring*. New York: Routledge, 2004.

Kart, Larry. *Jazz in Search of Itself*. New Haven: Yale University Press, 2004.

Kassabian, Anahid. *Hearing Film: Tracking Identifications in Contemporary Hollywood Film Music*. New York: Routledge, 2001.

Kelley, Ken. "A Conversation with the Real Woody Allen." *Rolling Stone*, July 1976, 34–40, 85–89. In *Woody Allen: Interviews*, edited by Robert E. Kapsis, 24–42. Jackson: University Press of Mississippi, 2016.

Kelly, Thomas Forrest. *Early Music: A Very Short Introduction*. New York: Oxford University Press, 2011.

Kennedy Center. "Arts Integration Resources." https://www.kennedycenter.org/education/resources-for-educators/classroom-resources/articles-and-how-tos/articles/collections/arts-integration-resources/what-is-arts-integration.

Kenyon, Nicholas, ed. *Authenticity and Early Music: A Symposium*. New York: Oxford University Press, 1988.

Ketchum, William E. III. "Fortnite's Travis Scott Concert Was Historic. But He's Not the Only Artist Getting Creative." Think, April 30, 2020. NBC. https://www.nbcnews.com/think/opinion/fortnite-s-travis-scott-concert-was-historic-he-s-not-ncna1195686.

Kindler, Anna M. "A Review of Rationales for Integrated Arts Programs." *Studies in Art Education* 29, no. 1 (Autumn 1987): 52–60.

Kipen, David. *The Schreiber Theory: A Radical Rewrite of American Film History*. Hoboken, NJ: Melville House, 2006.

Kivy, Peter. *Authenticities: Philosophical Reflections on Musical Performance*. Ithaca: Cornell University Press, 1995.

Klein, Joe. "Woody on the Town." *Gentlemen's Quarterly* 56, no. 2 (February 1986): 242–43. In *Woody Allen: Interviews*, edited by Robert E. Kapsis, 83–89. Jackson: University Press of Mississippi, 2016.

Kramer, Jonathan. "The Impact of Technology on the Musical Experience." College Music Society Symposium, 1997. https://www.music.org/index.php?option=com_content&view=article&id=2675:the-impact-of-technology-on-the-musical-experience&catid=220&Itemid=3665.

Krasilovsky, M. William, and Sidney Shemel. *This Business of Music: The Definitive Guide to the Music Industry*. 10th ed. New York: Billboard Books, 2007.

Kuijken, Barthold. *The Notation Is Not the Music: Reflections on Early Music Practice and Performance*. Bloomington: Indiana University Press, 2013.

"La La Land' Director Aimed to Make a Film Even Musical Skeptics Would Love." NPR, February 3, 2017. https://www.npr.org/2017/02/03/513235368/la-la-land-director-aimed-to-make-a-film-even-musical-skeptics-would-love.

Lack, Russell. *Twenty-Four Frames Under: A Buried History of Film Music*. London: Quartet Books, 1997.

Lahr, John. "The Imperfectionist." *New Yorker*, December 8, 1996, 68–83. In *Woody Allen: Interviews*, edited by Robert E. Kapsis, 131–51. Jackson: University Press of Mississippi, 2016.

Lang, Paul. *Musicology and Performance*. New Haven: Yale University Press, 1997.

Lattanzio, Ryan. "Mica Levi on Why Composing 'Under the Skin' Was 'Really Mental.'" *Indie Wire*, November 10, 2014. https://www.indiewire.com/2014/11/mica-levi-on-why-composing-under-the-skin-was-really-mental-190232/.

Laver, Mark. *Jazz Sells: Music, Marketing, and Meaning*. New York: Routledge, 2015.

Lawson, Colin, and Robin Stowell. *The Historical Performance of Music: An Introduction*. Cambridge: Cambridge University Press, 1999.

Lee, Spike. *Spike Lee's Gotta Have It: Inside Guerrilla Filmmaking*. New York: Simon & Schuster, 1997.

Lee, Spike, and Kaleem Aftab. *That's My Story and I'm Sticking to It*. London: W. W. Norton, 2005.

Lee, Spike, and Lisa Jones. *Mo' Better Blues*. New York: Simon & Schuster, 1990.

Lee, Spike, and Ralph Wiley. *By Any Means Necessary: The Trials and Tribulations of the Making of "Malcolm X."* New York: Hyperion, 1992.

Leech-Wilkinson, Daniel. *The Modern Invention of Medieval Music: Scholarship, Ideology, Performance.* Cambridge: Cambridge University Press, 2002.

Lees, Dominic. "Cinema and Authenticity: Anxieties in the Making of Historical Film. *Journal of Media Practice* 17, no. 2–3 (October 2016): 1–14.

Lees, Gene. *Cats of Any Color: Jazz, Black and White.* New York: Oxford University Press, 1995.

Lenin, Vladimir. "Directives on the Film Business." In *Collected Works*, Vol. 42 (New York: International, 1934): 388–89.

Lindo, Delroy. "Delroy Lindo on Spike Lee." In *Spike Lee: Interviews,* edited by Cynthia Fuchs, 161–77. Jackson: University Press of Mississippi, 2002.

Lipman, Ross. "Mingus, Cassavetes, and the Birth of a Jazz Cinema." *Journal of Film Music* 2, no. 2–4 (2010): 145–64.

Litowitz, Drew. "Trent Reznor and Atticus Ross: The Social Network." Consequence of Sound.net, October 20, 2010. https://consequenceofsound.net/2010/10/album-review-trent-reznor-and-atticus-ross-the-social-network-7/.

Lock, Graham, and David Murray, eds. *Thriving on a Riff: Jazz and Blues Influence in African American Literature and Film.* New York: Oxford University Press, 2009.

Lomanno, Mark. "Jazz in the Hollywood Machine: 'Whiplash,' Insider Anxiety, and Riffing Violence. *The Rhythm of Study*, March 1, 2015. http://rhythmofstudy.com/2015/03/01/whiplash-and-riffing-violence/.

Lopes, Paul. *The Rise of a Jazz Art World.* New York: Cambridge University Press, 2002.

Lopes, Paul. "Signifying Deviance and Transgression: Jazz in the Popular Imagination." *American Behavioral Scientist* 48, no. 11 (2005): 1468–81.

Lott, Eric. *Love and Theft: Blackface Minstrelsy and the American Working Class.* Oxford: Oxford University Press, 1993.

Lowery, David. "Music Streaming Rates 2018: Per Stream Rates Drop and YouTube's Value Gap Is Very Real." *All about Jazz*, February 8, 2019. https://news.allaboutjazz.com/musicstreaming-rates-2018-per-stream-rates-drop-and-youtubes-value-gap-is-very-real.

Lubiano, Wahneema. "But Compared to What? Reading Realism, Representation, and Essentialism in *School Daze, Do the Right Thing,* and the Spike Lee Discourse." In *The Spike Lee Reader,* edited by Paula Massood, 30–57. Philadelphia: Temple University Press, 2007.

Magee, Gayle Sherwood. *Robert Altman's Soundtracks: Film, Music, and Sound from 'M*A*S*H' to 'A Prairie Home Companion.'* New York: Oxford University Press, 2014.

Magee, Jeffrey. "Revisiting Fletcher Henderson's 'Copenhagen.'" *Journal of the American Musicological Society* 48, no. 1 (Spring 1995): 42–66.

Magee, Jeffrey. *The Uncrowned King of Swing: Fletcher Henderson and Big Band Jazz.* New York: Oxford University Press, 2005.

Magro, Anthony. *Contemporary Cat: Terence Blanchard with Special Guests.* Lanham, MD: Scarecrow Press, 2002.

Mahoney, Lesley. "Antonio Sánchez '97: The Making of the *Birdman* Score." Berklee, November 5, 2014. https://www.berklee.edu/news/antonio-sanchez-97-making-birdman-score.

Malle, Louis. *Malle on Malle.* Edited by Philip French. London: Faber & Faber, 1992.

Mancini, Henry. "Did They Mention the Music? (1989)." In *The Hollywood Film Music Reader,* edited by Mervyn Cooke, 189–208. New York: Oxford University Press, 2010.

Marich, Robert. *Marketing to Moviegoers: A Handbook of Strategies Used by Major Studios and Independents*. New York: Elsevier, 2005.

Marie, Michel. *The French New Wave: An Artistic School*. Translated by Richard Neupert. Oxford: Blackwell, 2003.

Marsalis, Wynton. "Music by Duke Ellington." Liner notes. *Anatomy of a Murder Soundtrack* (Columbia, 1999). CD.

Martin, Peter. *Music and the Sociological Gaze: Art Worlds and Cultural Production*. Manchester: Manchester University Press, 2006.

Martin, Rachel, and Nate Chinen. "How the Coronavirus Fallout Could Be Devastating to the Practice of Jazz." NPR, March 19, 2020. https://www.npr.org/2020/03/19/817342965/how-the-coronavirus-fallout-could-be-devastating-to-the-practice-of-jazz.

Martoccio, Angie, and Natalli Amato. "Coronavirus Cancellations: Festivals, Concerts, Tours, Films Affected by the Outbreak." *Rolling Stone*, March 10, 2020. https://www.rollingstone.com/music/music-news/coronavirus-cancellations-music-fests-concerts-tours-964575/.

Marx, Karl. *The Economic and Philosophic Manuscripts of 1844*. Edited by Dirk J. Struik. Translated by Martin Milligan. New York: International, 1964.

Mask, Mia, ed. *Contemporary Black American Cinema: Race, Gender, and Sexuality at the Movies*. New York: Routledge, 2012.

Massood, Paula, ed. *The Spike Lee Reader*. Philadelphia: Temple University Press, 2007.

Masters, Kim. "How Leonardo DiCaprio's *The Revenant* Shoot Became 'A Living Hell.'" *Hollywood Reporter*, July 22, 2015. http://www.hollywoodreporter.com/news/how-leonardo-dicaprios-revenant-shoot-810290.

Mayer, Vicki, Miranda J. Banks, and John Caldwell, eds. *Production Studies: Cultural Studies of Media Industries*. New York: Routledge, 2009.

McCollum, Maureen. "Behind 'La La Land,' a Long Relationship between a Director and a Composer." NPR, February 18, 2017. https://www.npr.org/2017/02/18/515848371/the-long-relationship-of-the-director-and-composer-from-la-la-land.

McCracken, Allison. *Real Men Don't Sing: Crooning in American Culture*. Durham, NC: Duke University Press, 2015.

McDonald, Tamar Jeffers. *Romantic Comedy: Boy Meets Girl Meets Genre*. New York: Columbia University Press, 2012.

McDonough, John. "The Chameleon Days of Dick Hyman." *Wall Street Journal*, December 30, 2009. http://www.wsj.com/articles/SB10001424052748704107204574475193134391938.

McGrath, Douglas. "If You Knew Woody like I Knew Woody." *New York Magazine*, October 17, 1994, 41–47. In *Woody Allen: Interviews*, edited by Robert E. Kapsis, 109–19. Jackson: University Press of Mississippi, 2016.

McGrath, Douglas. "Interview with Woody Allen." *Interview*, September 2008, 252–57. In *Woody Allen: Interviews*, edited by Robert E. Kapsis, 190–203. Jackson: University Press of Mississippi, 2016.

Medboe, Haftor, and Jose Dias. "Improvisation in the Digital Age: New Narratives in Jazz Promotion and Dissemination." *First Monday* 19, no. 10 (October 6, 2014). https://firstmonday.org/ojs/index.php/fm/article/view/5553/4132.

Meeker, David. *Jazz in the Movies: A Guide to Jazz Musicians, 1917–1977*. New Rochelle, NY: Arlington House, 1977.

Mera, Miguel. "Materializing Film Music." In *Cambridge Companion to Film Music*, edited by Mervyn Cooke and Fiona Ford, 157–72. Cambridge: Cambridge University Press, 2016.

Messina, Frank John, and Mary Ann Stankiewicz. "A Critique of the Integrated Arts Experience: Its Relation to Learning Theory and Its Pedagogical Value (Abstract and Review)." *Review of Research in Visual Arts Education* 6, no. 1 (Winter 1979): 45–50.

Micallef, Ken. "Antonio Sanchez: Flying High." *DownBeat* 82, no. 7 (2015): 24–28.

Michelmore, Guy. "A Producer's Guide to Working with Live Orchestra." Guy Michelmore .com. https://guymichelmore.com/2017/04/11/a-producers-guide-to-working-with -live-orchestra/#:~:text=How%20much%20does%20it%20does,and%20studio%20is%20 around%20%24100%2C000.

"Mid-Year Report: U.S. 2019." Nielsen Music. https://www.nielsen.com/wpcontent/uploads/ sites/3/2019/06/nielsen-us-music-mid-year-report-2019.pdf.

Miller, Julie. "How Jazz Drummer Antonio Sanchez Improvised the Birdman Score." *Vanity Fair Hollywood*, November 7, 2014. https://www.vanityfair.com/hollywood/2014/11/ birdman-score-antonio-sanchez.

Milkowski, Bill. "Tragic Symphony: Terence Blanchard Scores the Aftermath of Hurricane Katrina with Empathy and Grace." *JazzTimes* 37, no. 7 (September 2007): 52–56, 95.

Mitchell, Elvis. "Alejandro González Iñárritu." *Interview*, October 8, 2014. https://www.inte rviewmagazine.com/film/alejandro-gonzalez-inarritu.

Monson, Ingrid. *Saying Something: Jazz Improvisation and Interaction*. Chicago: University of Chicago Press, 1996.

"The Monster That Ate Hollywood: Interview, Lucy Fisher." PBS Frontline, November 2001. http://www.pbs.org/wgbh/pages/frontline/shows/hollywood/interviews/fisher.html.

Moore, Jason. "Melissa Harris-Perry Asks Terence Blanchard What Role Music Has in Social Activism; His Answer: Impeccable." *Atlanta Black Star*, June 3, 2015. http:// atlantablackstar.com/2015/06/03/melissa-harris-perry-ask-terrence-roll-music-social -activism-answer-impeccable/.

Morgan, David. *Knowing the Score: Film Composers Talk about the Art, Craft, Blood, Sweat and Tears of Writing for the Cinema*. New York: HarperCollins, 2000.

Moss, Robert F. "Creators on Creating: Woody Allen." *Saturday Review* 7 (November 1980): 40–44. In *Woody Allen: Interviews*, edited by Robert E. Kapsis, 60–66. Jackson: University Press of Mississippi, 2016.

Mundy, Robert, and Stephen Mamber. "Woody Allen Interview." *Cinema* (Winter 1972/73): 14–21. In *Woody Allen: Interviews*, edited by Robert E. Kapsis, 3–20. Jackson: University Press of Mississippi, 2016.

Naremore, James. *Acting in the Cinema*. Berkeley: University of California Press, 1988.

National Education Association. *Preparing 21st Century Students for a Global Society: An Educator's Guide to the "Four C's."* http://www.nea.org/assets/docs/A-Guide-to-Four-Cs .pdf.

National Endowment for the Arts. "Examples of Arts in Healthcare Programs." https:// www.arts.gov/accessibility/accessibility-resources/leadership-initiatives/arts-healthcare/ arts-endowment-issues-0.

Neupert, Richard. *A History of the French New Wave Cinema*. 2nd ed. Madison: University of Wisconsin Press, 2007.

Newell, William H., and Julie Thompson Klein. "Interdisciplinary Studies into the 21st Century." *Journal of General Education* 45, no. 2 (1996): 152–69.

Nielsen. "2014 Nielsen Music U.S. Report." http://so.thejazzline.com/tjl/uploads/2015/03/nielsen-2014-year-end-music-report-us.pdf.

Nielsen. "Streaming Consumption Rises in U.S. Markets with Early Stay-at-Home Orders during Covid-19." April 22, 2020. https://www.nielsen.com/us/en/insights/article/2020/streaming-consumption-rises-in-u-s-markets-with-early-stay-at-home-orders-during-covid-19/.

Noble, Bob. "Interview with Phil Ek." Hit Quarters, May 25, 2009. http://www.hitquarters.com/index.php3?page=intrview/opar/intrview_Phil_Ek_Interview.html.

Nyce, Ben. *Scorsese Up Close: A Study of the Films*. Lanham, MD: Scarecrow Press, 2004.

Ohmer, Susan. *George Gallup in Hollywood*. New York: Columbia University Press, 2006.

Olenski, Steve. "What Was Old Is New Again—The Power of Nostalgia Marketing." *Forbes*, August 14, 2015. https://www.forbes.com/sites/steveolenski/2015/08/14/what-was-old-is-new-again-the-power-of-nostalgia-marketing/?sh=5a536f086881.

O'Meally, Robert, ed. *The Jazz Cadence of American Culture*. New York: Columbia University Press, 1998.

O'Meally, Robert, Brent Hayes Edwards, and Farah Jasmine Griffin, eds. *Uptown Conversation: The New Jazz Studies*. New York: Columbia University Press, 2004.

Ortner, Sherry. *Not Hollywood: Independent Film at the Twilight of the American Dream*. Durham, NC: Duke University Press, 2013.

Patterson, John. "Alan Rudolph: 'People Just Don't Surrender to My Movies, Ever.'" *Guardian*, April 30, 2018. https://www.theguardian.com/film/2018/apr/30/alan-rudolph-film-robert-altman-interview.

Perez, Miguel Angel. *Hollywood Film Music: Cramping the Composer's Style*. Departamento de Filología Inglesa, Universidad de Alicante, 2004.

Peterson, Richard. *Creating Country Music: Fabricating Authenticity*. Chicago: University of Chicago Press, 1997.

Phillips, Kyna, and Deena Zaru. "Human Toll of Covid-19 Touches Every Corner of the Jazz World." ABC, June 12, 2020. https://abcnews.go.com/Entertainment/human-toll-covid-19-touches-corner-jazz-world/story?id=71178081.

Piazza, Tom. "Black and Tan Fantasy." Review. *New Republic*, July 11, 1988, 36–39.

Pillai, Nicolas. *Jazz as Visual Language: Film, Television, and the Dissonant Image*. London: I. B. Tauris, 2017.

Pond, Steve. "How *Birdman* Composer Improvised the Year's Most Audacious Film Score." *The Wrap: Covering Hollywood*, October 19, 2014. http://www.thewrap.com/how-birdman-composer-improvised-the-years-most-audacious-film-score/.

Porter, Eric. *What Is This Thing Called Jazz?: African American Musicians as Artists, Critics, and Activists*. Berkeley: University of California Press, 2002.

Powdermaker, Hortense. *Hollywood: The Dream Factory: An Anthropologist Looks at the Movie-Makers*. New York: Little, Brown, 1950.

Radford, Ivan. "*Birdman, Whiplash*, and the Sound of Drums." Den of Geek, February 23, 2015. http://www.denofgeek.com/us/movies/whiplash/243978/birdman-whiplash-and-the-sound-of-drums.

Raeburn, Bruce Boyd. "Jamming with Disaster: New Orleans Jazz in the Aftermath of Hurricane Katrina." In *Forces of Nature and Cultural Responses*, edited by Katrin Pfeifer and Niki Pfeifer, 169–84. Dordrecht, Netherlands: Springer, 2013.

Rathore, Elia. "Living in the Age of Political Memes." *New York Times*, April 23, 2019. https://www.nytimes.com/2019/04/23/style/india-pakistan-political-memes.html.

Reay, Pauline. *Music in Film: Soundtracks and Synergy*. New York: Wallflower, 2004.

Reich, Howard. "With Little or No Safety Net, Jazz Musicians Watch Their Gigs Disappear as Coronavirus Spreads." *Chicago Tribune*, March 18, 2020. https://www.chicagotribune.com/coronavirus/ct-ent-jazz-musicians-reich-coronavirus-0322-20200318-xmeg67zy5n bblpdj5flfd7oqfe-story.html.

Richolson, Janice Mosier. "He's Gotta Have It: An Interview with Spike Lee." In *Spike Lee: Interviews*, edited by Cynthia Fuchs, 25–34. Jackson: University Press of Mississippi, 2002.

"Risk." *Economic Times*. http://economictimes.indiatimes.com/definition/risk.

Robinson, Jason. "The Challenge of the Changing Same: The Jazz Avant-Garde of the 1960s, the Black Aesthetic, and the Black Arts Movement." *Critical Studies in Improvisation* 1, no. 2 (September 8, 2005). https://www.criticalimprov.com/index.php/csieci/article/download/17/47?inline=1.

Rosa, Christopher. "These Are the Actors Who Now Regret Working with Woody Allen—and the Ones Who Don't." *Glamour*, September 11, 2020.

Rosten, Leo C. *Hollywood: The Movie Colony, the Movie Makers*. New York: Harcourt Brace, 1941.

Ryan, Bill. *Making Capital from Culture: The Corporate Form of Capitalist Cultural Production*. Berlin: Walter de Gruyter, 1992.

Ryzick, Melena. "Ticking Watch. Boat Engine. Slowness. The Secrets of the 'Dunkirk' Score." *New York Times*, July 26, 2017. https://www.nytimes.com/2017/07/26/movies/the-secrets-of-the-dunkirk-score-christopher-nolan.html?auth=login-google.

Sadlier, Allison. "Americans Are Streaming 8 hours a Day During Coronavirus Lockdown." *New York Post*, April 14, 2020. https://nypost.com/2020/04/14/average-american-streaming-content-8-hours-a-day-during-covid-19-according-to-new-research/.

Salamone, Frank A. *The Culture of Jazz*. Lanham, MD: University Press of America, 2009.

Sandke, Randall. *Where the Dark and the Light Folks Meet: Race and the Mythology, Politics, and Business of Jazz*. Lanham, MD: Scarecrow Press, 2010.

Sarris, Andrew. *The American Cinema: Directors and Directions, 1929–1968*. New York: Da Capo Press, 1996.

Sarris, Andrew. "Notes on Auteur Theory in 1962." In *Film Theory and Criticism: Introductory Readings*, edited by Leo Braudy and Marshall Cohen, 515–18. New York: Oxford University Press, 2009.

Schelle, Michael. *The Score: Interviews with Film Composers*. Los Angeles: Silman-James Press, 1999.

Scheurer, Timothy. *Music and Mythmaking in Film: Genre and the Role of the Composer*. Jefferson, NC: McFarland, 2008.

Scott, A. O. "My Woody Allen Problem." *New York Times*, January 31, 2018. https://www.nytimes.com/2018/01/31/movies/woody-allen.html.

Sedgwick, John, and Michael Pokorny, eds. *An Economic History of Film*. New York: Routledge, 2005.

Sharf, Zack. "Ava DuVernay Fires Back at Men Who Aren't Happy She Hires Female 'Queen Sugar' Directors: 'Sue Me.'" *Indie Wire*, May 4, 2018. https://www.indiewire.com/2018/05/ava-duvernay-men-unhappy-women-queen-sugar-directors-1201960610/.

Sherman, Bernard. *Inside Early Music: Conversations with Performers*. Oxford: Oxford University Press, 1997.

Siegel, Tatiana. "Only Featured Black Actress in a Woody Allen Film Defends His All-White Casts (Q&A). *Hollywood Reporter*, August 7, 2015. https://www.hollywoodreporter.com/news/hazelle-goodman-woody-allen-all-813921.

Small, Christopher. *Musicking: The Meanings of Performing and Listening*. Hanover, NH: University Press of New England, 1998.

Smith, Jeff. *The Sounds of Commerce: Marketing Popular Film Music*. New York: Columbia University Press, 1998.

Spera, Keith. *Groove, Interrupted: Loss, Renewal, and the Music of New Orleans*. New York: St. Martin's Press, 2011.

Spera, Keith. "Terence Blanchard Aimed for a Universal Feeling with 'A Tale of God's Will': Katrina and the Arts." *Times Picayune*, August 24 , 2015. http://www.nola.com/katrina/index.ssf/2015/08/terence_blanchard_katrina_a_ta.html.

"Spike Lee on Gentrification, Jazz, and How He Got His Start in Film." NPR, February 15, 2019. https://www.npr.org/2019/02/15/694696224/spike-lee-on-gentrification-jazz-and-how-he-got-his-start-in-film.

Stahl, Matt. "Privilege and Distinction in Production Worlds: Copyright, Collective Bargaining, and Working Conditions in Media Making." In *Production Studies: Cultural Studies of Media Industries*, edited by Vicki Mayer et al, 54–67. New York: Routledge, 2009.

Stahl, Matt. *Unfree Masters: Recording Artists and the Politics of Work*. Durham, NC: Duke University Press, 2013.

Stanbridge, Alan. "From the Margins to the Mainstream: Jazz, Social Relations, and Discourses of Value." *Critical Studies in Improvisation* 4, no. 1 (2008). https://journal.lib.uoguelph.ca/index.php/csieci/article/viewArticle/361/960.

Stanfield, Peter. *Body and Soul: Jazz and Blues in American Film, 1927–63*. Urbana: University of Illinois Press, 2005.

Sterritt, David. *Spike Lee's America*. Cambridge, UK: Polity Press, 2013.

Stewart, Susan. "Notes on Distressed Genres." *Journal of American Folklore* 104, no. 411 (Winter 1991): 5–31.

Stewart, Susan. *On Longing: Narratives of the Miniature, the Gigantic, the Souvenir, the Collection*. Durham, NC: Duke University Press, 1993.

Stratemann, Klaus. *Duke Ellington, Day by Day and Film by Film*. Copenhagen: Jazz Media, 1992.

Sullivan, John L. "Leo C. Rosten's Hollywood: Power, Status, and the Primacy of Economic and Social Networks in Cultural Production." In *Production Studies: Cultural Studies of Media Industries*, edited by Vicki Mayer et al., 47–61. New York: Routledge, 2009.

Swinson, Brock. "A Film within a Film: Robert Budreau on *Born to Be Blue*." *Creative Screenwriting*, May 17, 2016. https://creativescreenwriting.com/a-film-within-a-film-robert-budreau-on-born-to-be-blue/.

Szczerpanik, Petr, and Patrick Vonderau, eds. *Behind the Screen: Inside European Production Cultures*. New York: Palgrave Macmillan, 2013.

Tagg, Philip, and Bob Clarida. *Ten Little Tunes: Towards a Musicology of the Mass Media*. New York: Mass Media Music Scholars Press, 2003.

Tapley, Kristopher. "Oscar-Winning Cinematographer Emmanuel Lubezki Details the 'Dance' of Filming Birdman." HitFix, December 20, 2014. http://uproxx.com/hitfix/oscar-winning-cinematographer-emmanuel-lubezki-details-the-dance-of-filming-birdman/.

Taruskin, Richard. *Text and Act: Essays on Musical Performance*. New York: Oxford University Press, 1995.

Thompson, David, and Ian Christie, eds. *Scorsese on Scorsese*. London: Faber, 2003.

Thompson, John. "Some Issues in Historically Informed Qin Performance." http://www.silkqin.com/08anal/hip.htm.

Thorne, Will, and Kate Aurthur. "All the Shows and Movies Shut Down or Delayed Because of Coronavirus." *Variety*, March 12, 2020. https://variety.com/2020/film/news/films-tv-delayed-coronavirus-canceled-1203532033/.

Tiedemann, Garrett. "Which Comes First, the Movie or the Music?" *Classical MPR*, April 5, 2015. https://www.classicalmpr.org/story/2014/11/05/film-score-picture.

Townsend, Peter. *Jazz in American Culture*. Jackson: University Press of Mississippi, 2000.

Toynbee, Jason. *Making Popular Music: Musicians, Creativity, and Institutions*. New York: Oxford University Press, 2000.

"Travis Scott and Fortnite Present: Astronomical." YouTube. April 26, 2020. https://www.youtube.com/watch?v=wYeFAlVC8qU.

Truffaut, François. "Une certaine tendance du cinéma français." *Cahiers du cinéma* 6, no. 31 (January 1954): 15–29.

Tucker, Sherrie. "Deconstructing the Jazz Tradition: The 'Subjectless Subject' of New Jazz Studies." In *Jazz/Not Jazz: The Music and Its Boundaries*, edited by David Ake et al., 264–84. Berkeley: University of California Press, 2012.

UCLA College Social Sciences. "Hollywood Diversity Report 2019: Old Story, New Beginning." https://socialsciences.ucla.edu/wp-content/uploads/2019/02/UCLA-Hollywood-Diversity-Report-2019-2-21-2019.pdf.

Ugwu, Reggie. "The Hashtag That Changed the Oscars: An Oral History." *New York Times*, February 6, 2020. https://www.nytimes.com/2020/02/06/movies/oscarssowhite-history.html.

Upton, Elizabeth. "Concepts of Authenticity in Early Music and Popular Music Communities." *Ethnomusicology Review* 17 (February 23, 2012): 1–13.

US Congress. House. A Concurrent Resolution Expressing the Sense of Congress Respecting the Designation of Jazz as a Rare and Valuable National American Treasure. H. R. Res 57. 100th Congress. Introduced in House March 3, 1987. https://www.congress.gov/bill/100th-congress/house-concurrent-resolution/57.

Vest, Jason. *Spike Lee: Finding the Story and Forcing the Issue*. Santa Barbara, CA: Praeger, 2014.

Wager, Jans B. *Jazz and Cocktails: Rethinking Race and the Sound of Film Noir*. Austin: University of Texas Press, 2017.

Waksman, Steve. *Instruments of Desire: The Electric Guitar and the Shaping of Musical Experience*. Cambridge: Harvard University Press, 1999.

Wallace, Michele. "Spike Lee and Black Women." In *The Spike Lee Reader*, edited by Paula Massood, 23–29. Philadelphia: Temple University Press, 2007.

Webster, Andrew. "More than 12 Million People Attended Travis Scott's Fortnite Concert." *The Verge*, April 23, 2020. https://www.theverge.com/2020/4/23/21233946/travis-scott-fortnite-concert-astronomical-record-breaking-player-count.

Weiner, Natalie. "Terence Blanchard on Ferguson vs. Waco, Spike Lee's 'Chiraq,' and His New Album 'Breathless.'" *Billboard*, May 27, 2015. http://www.billboard.com/articles/news/6576084/terence-blanchard-breathless-ferguson-chiraq-new-album.

Wennekes, Emile, and Emilio Audissino, eds. *Cinema Changes: Incorporations of Jazz in the Film Soundtrack*. Turnhout, Belgium: Brepols, 2019.

"*When The Levees Broke: A Requiem in Four Acts*, Synopsis." HBO Documentaries. http://www.hbo.com/documentaries/when-the-levees-broke-a-requiem-in-four-acts/synopsis.html. Accessed December 5, 2013.

Williams, Justin A. *Rhymin' and Stealin': Musical Borrowing in Hip-Hop*. Ann Arbor: University of Michigan Press, 2013.

Wilson, John S. "Allen Plans Year-Round Jazz Playing." *New York Times*, June 4, 1984. http://www.nytimes.com/1984/06/04/arts/allen-plans-year-round-jazz-playing.html?pagewanted=all.

Wollen, Peter. "The Auteur Theory." *Signs and Meaning in the Cinema*. 3rd ed. Bloomington: Indiana University Press, 1972.

X, Malcolm, and Alex Haley. *The Autobiography of Malcolm X*. New York: Grove Press, 1965.

Yanow, Scott. *Jazz on Film: The Complete Story of the Musicians & Music Onscreen*. San Francisco: Backbeat Books, 2004.

Yanow, Scott. "Terence Blanchard: *The Malcolm X Jazz Suite*." AllMusic. http://www.allmusic.com/album/the-malcolm-x-jazz-suite-mw0000618632.

Zafirau, Stephen. "Audience Knowledge and the Everyday Lives of Cultural Producers in Hollywood." In *Production Studies: Cultural Studies of Media Industries*, edited by Vicki Mayer, Miranda J. Banks, and John Caldwell, 198–210. New York: Routledge, 2009.

Zinsser, William. "Doin' the Chameleon." *The Atlantic*, October 1995, 98–108.

Zirpolo, Michael. "Get Rhythm in Your Feet: A Profile of Vince Giordano and the Nighthawks." *IAJRC Journal* (June 1, 2012): 43.

SELECT FILMOGRAPHY

Allen, Woody, dir. *Hannah and Her Sisters*. 1986. Santa Monica, CA: MGM, 2001. DVD.

Allen, Woody, dir. *Manhattan*. 1979. Culver City, CA: MGM, 2000. DVD.

Allen, Woody, dir. *Midnight in Paris*. Culver City, CA: Sony Pictures, 2011. DVD.

Allen, Woody, dir. *Zelig*. 1983. Santa Monica, CA: MGM, 2001. DVD.

Chazelle, Damien, dir. *Whiplash*. 2014. Culver City, CA: Sony, 2015. DVD.

Cheadle, Don, dir. *Miles Ahead*. 2015. Culver City, CA: Sony, 2016. DVD.

Iñárritu, Alejandro González, dir. *Birdman or (the Unexpected Virtue of Ignorance)*. 2014. Beverly Hills, CA: 20th Century Fox, 2015. DVD.

Lee, Spike, dir. *Malcolm X*. 1992. Burbank, CA: Warner, 2000. DVD.

Lee, Spike, dir. *Mo' Better Blues*. 1990. Universal City, CA: Universal Studios, 2000. DVD.

Lee, Spike, dir. *When the Levees Broke: A Requiem for Katrina*. New York: HBO, 2006. DVD.

Malle, Louis, dir. *Ascenseur pour l'échafaud*. 1958. Irvington, NY: Criterion Collection, 2006.

BIBLIOGRAPHY 201

Preminger, Otto, dir. *Anatomy of a Murder*. 1959. Burbank, CA: Columbia TriStar, 2000. DVD.
Rudolph, Alan, dir. *Afterglow*. 1997. Studio City, CA: Moonstone Entertainment, 1997. DVD.

SELECT DISCOGRAPHY

Blanchard, Terence. *Jazz in Film*. New York: Sony Classical, 1999.
Blanchard, Terence. *The Malcolm X Jazz Suite*. New York: Columbia, 1993.
Blanchard, Terence. *A Tale of God's Will: A Requiem for Katrina*. New York: Blue Note, 2007.
Davis, Miles. *Ascenseur pour l'échafaud: Complete Recordings*. New York: Polygram, 1988.
Hyman, Dick, and Various Artists. *Sweet and Lowdown: Music from the Motion Picture*. New York: Sony Classical, 1999.
Isham, Mark, featuring Charles Lloyd, Gary Burton, Geri Allen, and Sid Page. *Afterglow: Music from the Motion Picture*. New York: Columbia/Sony, 1998.
Isham, Mark. *Blue Sun*. New York: Columbia/Sony, 1995.
Lee, Bill, and the Branford Marsalis Quintet featuring Terence Blanchard and Cynda Williams. *Music from Mo' Better Blues*. New York: Columbia, 1990.
Sánchez, Antonio. *Birdman, or (The Unexpected Virtue of Ignorance): Original Motion Picture Soundtrack*. Los Angeles: Milan Records, 2014.

INTERVIEWS

Blanchard, Terence. Interview by the author. June 20, 2015. Washington, DC.
Blanchard, Terence. Interview by the author. August 25, 2015, by telephone.
Cantor, Allison. Interview by the author. December 15, 2014. Los Angeles, CA.
Cunningham, Adrian. Interview by the author. October 27, 2014, by telephone.
Giordano, Vince. Interview by the author. September 29, 2014. New York, NY.
Giordano, Vince. Interview by the author. October 17, 2014, by telephone.
Giordano, Vince. Interview by the author. March 26, 2016, by telephone.
Hyman, Dick. Interview by the author. March 10, 2015. Venice, FL.
Isham, Mark. Interview by the author. December 15, 2014. Los Angeles, CA.
Isham, Mark. Interview by the author. December 17, 2014. Los Angeles, CA.
Kirchner, Bill. Interview by the author. October 29, 2015, by telephone.
Lerman, Stewart. Interview by the author. November 21, 2014, by telephone.
Lopeman, Mark. Interview by the author. October 11, 2014, by telephone.

INDEX

Page numbers in **bold** indicate illustrations.

Academy Awards: African American re-
cipients, 78; Best Original Score, 54–55,
117, 149–50, 167n16; categories, 15, 28;
#OscarsSoWhite movement, 37–38
activism. *See* musical activism
Adams, John, 54
adaptation scores, 32, 45
African Americans: creativity and artistic
expression of, 75, 84–97, 117, 142; entrepreneurship in film industry, 82–84;
jazz and, 75, 86–90, 173n42; richness of
culture, 77–82, 172n11. *See also* race
Ake, David, *Jazz/Not Jazz*, 12
Alden, Howard, 135, 139
Ali, Lorraine, 53
"alienation effect," 4, 21
Allain, Stephanie, 83
Allen, Geri, 70
Allen, Woody, 6, 24, 118–43; as actor,
122–24; authenticity and, 125, 131–32,
136, 141–42; branding of, 15, 123; career,
121–22; characters of, 120–21, 124, 142,
180n65; clarinet and, 127–28; compilation soundtracks of, 125–26, 129; creative approach of, 121–22; Eddy Davis
Jazz Band and, 127; escapism of, 129–30;
film themes of, 125, 129; Hyman and, 38,
134–42, **137**; improvisation and, 134, 142;
as independent auteur/maverick, 15–16,
121–22; jazz and, 125–33, 142; magic and,
127, 130; New York City and, 119–21,
177n12; nostalgia and, 130–33; original
scoring for, 133–34; race and, 120; risk
and, 121–22; scandal of, 123–24, 177n21;
themes of, 125

Allen, Woody, works by: *Annie Hall*,
128, 133, 142; *Another Woman*, 121;
Apropos of Nothing (memoir), 124,
126; *Bananas*, 133; *Blue Jasmine*, 121,
142; *Broadway Danny Rose*, 137; *Bullets
over Broadway*, 137; *Chiraq*, 77; *Crimes
and Misdemeanors*, 121; *The Curse of
the Jade Scorpion*, 137, 139, 142; *Death*,
125; *Deconstructing Harry*, 120, 125;
Everyone Says I Love You, 121, 137;
*Everything You Always Wanted to
Know about Sex* (*But Were Afraid to
Ask)*, 136–37; *Hannah and Her Sisters*,
118–19, 137; *Husbands and Wives*, 121;
Interiors, 121; *Love and Death*, 125;
Manhattan, 118–19, 129, 137, 142; *Match
Point*, 121; *Melinda and Melinda*, 120,
137; *Midnight in Paris*, 129, 131; *Mighty
Aphrodite*, 137; *The Purple Rose of
Cairo*, 129–30, 137; *Radio Days*, 131, 137;
A Rainy Day in New York, 124; *Rifkin's
Festival*, 124; *September*, 121; *Sleeper*,
133–34, 142; *Stardust Memories*, 123,
125, 129, 133, 137; *Sweet and Lowdown*,
137, 139, 142; *Take the Money and Run*,
133–34; *Vicky Cristina Barcelona*, 120;
Zelig, 136–39, **138**
Altman, Robert, 66, 71, 170n70
Anderson, Paul Thomas, 149
Andrew, Geoff, 52
Arlen, Harold, 135
Armstrong, Louis, 12, 90, 126–28, 130, 133,
142
Art Blakey's Jazz Messengers, 75
art world theory, 15, 26–28

INDEX

Astaire, Fred, 130

audiences: Allen shaping perceptions and expectations of, 121, 123–24; authenticity in film and, 18, 54, 99; challenges presented by jazz/film intersections for, 11; diversity in, 38, 74, 78, 89–90, 98; expectations of, 11; haptic music and audience response, 59; jazz as signifier for, 19–20, 148; jazz exposure from films, 16, 18, 97; Lee creating challenges for, 80–82; live performance of jazz and, 155; musical score's effect on emotions of, 47, 104, 153–54; of streaming services, 157–58

Audissino, Emilio, *Cinema Changes*, 7

Auricle Time Processor, 35–36

Austin, Gene, 151

Austin, J. L., 16

auteur theory, 14–15, 162n29, 162n32

authenticity, 16–19; Allen and, 131–32, 136, 141; Blanchard and, 98–99, 117; blues and, 114–15; definition of, 16–17; historically informed performance and, 139–41, **140**, 179n61; Hyman and, 135, 138–39; Iñárritu and, 52–54, 59–60, 65, 72; jazz and, 31, 40; Lee and, 74, 88–89, 92–93, 95, 117; Rudolph and, 52–53, 67, 72

autonomy, 8, 22–23, 28, 36, 39, 47, 61, 100, 164n4

avant-garde jazz, 17–18, 149

Bagneris, Vernel, "One Mo' Time," 144

Baker, Chet, 145

Baker, Sarah, 22

Baldwin, Alec, 124

Baldwin, James, 101–2

Baraka, Amiri (LeRoi Jones): *Blues People*, 115; "Spike Lee at the Movies," 81

Baron, Kenny, 90

Barrow, Geoff, scores of, 149

Barth, Bruce, 107–8

Barthes, Roland, "The Death of the Author," 14

bebop, 10, 12, 18, 49–50, 59, 90

Bechet, Sidney, 125–29; "Si tu vois ma mère," 129

Becker, Howard, 15, 52; *Art Worlds*, 26, 161n19

Beethoven, Ludwig van, 134

Beiderbecke, Bix, 136

Belafonte, Harry, 78

Bergman, Ingmar, 121, 130

Berlin, Irving, 130, 135

Berliner, Paul, *Thinking in Jazz*, 17

Bernstein, Elmer, scores of, 50

Berry, Halle, 84

Betty Boop, 138

Betty X, 102

big band, 105–6

Billboard charts, 109, 158

biopics, 5, 144–45, 147

Birdman (Iñárritu), 23–24, 53–66; artistic accomplishment of, 73; Best Original Score ineligibility, 54–55, 167n16; characters/plot, 55–56; conception of, 54–55; improvised score in, 62–65; jazz component of, 52; live aesthetic in, 59–60, 169n36; preproduction development of, 56–57; reception of, 54, 73, 153; semiotic meanings in, 60–62, 169n38; significance of, 65–66; soundtrack uniqueness, 54–55; structure/movement/pacing in, 57–58, 168n32

Biskind, Peter, 121

Black culture. *See* African Americans

Black Lives Matter movement, 76

blackface minstrelsy. *See* minstrelsy

Blake, Eubie, 134–35

Blakey, Art, *Les liaisons dangereuses* (score), 49

Blanchard, Terence, 24, 74–77, 95–117; authenticity and, 98–99, 117; awards and honors, 75, 116–17, 171n2; career, 8, 75–77, 90, 116–17, 173n44; creative autonomy of, 100; creative process of, 107; on creativity vs. time constraints, 43; jazz and, 13, 74, 76, 98–99, 175n69; Lee and, 74–76, 77, 95–96, 100–101, 174n57, 175n73; Morris and, 34; musician network of, 32, 77; New Orleans and, 75, 112–13; social justice and musical activism of, 75–76, 97–98, 101, 112–13; Terence Blanchard Quintet, 113, 176n101; trumpet and, 113–16

Blanchard, Terence, works by: "Betty's Theme," 108; "Blues for Malcolm," 108; *Breathless*, 75–76; *Champion*, 76; "Dear Mom," 116; *Fire Shut Up in My Bones*, 76; "Funeral Dirge," 111–13, **111**; "Ghost of Betsy," 116; "Ghost of Congo Square," 116; "Ghost of 1927," 116; "Levees," 111–14, **111**; "Malcolm at Peace," 108–9; "Malcolm Makes Hajj," 108; *Malcolm X* (score), 103–6, 176n90; *The Malcolm X Jazz Suite*, 75, 101, 107–9; "Malcolm's Theme," reprises of, 12, 105–6, 108–9, 176n89; "Melody for Laura," 106, 108; *Mo' Better Blues* (score), 95–96; "The Nation," 108; "The Opening," 108; "Perpetuity," 108–9; *A Tale of God's Will: A Requiem for Katrina*, 75, 101, 113–16, 176n102; "Theme for Elijah," 108–9; "Using Music to Underscore Three Words: I Can't Breathe" (essay), 75–76; "Wading Through," 111–13, **111**; "The Water," 111–13, **111**; *When the Levees Broke* (score), 111–12

Blauner, Robert, 21–22

Blaxploitation era, 78, 172n6

Blue Note records, 27, 113, 116

blues, 18, 90, 99, 106, 114–15, 141

Bolden, Buddy, 144–45

Borne, Steve, 70

Bourdieu, Pierre, 22

Boyle, Lara Flynn, 68

Braff, Ruby, 135

Branford Marsalis Quartet, 90, 96–97, 174n60

Brecker, Michael, 55

Breskin, David, 83

Brown, Andy, 155–56

Brown, Effie, 83

Burton, Gary, 70

Burton, Tim, 100

Butler, David, *Jazz Noir*, 7

Caine, Michael, 124

Caldwell, John, 14; *Production Culture*, 7

Canby, Vincent, 121

Cantor, Allison, 35

Captain Autonomous-Anonymous, 66

Carmichael, Hoagy, 126

Carroll, Kathleen, 124

Carter, Benny, 5

Carter, Ruth, 85

Cassavetes, John, *Shadows*, 50

Caudle, Caleb, *Better Hurry Up*, 155

Chalamet, Timothée, 124

Champlin, Charles, 123

Chaplin, Charlie, *The Kid*, 153

Charlap, Bill, 135

Charles, Ray, 103

Chazelle, Damien: *La La Land*, 6, 38, 50, 144–45, 147; *Whiplash*, 6, 38, 50, 144–45, 147

Cheadle, Don: *The Hippopotamus*, 73; *Miles Ahead*, 5, 73, 144, 147, 171n73, 180n5

choreography, 56, 65–66

Christie, Julie, 68

Ciment, Michel, 129

cinematography, 56–57, 84–85, 137, 168n31

Clarke, Kenny, 48

Coleman, Ornette: "Lonely Woman," 97; *Naked Lunch* (score), 12, 50

collaboration in jazz-film, 23, 26–47; behind-the-scenes examination of, 4, 8–11; budgeting, 41–42; composers and musicians, 32; compromise in, 46–47; directorial investment and, 13–16; director/producer, role of, 29–30; editing, 44–45; hierarchical structure of, 29–38, **29**; implications for jazz specifically, 152–59; inner circle and networking, 36–38; inter-arts collaborations, 152; intersection of art and labor, 38–47; intersection of film personnel and jazz artists, 27–28; music engineer and music editor, role of, 33–34; music rights,

45–46; music supervisors, role of, 30–31; overview, 26–28; schedule/timeline, 42–44; support positions and technology, 35–36. *See also* creativity/creative labor/creative agency; *and specific film directors and film composers*

Coltrane, John, 90; "Acknowledgment" (*A Love Supreme*, Part I), 97; "Alabama," 75–76, 97–98; "Tunji," 97

compilation soundtracks, 5, 32, 125–26, 143, 160n16

"Concert for Hurricane Relief, A" (TV special), 110–11, 176n98

Confrey, Zez, 135

Cooke, Mervyn, 3–4

Cooke, Sam, 74, 87, 103

cool jazz, 12, 68

Coppola, Francis Ford, *Apocalypse Now*, 85

Copyright Act (1976), 45

Corea, Chick, 55

Corigliano, John, 40, 44

COVID-19 pandemic, 154–57, 182n28

Cox, Arnie, 59

creativity/creative labor/creative agency, 4–11, 21–23; of Black artists, 75, 84–86, 88–90, 94, 117, 142; delegation of, 36; director/producer and, 13–15, 29–30, 67; experimental film scoring and, 150, 152; film composers and, 11, 24, 41, 116; jazz artists and, 5, 11, 13, 27–28, 39, 72–73, 156; labor as art, 46–47; music engineer and music editor and, 33–34; music supervisors and, 31; "selling out" vs., 40; strategies for jazz's future and, 158; time constraints on, 42–44. *See also* autonomy; improvisation; *and specific film composers and jazz artists*

crime jazz, 21, 61

Cristofer, Michael, 76

Criterion Collection, 48

Cronenberg, David, *Naked Lunch*, 12, 50

Crosby, Bing, 151

Crouch, Stanley, 4

Culp, Jerome McCristal, Jr., 120

culture. *See* African Americans; popular culture

culture industry: art as labor, 39–41; creativity, labor, and agency in, 11, 22–23, 28, 47, 72; literature studies of, 7. *See also* authenticity; creativity/creative labor/ creative agency; risk

Curtiz, Michael, *Young Man with a Horn*, 91–92, 145

Dandridge, Dorothy, 78

Daniels, Lee: *Precious*, 79–80; *The United States vs. Billie Holiday*, 146

Danska, Herbert, *Sweet Love, Bitter*, 92

Davis, Miles: "All Blues," 97; *Ascenseur pour l'échafaud* (score), 16, 48–49, **49**, 73, 153; biopic on, 147; criticism of, 40–41; *Kind of Blue*, 67–68, 73; musical activism of, 90; myth of, 145; scores of, 5

Davis, Troy, 108

Desplat, Alexandre, 150

DeVeaux, Scott, 10, 17–18; "Constructing the Jazz Tradition," 13

Dias, José, 157–58

Dick, Kirby, *Allen v. Farrow* (documentary), 124

Dickerson, Ernest, 85

Dickerson, Roger, 75

Disconforme SL, 126

Disney+, 154, 181n21

Doctor, Jenny, *Watching Jazz*, 7

Dodds, Johnny, 126–27

Donnelley, K. J., *Film Music*, 10, 161n21

drums, 61–62

dual authenticity, 139–42, **140**, 179n61

Duke Ellington Orchestra, 126

Dutton, Denis, 16–17, 140, 162n35

DuVernay, Ava, 37, 83

Eastwood, Clint, 6; *Bird*, 50, 91–92, 95, 144

Eddy Davis Jazz Band, 127

Edison, Thomas, 79

Ek, Phil, 33

Elfman, Danny, 100, 150

Ellington, Duke: Allen and, 125–26, 142; *Anatomy of a Murder* (score), 3–5, 16, 50, 153; Blanchard on, 98; criticism of,

40–41; "Flirtibird," 3–4, 160n1; Hyman and, 135; influence of, 105, 109; musical activism of, 90

Ellison, Ralph, *Invisible Man*, 85

Elsdon, Peter, *Watching Jazz*, 7

Esposito, Giancarlo, 95

Evans, Bill, 135

Evans, David, 114–15

experimental film scoring, 148–52

expressive/experiential authenticity, 140–41, **140**, 179n61

factual authenticity, 140–41, **140**

Farrakhan, Louis, 102

Farrow, Dylan, 123–24, 177n21

Farrow, Mia, 123–24, 130, 137

Farrow, Moses, 123

Farrow, Satchel Ronan, 123

Faulkner, Robert: *Hollywood Studio Musicians*, 31, 37, 40; *Music on Demand*, 7, 22, 36–37, 39, 41, 47

Fellini, Federico, 121

film and jazz. *See* collaboration in jazz-film; jazz and film

film criticism/critics, 14

film festivals, 154

film industry: art as labor, 39–41; commercial risk in, 19–21, 166n7; COVID-19's effect on, 154–55, 182n28; hierarchical structure of, 29–38, **29**; influence of, 79; inner circle and networking, 36–38; overview, 26–28; race and gender in, 37–38, 82–84, 161n28, 163n47. *See also specific positions in film hierarchy*

film noir, 21, 61

Finale (music notation software), 35

Fischer, Fred, "Chicago (That Toddlin' Town)," 138–39

Fishburne, Larry, 84

Fitzgerald, Ella, 74, 87

Fleming, Michael, 95

Flory, Dan, 80

Ford, John, 67

40 Acres and a Mule Filmworks, 79, 83

Franklin, Aretha, 103

free jazz, 12, 50

French New Wave, 14, 21, 48–50, 72, 166n3

Frith, Simon, 20, 61, 163n48, 169n39

Fuller, Charles, 101

Furie, Sidney J., *Lady Sings the Blues*, 92

Gabbard, Krin, 10; *Jammin' at the Margins*, 3–4, 7, 51, 92; *Jazz Among the Discourses*, 7; *Representing Jazz*, 7

Galifianakis, Zach, 66

Gans, Herbert, 40

Garner, Eric, 75

Garner, Erroll, 136

Garrett, Charles Hiroshi, *Jazz/Not Jazz*, 12

gender, 14, 37, 161n28

Gershwin, George, *Rhapsody in Blue*, 119, 129

Gerwig, Greta, 124

Getz, Stan, 12

Giddins, Gary, 73

Gillespie, Dizzy, 90, 108, 135

Giordano, Vince, 31, 34, 43, 45–46, 139

Glazer, Jonathan, 149

Glenn Miller Orchestra. *See* Miller, Glenn

Godard, Jean-Luc, *Breathless*, 49

Godsall, Jonathan, 59

Goldmark, Daniel, *Jazz/Not Jazz*, 12

González Iñárritu, Alejandro. *See* Iñárritu, Alejandro González

Goodman, Benny, 135

Goodman, Hazelle, 120–21

Gorbman, Claudia, 103–5, 129, 175n85

Grammy Awards, 75, 116

Greenwood, Jonny, scores of, 148–49

Gridley, Mark, 10

Griffith, Emile, 76

Gross, Jenna, 132

Grusin, Dave, *The Fabulous Baker Boys* (score), 50, 166n5

Haley, Alex, *Autobiography of Malcolm X*, 101–2, 175n77

Hall, Rebecca, 124

Hall, Stefan, 157

Hamlisch, Marvin, scores of, 133–34

Hampton, Lionel, 75, 103
Hancock, Herbie, 8, 16, 40–41, 161n17
Handy, W. C., "Harlem Blues," 94
haptic music, 59
hard bop, 90
Harrison, Barbara Grizutti, "Spike Lee Hates Your Cracker Ass," 81
Harrison, Donald, 75, 95
Harry James Orchestra, 126
Hart, Lorenz, "Bewitched, Bothered, and Bewildered," 118, 133, 139
Harvey, Adam, *Soundtracks of Woody Allen*, 125
HBO (Home Box Office), 46, 110, 149
Heile, Björn, *Watching Jazz*, 7
Hemingway, Anthony, *Red Tails*, 76–77
Hemingway, Ernest, 131
Henderson, Joe, 117
Hentoff, Nat, 137
Hesmondhalgh, David, 22, 28
Higgins, Billy, 70
Hinton, Milt, 135
hip-hop, 144–45, 151
Hirsch, Paul, 39
historically informed compositions (HIC), 137
historically informed performance (HIP), 31, 139–42, **140**, 179n59, 179n61
Hjort, Mette, *Film and Risk*, 19
Hodges, Johnny, 3
Holiday, Billie, 90, 103, 130, 132
Hollywood, 37–38, 47–48, 77–78; royalty, 38
hooks, bell, 81
Hope, Bob, 130
Horner, James, 150
horror films, 149
Hubai, Gergely, *Torn Music*, 41
Hunter, Alberta, 71
Hurricane Katrina, 109–10
Hurst, Robert, 90
Hurston, Zora Neale, 85
Hurwitz, Justin, 38
Hutchings, Shabaka, 156
Hyman, Dick, 24, 134–42; Allen and, 38, 134–36, **137**; authenticity and, 135,

138–39; cameo roles, 136, 139, 179n55; career, 8, 134–35; historically informed compositions of, 136–39, 141–42, 180n63; on improvised soundtracks, 51; as jazz artist, 13; musician network of, 32
Hyman, Dick, works by: *Century of Jazz Piano*, 135; "Chameleon Days," 138, **138**; "Doin' the Chameleon," 138; *Hannah and Her Sisters* (score), 118–19; "How High the Moon" (arr.), 139; "Leonard the Lizard," 138; "Reptile Eyes," 138; *Zelig* (score), 136–39

Ichaso, Leo, *Sugar Hill*, 76
improvisation: Allen and, 134, 142; Iñárritu and, 52, 55, 59, 71–73; jazz and, 17, 21, 25, 27, 146, 169n37; jazz soundtracks and, 20, 48–53, 68–73, 153–54, 166n1; Lee and, 86; Rudolph and, 52, 68, 71–73
Impulse! Records, 27
Iñárritu, Alejandro González, 51–66; authenticity and, 52–53, 54, 59–60, 65, 72; awards and honors, 53, 167n12; career, 53; cinematic approach of, 57–58, 168n32; improvisation and, 52, 55, 59, 71–73; as independent auteur/maverick, 15–16, 51–54, 167n14; jazz and, 52, 142; risk and, 52, 72; Sánchez and, 38, 51–53, 55, 71–72, 167n17
Iñárritu, Alejandro González, works by: *The Revenant*, 53, 73, 167n14. See also *Birdman*
independent filmmakers, 15–16, 30, 51, 162n34
Isham, Mark, 66–71; artistic development of, 73; Cantor and, 35; career, 8, 66, 161n18; Dechter and, 35; on economic reward, 40; as jazz artist, 13; risk and, 71; Rudolph and, 38, 51–53, 66–67, **67**, 71–72; on scores/casting, 32; trumpet and, 68–69
Isham, Mark, works by: *Afterglow* (score), 23, 66, **67**, 68–71; *Blue Sun* (quintet album), 68–69; *Vapor Drawings* (album), 67

Jackpot Records, 126
Jackson, Janet, 83
Jackson, Samuel L., 84
James, Harry, 125–26
jazz and film, 6–23; authenticity and, 16–19; behind-the-scenes examination of, 4, 8–11; directorial investment in, 13–16; golden era of jazz scores, 5, 21, 89; implications for future, 24–25, 152–59; jazz definition in, 12–13; resurgence of, 144–48; risk in, 19–21. *See also* collaboration in jazz-film; media and music collaboration; *and specific film directors and film composers*
jazz biopics, 5, 144, 147
jazz criticism/critics, 40
Jazz in July concert, 135
Jazz Preservation Act (1987), 18
Jewison, Norman, 101–2, 175n80
Johansson, Scarlett, 124, 149
Johnson, Bunk, 126
Johnson, James P., 135; "Charleston," 138
Jones, LeRoi. *See* Baraka, Amiri
Jones, Norah, 156
Jones, Quincy, 5
Joplin, Scott, 135
Jordan, Louis, 103
Jordan, Michael, 83

Kael, Pauline, 14
Kane, Helen, 138
Kaplan, Fred, 129
Karlin, Fred, *On the Track*, 7, 30, 33, 42, 44
Kart, Larry, *Jazz in Search of Itself*, 12
Kazan, Elia, *A Streetcar Named Desire*, 12, 49, 61, 169n40
Keaton, Diane, 124, 133
Keaton, Michael, 55, 65, 168n20
Kern, Jerome, 126–27
Kilik, John, 103
King, Regina, *One Night in Miami*, 77
Kirchner, Bill, 20
Kirkland, Kenny, 90
Kivy, Peter, *Authenticities*, 17
Klein, Joe, 119

Konitz, Lee, 156
Kopple, Barbara, *Wild Man Blues*, 127–28
Kravitz, Zoe, 120
Krim, Arthur, 122

Le Poste Parisien, 48
Lee, Bill: *Mo' Better Blues* (score), 93–95; Spike as son of, 74, 87
Lee, Cinqué, 87
Lee, Joie, 87, 91, 93
Lee, Spike, 6, 24, 77–97; African American culture and, 77–82; authenticity and, 74, 88–89, 92–93, 95, 117; Black creativity/artistic expression and, 84–86; Blanchard and, 74, 76, 77, 95–96, 100–101, 117; business ventures and branding of, 15, 83; criticism of, 81–82; entrepreneurship and, 82–84; father (Bill Lee) and, 74, 91; 40 Acres and a Mule Filmworks and, 79, 83; Hollywood and, 84, 92, 102; improvisation and, 86; as independent auteur/maverick, 15–16, 77–78; jazz/jazz musicians and, 86–90, 91–93, 94–97, 142; on legacy, 74; publications of, 83, 172n24; signature shot technique, 85, 173n31; women portrayals by, 81, 93
Lee, Spike, works by: *Bamboozled*, 77, 79, 80, 85; *BlacKkKlansman*, 77, 117, 171n5; *Clockers*, 76–77; *Crooklyn*, 77, 87–88; *Da 5 Bloods*, 76–77, 85; *Do the Right Thing*, 76, 80, 87; *4 Little Girls*, 76–77, 101; *Get on the Bus*, 77; *Inside Man*, 77; *Jim Brown: All American*, 77; *Jungle Fever*, 77, 86–87, 100; *Miracle at St. Anna*, 76–77; *School Daze*, 76, 80, 87; *She Hate Me*, 77; *She's Gotta Have It*, 87–88; *Spike Lee's Gotta Have It* (text), 83; *Summer of Sam*, 77; *25th Hour*, 77; *Uplift the Race* (text), 83; *When the Levees Broke: A Requiem in Four Acts*, 76, 101, 109–13, 176n96. See also *Malcolm X*; *Mo' Better Blues*
Lees, Gene, 18
leitmotifs, 47, 104–5
Lemmons, Kasi: *Eve's Bayou*, 77; *Fire Shut Up in My Bones*, 76; *Harriet*, 77

Lenin, Vladimir, 79
Lerman, Stewart, 31
Levi, Mica, scores of, 149
Lewis, George, 126, 128
Lewis, John: *Sait-on jamais* (score), 49; "Skating in Central Park," 106
licensing, 31–32, 42, 136, 139, 160n16
Lincoln, Abbey, 18
Litowitz, Drew, 149
Littleton, Jeff, 70
Lloyd, Charles, 70
Lopeman, Mark, 31, 45
Lopes, Paul, 10
Lott, Eric, *Love and Theft*, 78, 178n29
Lowe, Mundell, 136
Lubezki, Emmanuel, 56, 168n31
Lubiano, Wahneema, 81
Luhrmann, Baz, *The Great Gatsby*, 144, 180n3
Lumet, Sidney, 101
Lunacharsky, Anatoly, 79

magic, 127, 130
Mahler, Gustav, 54
Malcolm X, 101–2, 107, 109
Malcolm X (Lee), 101–6; background, 101–2; character stereotypes in, 81, 172n18; commission of, 102, 175n81; "Malcolm's Theme," reprises of, 105–6, 108–9, 176n89; score for, 103–6, 176n90
Malle, Louis, 72; *Ascenseur pour l'échafaud* (*Elevator to the Gallows*), 16, 48–49, **49**, 73, 153
Mamet, David, 101
Mancini, Henry, 44; *The Pink Panther* (score), 21, 153
Manhattan, New York City, 119–20
Marsalis, Branford: Branford Marsalis Quartet, 90, 96–97, 174n60; criticism of, 40–41; Lee and, 93, 95; New Orleans and, 75
Marsalis, Branford, works by: "Beneath the Underdog," 94; "Knocked Out of the Box," 94; "Pop Top 40," 94; "Say Hey," 94
Marsalis, Ellis, 75, 156
Marsalis, Wynton, 4, 75, 109, 139, 180n2

Martin, Darnell: *Cadillac Records*, 76; *Their Eyes Were Watching God*, 76
Marx, Karl, 21, 163n50
Mask, Mia, 85
Massood, Paula, 83–85
Mateen, Tarus, 107
maverick filmmakers, 15–16, 21, 52, 166n9
Mayer, Vicki, 14
McCracken, Allison, *Real Men Don't Sing*, 151
McCristal Culp, Jerome, Jr., 120
McQueen, Steve, *12 Years a Slave*, 79, 149
Medbøe, Haftor, 157–58
media and music collaboration, 146, 154, 156–58
Meeker, David, *Jazz in the Movies*, 12
Mendes, Sam, 100
Mera, Miguel, 59
Metheny, Pat, 55
Method Acting, 18
#MeToo movement, 123–24
Mezzrow, Mezz, 127
Michael's Pub, New York City, 127
Micheaux, Oscar, 78
Michelmore, Guy, scores of, 151
Michelot, Pierre, 48
Mickey Mousing, 64–65, 170n46
Milkowski, Bill, 116
Miller, Glenn: "In the Mood," 126, 131; "Moonlight Serenade," 129
Miller, Jonny Lee, 68
Mills Brothers, 131
Mingus, Charles, 90; "Goodbye Pork Pie Hat," 97; *Shadows* (score), 50
minstrelsy, 61, 78, 127, 178n29
Mitchell, Elvis, 54
Mo' Better Blues (Lee), 90–97; characters/plot, 81, 91–94, 174n48, 174n52, 174n54; controversy over, 93; jazz in, 90–91, 94–97, **96**, 174n61; realism in, 93–96
modal jazz, 12, 90
Monk, Thelonious, *Les liaisons dangereuses* (score), 49
Monson, Ingrid, *Saying Something*, 17
Moreau, Jeanne, 48

Morgan, David, *Knowing the Score*, 7
Morris, Marvin, 34
Morton, Jelly Roll, 126, 136
Mos Def, 87
Muhammad, Elijah, 105, 108
Murch, Walter, 54
Murray, Albert, 18
music industry, 27, 154–57
musical activism, 75–76, 90, 97–98, 111–13

Nagin, Ray, 109–10
Nation of Islam (NOI), 102, 105, 108
neo-minstrelsy, 80
neoromanticism, 5, 145, 150
New Black Music, 18
New Jazz Studies, 7, 13, 161n26
New Orleans, 75, 109–16; jazz, 126–28, 130, 133–34, 141–42
New Wave, 14, 21, 48–50, 72, 166n3
New York City in Allen's work, 119–21
New York Jazz Repertory Company, 135
Newman, Thomas, 100, 150
Newsome, Sam, 107–9
Nielsen: on streaming's popularity, 154; U.S. Music Mid-Year Report (2019), 27
Nighthawks Orchestra, 31, 45
92nd Street Y, New York City, 135
noir films, 21, 61, 89
Nolan, Christopher, *Dunkirk*, 150
Nolte, Nick, 68
nominal/factual authenticity, 140–41, **140**
North, Alex, *A Streetcar Named Desire* (score), 12, 49, 61, 169n40
Northwest Sinfonia, 113
Norton, Edward, 65–66
nostalgia, 131–33
Nunn, Bill, 94, 95

Ochs, Phil, 75
Orion Pictures, 122
Oscar Micheaux Corporation, 78
Oscars. *See* Academy Awards

Page, Sid, 70
Palomar Productions, 134

Parker, Charlie, 92, 108, 135, 145
Parks, Gordon, *The Learning Tree*, 78
Peele, Jordan, 83
Penn, Leo, *A Man Called Adam*, 91
Peplowski, Ken, 135
period films, 5–6, 31, 33
Perl, Arnold, 101, 102
Perry, Tyler, *Why Did I Get Married?*, 79
Piazza, Tom, 4
Pillai, Nicolas, *Jazz as Visual Language*, 4, 7
Pixar Animation Studios, *Soul*, 146
Pizzarelli, Bucky, 135, 156
Poitier, Sidney, 78
Pokorny, Michael, *An Economic History of Film*, 19
Pond, Steve, 62
pop scoring, 5, 160n16
popular culture, 21, 40, 61, 67, 145–46, 157
Porter, Cole, 125–27, 130, 135–36
Porter, Eric, *What Is This Thing Called Jazz?*, 12
Portishead, 149
Poster, Randall, 31
postproduction, 26, 32, 56, 168n22
Powdermaker, Hortense, 14
Powell, Bud, 135, 136
Preminger, Otto: *Anatomy of a Murder*, 3–5, 16, 50, 153; *The Man with the Golden Arm*, 50, 91, 145
Previn, Soon-Yi, 123
Price, Stephen, *Gravity* (score), 47
Prince-Bythewood, Gina, *Love and Basketball*, 76
Pritzker, Daniel, *Bolden*, 5, 144, 180n2
psychological thriller films, 71, 149, 151
Public Enemy, 87

Quadrani, Alexia, 154
Questel, Mae, 138

race, 17–18, 20, 37–38, 78–80, 127, 163n47. *See also* musical activism
Rachmaninoff, Sergei, 54
Radiohead, 148

ragtime, 135

Ravel, Maurice, 54

Redman, Don, 127

Rees, Dee, *Bessie*, 5, 144

Reinhardt, Django, "I'll See You in My Dreams," 139

Revell, Graeme, *Lara Croft: Tomb Raider* (score), 42–43

Reznor, Trent, scores of, 149

Ribot, Marc, scores of, 153–54

Rich, Mattie, *The Inkwell*, 76

Riseborough, Andrea, 65

risk: Allen and, 121–22; film industry and, 19–21, 27, 79–80, 101, 166n7; improvised scores and, 51; Iñárritu and, 52, 72; Rudolph and, 52, 71–72

Roach, Max, *Freedom Now Suite*, 98

Rodgers, Richard, "Bewitched, Bothered, and Bewildered," 118, 133, 139

Rogers, Ginger, 130

Roney, Wallace, 156

Rosenblum, Ralph, 134

Ross, Atticus, scores of, 149

Rosten, Leo C., 14

Rudolph, Alan, 66–71; Altman and, 66, 71, 170n70; authenticity and, 52–53, 67, 72; career, 66; editing and, 71; improvisation and, 52, 68, 71–73; as independent auteur/maverick, 15–16, 51–52; Isham and, 38, 66–68, **67**; jazz and, 52, 67–68, 142; risk and, 52, 71–72

Rudolph, Alan, works by: *Afterglow*, 23–24, 52, 68–71, 73; *Breakfast of Champions*, 67; *Love at Large*, 67; *Made in Heaven*, 67; *The Moderns*, 67; *Mrs. Parker and the Vicious Circle*, 67; *Ray Meets Helen*, 66; *Remember My Name*, 71; *The Secret Lives of Dentists*, 66; *Trixie*, 67; *Trouble in Mind*, 67

Ryan, Bill, 22

Salamone, Frank A., 17

Salvant, Cécile McLorin, 156

Sánchez, Antonio, 53–66; artistic development of, 55, 73; *Birdman* (score), 23–24,

59–65, 169n36; career, 8, 55, 73; creative approach of, 62–66; Iñárritu and, 38, 51–53, 55, 71–72, 167n17; as jazz artist, 13, 55; musician network of, 32, 55

Sandke, Randy, 18, 135

Sarris, Andrew, 14, 162n29

Schelle Michael, 76

sci-fi films, 149, 151

Scorsese, Martin, 19, 122

Scott, A. O., "My Woody Allen Problem," 123–24

Scott, Travis, 157

Sedgwick, John, *An Economic History of Film*, 19

Sedric, Gene, 127

"selling out," 40

Shabazz, Betty, 102

Shepard Tone technique, 150

Shepp, Archie, 18

Shore, Howard, 5, 150; *Naked Lunch* (score), 50

Shorter, Wayne, "Footprints," 97, 108

Sibelius (software), 35

silent films, 153–54

Sinatra, Frank, 131

Singleton, John, *Boyz in da Hood*, 79

16th Street Baptist Church bombing, 97

Smith, Bessie, 144–45

Smith, Jada Pinkett, 38, 84

Smith, Jeff, *The Sounds of Commerce*, 19

Smith, Nate, 169n36

Smith, Will, 38

Snipes, Wesley, 84, 93, 95–96

social justice activism. *See* musical activism

social media, 156–57

Solal, Martial, *Breathless* (score), 49

Sontag, Susan, 137

Spielberg, Steven, 100, 122

Spike's Joint, 83

spotting sessions, 32, 33

Stahl, Matt, 45–46; *Unfree Masters*, 7, 22–23

Stanfield, Peter, *Body and Soul*, 7

Sterritt, David, 78

Stetson, Colin, scores of, 149

Stewart, Susan, *On Longing*, 132

Steyermark, Alex, 86
Stone, Emma, 65, 145
Strayhorn, Billy, 4
streaming media, 154, 181n21
Streamline Music Scoring System, 36
stride, 135, 141
Sullivan, John L., 22
Sunnyside Records, 27
swing, 12, 90, 130, 135

Tavernier, Bertrand, *Round Midnight*, 16, 50, 91–92, 144
Tchaikovsky, Peter Ilich, 54
technological development, 24–25, 33, 130, 146, 149–52, 157–58
television: Black culture and stories on, 146; series with jazz soundtracks, 21, 31, 45, 61
temp tracks, 33, 164n18
Terence Blanchard Quintet, 113, 176n101
#TimesUp movement, 124
Tin Pan Alley, 130, 135
Tobin, Yann, 129
Toynbee, Jason, 22, 163n54
Triangle Music, 126
Truffaut, François, "Une certaine tendance du cinéma français," 14

UCLA Division of Social Sciences, *Hollywood Diversity Report* (2019), 37
unions, 42, 84
Urtreger, René, 48

Vadim, Roger, 49
Varèse Sarabande, 126
Verve Records, 27
Vest, Jason, 101
Vick, Harold, 76
Victor Records, 138
video games, 158
Von Sternberg, Josef, *The Docks of New York*, 153

Wager, Jans B., *Jazz and Cocktails*, 3–4, 7
Waksman, Steve, *Instruments of Desire*, 151
Wallace, Michelle, 81
Waller, Fats, 127, 135, 136
Warner Bros., 101–2, 175nn80–81
Washington, Denzel, 76, 84, 91, 95–96, **96**, 102
Watts, Jeff "Tain," 90, 95
Watts, Naomi, 65
Wein, George, 135
Wennekes, Emile, 59; *Cinema Changes*, 7
Wilen, Barney, 48
Williams, Cynda, 93
Williams, John, 5, 47, 100, 150
Willis, Gordon, 137
Wilson, August, 145
Wilson, Teddy, 135
Windham Hill Records, 67
Winfrey, Oprah, 83
Winslet, Kate, 124
Wolfe, George C., *Ma Rainey's Black Bottom*, 145
women in film, 37, 161n28
work for hire, 45–46
Worth, Marvin, 101
Wright, Rayburn, *On the Track*, 7, 30, 33, 42, 44

X, Betty, 102
X, Malcolm, 101–2, 107, 109. See also *Malcolm X* (Lee)

Yanow, Scott, 109

Zawinul, Joe, "Mercy, Mercy, Mercy," 97
Zelig, Leonard, 137
Ziering, Amy, *Allen v. Farrow* (documentary), 124
Zimmer, Hans: neoromantic style of, 5; scores of, 149–50
Zinsser, William, 135

ABOUT THE AUTHOR

Credit: Andrew A. Carlson

Gretchen L. Carlson, PhD, is a musicologist and professor of music history and culture at Towson University, where she teaches courses in jazz, film music, popular music, and music in American culture, among others. She has authored several publications focusing on jazz and film, featured in the *Journal of the Society for American Music* and *Jazz and Culture*. An active pianist, Carlson balances her research and teaching with solo and collaborative performance and maintains a private piano studio.